# The Aesthetics of Movement

Photographs by Eadweard Muybridge

# The Aesthetics of Movement

Paul Souriau    Translated and edited by Manon Souriau

Foreword by Francis Sparshott

The University of Massachusetts Press    Amherst, 1983

"Woman removing jar from shoulder" is reprinted
with the kind permission of the Smith College Museum
of Art, Northampton, Massachusetts.
Gift of the Philadelphia Commercial Museum, 1950.
All other photographs are reprinted with permission of
The Metropolitan Museum of Art, New York City.
Copyright © 1887 by Eadweard Muybridge.

Copyright © 1983 by
The University of Massachusetts Press
All rights reserved
Printed in the United States of America
Library of Congress Cataloging in Publication Data
Souriau, Paul, 1852–1926.
The aesthetics of movement.
Translation of: L'esthétique du mouvement.
Includes index.
1. Movement, Aesthetics of.   I. Souriau, Manon.
II. Title.
BH301.M6S613 1983   612'.76'01   83–10366
ISBN 0-87023-412-9

# Contents

# List of Illustrations

# Foreword

If you look for Paul Souriau in the index to Raymond Bayer's *Histoire de l'esthétique,* you will find him, but in the text he figures only as the father of Etienne, who became a dominant figure in European aesthetics for several decades. In Bayer's *L'esthétique mondiale au XX<sup>e</sup> siècle* he plays the same modest part; Bayer does identify him further as the author of one book, but it is *La beauté rationelle* of 1904.[1] Nowhere in either volume is there any information about his work; and nowhere in the accounts of French aesthetic movements of the day is there any indication of any trend to which *The Aesthetics of Movement* might be assigned. But the debates to which it contributes were lively ones in their day, and the book itself is written with great charm and imaginative power. It has never lacked admirers and, though its science is that of a bygone age, nothing has been written to replace it. The current surge of interest in dance makes the appearance of Manon Souriau's fine translation especially welcome.

Souriau's argument is subtle and intricate, and, as he says in his introduction, not easy to sort out and summarize. The intention is to differentiate the subjective from the objective elements in the delight we take in moving and in observing the movements of humans and animals. The underlying scheme is that of Immanuel Kant's *Critique of Judgment* of 1790. Kant had in effect distinguished three phases of aesthetic pleasure. First there is the merely subjective, sensuous delight in appearances—in colors and sounds. Then there is the delight in the appreciation of perfection in form and functionality in move-

ment. Finally, there is the pure aesthetic judgment, the delighted recognition of beauty as such, in which we abstract from all actual concepts and functions and take delight in pure form, in the "purposiveness without purpose" of something that strikes our imaginations as being just right as it is. Francis Hutcheson, who greatly influenced Kant, had in 1725 ascribed the delight we take in animal movement to an innate sense of beauty that manifested itself as an immediate recognition of efficiency in design and economy in movement; and Herbert Spencer, in an immensely influential formulation to which Souriau refers, had more recently equated the quality of gracefulness with visible economy of effort in human and animal motion.[2] What Souriau does is take the Kantian scheme, use Spencer's formulation as a key to its application in the realm of movement, correlate its three phases with three phases of consciousness in the production of movement, and find a new equivalent for the pure aesthetic judgment and its objects. In doing this he substitutes scientific objectivity for the epistemic imperatives that animated Kant's own inquiries: everything is translated into terms of the physiology and psychology of the day, in the manner of his contemporary neo-Kantians at Marburg and especially the founder of that school, Hermann Cohen.[3]

The physiological determinants of movement, which preoccupy today's kinesiology textbooks, are set aside as only indirectly relevant to our appreciation of movement. What is directly relevant are the psychological determinants. At the lowest level among these are the pleasures and pains felt in moving, which are a function of muscular effort and release. They are basic and ineluctable, but they tell us nothing about the objective quality of the movement we are experiencing.

That quality depends rather on efficiency, on economy of effort in relation to a given task. Every animal is an artist, says Souriau, in the intelligent economy with which it performs complex bodily functions. But to achieve such economy is not the highest use of intelligence in action, for a sense of ease may be deceptive. Something not obvious, something hard to learn and not immediately comfortable, may serve better. The most rewarding movements in the long run are those that secure greater economies in the accomplishing of remoter objectives. So we go beyond efficiency to an articulate effectiveness.

From the spectator's point of view, our immediate gratification in the observation of movement reflects the curious physiology of our sense organs, with its immediate consequences in the form of perception thresholds, afterimages, and such. Like the feelings produced by muscular tension and relaxation, these are basic and ineluctable, but they tell us nothing about the real qualities of movements. To judge such qualities we rely on the recognized efficiency of movement, the animal ease of which Spencer spoke. But the easiest movement is not, after all, the most graceful. We appreciate movement as expressive of the mover's will. The most beautiful movement is accordingly not the most efficient but that which is eloquent of efficiency: movement clearly articulated by the mover to make its structure evident, to give it a perceptible purposiveness independent of any extraneous purpose it might have. Such movement answers to, and is a special form of, the articulate effectiveness that is the finest form of movement from the mover's point of view. The symmetry of Souriau's account, if I have read it aright, is complete but by no means simple.

The paradigm of beautiful movement, analyzed and reconstituted, is not that of the dancer but that of the gymnast. Ballet choreography is censured for its regimentation, and hints for choreographers are derived from the psychology of movement perception, but dance as an art of movement is not mentioned. Animals, we noted, are artists of movement; but it appears that dancers are not. This should be shocking, but it is not surprising. Gymnastics was of immense social importance in Souriau's day, but artistic dance was not. Ted Shawn's account of the situation in *Every Little Movement* is instructive here—granted that it is a partisan statement, it is not an uninformed one. Ballet in France at the end of the nineteenth century, he writes, "was frankly a spectacle, not highly honored even as a great theater art," and its practitioners and audiences were preoccupied with technique—that is, with gymnastics, and a form of gymnastics not governed by gymnastic principles; and the only other form of dancing presented for display was crassly commercial show dancing.[4] What makes Shawn's account particularly interesting from our point of view is his contention that all modern dance in America and Europe is derived, not from the development of any dance tradition, but precisely from the sort of theoretical analysis of body movement that Souriau is concerned with. The association of modern dance with physical education departments in colleges, which strikes today's student of aesthetics as so extraordinary, is no accident: the origins of that dance have far more to do with gymnastics than they have with any established art practice.

Ted Shawn's specific thesis is that all modern dance stems from the particular form of movement analysis worked out by François Delsarte, who lectured on "applied aesthetics" in Paris from 1839 until his death in 1871. Delsarte's system was introduced and popularized in America by Steele Mackay, and it is plausible enough that American modern dance owes a lot to him; but the thesis requires that Rudolph von Laban's movement analysis was also Delsartian in inspiration, and this is much harder to believe. My very limited information would suggest rather that Laban's work was a straightforward development of the system of exercise worked out by Adolph Spiess (1810–1858), who was primarily responsible for developing gymnastics as a part of the school curriculum.[5] Delsarte himself was not involved in the development of gymnastics and not interested in dance, and he had no dancers among his students: he was interested primarily in voice training and secondarily in the technique of stage acting. What made him especially suitable as an adoptive godparent for modern dance was a combination of three things: a wide-ranging empirical study of how people in different situations actually do move; an easily remembered and suggestive system of "principles" for analyzing movements; and a line of inspirational patter suitable for filling dancers with convictions about the importance of their work. School histories of physical education still dismiss him, as Shawn complains, as "unscientific," but the notion of science by which he is condemned seems to amount to no more than the accumulation of verified data without much regard to its theoretical significance.

Delsarte's work is of direct relevance to us here precisely because Souriau never mentions him. They appear to represent independent manifestations of what seems to have been a preoccupation of the nineteenth century generally: the establishing and describing of the true facts of animal locomotion in general and human locomotion in particular. The forms this interest took were as various as the motives that inspired it. It is a complex story and, if it has been told, I do not know who

has told it. But it does seem that by 1860 Delsarte, whatever his earlier fame, had fallen into obscurity. The new center of interest was the empirical investigation of the mechanics of movement, and the technology associated with that investigation. Jules Marey, on whom Souriau chiefly relies (Souriau's approach to physiology, with its heavy emphasis on muscles, is essentially that of Marey's *Animal Mechanism* [1873], and contrasts with Pettigrew's emphasis on the limbs as systems of levers), relied on recording devices attached to the moving animal, and his concerns seem to have been biological.[6] James Bell Pettigrew, interacting with Marey, is preoccupied with figure-of-eight movements in animal locomotion and their applicability to flexible-wing designs for flying machines.[7] This interest in human flight surfaces near the end of Souriau's book, where he is badly let down by his ignorance of the part played by thermal currents in soaring. His denigration of the screw propeller as a means to mechanical flight, which to our hindsight may seem strange, makes sense in the day of Marey and Pettigrew, when research centered on the behavior of kites. The interaction of wing and air was indeed the heart of the matter, as we realize when we reflect that the key to the Wright brothers' eventual triumph was not the harnessing of a screw propeller to a light engine—that principle was already used in Stringfellow's model of 1868—but was precisely the development of a mechanical equivalent for the flexible wing, which proved essential to stability even though useless for propulsion.

Meanwhile, Eadweard Muybridge, whose astonishing work complements Souriau's text in this translation, shared neither Marey's scientific interests nor Pettigrew's hopes for aviation. He was interested in photography as an art and a technique, as a means to showmanship, and as an aid to artists. His work belongs in the context of the long series of devices developed in his time to produce the illusion of motion by means of a succession of images, and of the search for chemicals that would permit exposure times short enough to capture on a photographic plate a sharp image of a rapidly moving object.[8] Thomas Eakins, the sports painter, was one of the main sponsors of Muybridge's work in Philadelphia; and, though we now think of Muybridge primarily as a revealer of animal locomotion, which was indeed his lasting contribution, the long series of photographs of the human figure in motion, together with his complaint that the only women who would allow themselves to be photographed in naked motion were so ill-bred that their movements were not truly graceful, suggest that his devotion to pure science was not a monomania.[9] The proper representation of movement in art is, of course, one of Souriau's concerns—he says things that could serve as descriptions of works produced by Italian futurists around 1910 —and the very fact that how to depict movement suddenly appeared as an unsolved problem after artists had been doing it for millennia is significant testimony to the way in which the nature of movement had become a theme in nineteenth-century thought.

The intense flurry of activity in the investigation of movement in the years following 1865, which is the immediate context of Souriau's reflection, is diverse in methods and interests. But it is uniformly hard-nosed in approach, in that the immediate task is seen as ascertaining the material facts about how bodies move. In this, as we have said, it belongs to a different world from that of Delsarte. But our initial analysis of Souriau's argument revealed a double emphasis. At one extreme we have the admittedly fundamental facts about move-

ment and perception. But objective beauty is not to be sought there: it belongs to the gymnast, whose movements represent a double rationality, in the devising of new and more efficient ways to move and in the articulation of such movements for presentation to a spectator. Souriau thus places himself in a very different context, that of gymnastics.

The growth of gymnastics in the nineteenth century is a remarkable story. It is not a French one, except in its origins, when it goes back to the publication of Rousseau's *Émile* in 1762. Rousseau there presents what is for practical purposes a new philosophy of education, based on Condillac's reworking of John Locke's account of the workings of human reason. The proper use of the reason depends on the development of the sense organs and their use in the activity of a healthy body. To make education center on the transmission of information and methods in a classroom is therefore radically wrong. These ideas are developed into an ideal curriculum by Guts-Muths, Pestalozzi, and others at the turn of the century; and the ideal of humanity they represent plays an important part in the thinking and practice of educational authorities, especially in Germanic and Scandinavian countries, throughout the nineteenth century. And at least until the middle of the century, when outdoor games became more popular, the physical basis of the system was, essentially, gymnastics. Until about 1860 gymnastics and physical education generally were a focus of interest and debate, with heavy government involvement.[10]

The part played by gymnastics in nineteenth-century social and political thought and practice was ambivalent, to say the least. On the one hand, the Rousseauian ideal of the healthy autonomous thinker, as cultivated in the *Turnvereinen,* became the symbol of German national unity and independence, and as such was suppressed in the reactionary aftermath of the Congress of Vienna. But, on the other hand, the introduction of mass citizen armies in the Napoleonic wars gave governments a new interest in the physical well-being of their subjects; and the rise of the factory, with its body-deforming employments, made a corrective regime of physical culture obviously desirable. Gymnastics thus, in its two aspects, becomes a symbol both of personal liberation and of military-industrial servitude. It is in the light of this double aspect that the complex contrast in Souriau's thought between the objective beauty of gymnastic rationality and the merely factual necessity imposed by the bodily mechanism has to be understood.

The analysis of bodily movement itself has a darker side, on which we have already touched by implication. Industrialization as such demands movement analysis. In the end, the human being becomes just one more moving part in the industrial process. In the "systems approach" to production, human software is integrated into the hardware. And, though the phrase "systems approach" is itself a more recent coinage, the manifesto of the movement itself, under the name "scientific management," was published by F. W. Taylor as *Differential Piece Rate* in 1895, just six years after Souriau's book appeared.[11]

It was inevitable that interest should turn to the mechanisms of animal and human movement, to the structures and operations of living bodies, because the essence of the industrial revolution was precisely the introduction of machines to perform complex tasks—tasks that accordingly had to be analyzed. The extraordinary eighteenth-century vogue for automata, inaugurated by Jacques de Vaucanson, was a portent; and the title of Marey's book, *La machine animale*, was perhaps its fulfillment.[12] But in any case, the properties of materials and their

capabilities had to be an obsession of the machine age, which was also a "scientific" age based on an understanding of "science" according to which everything had to be taken apart and put back together again. Souriau's gymnast, who shows his rationality and achieves grace and beauty by taking himself to pieces and reassembling himself, is a noble vision of its time.

Although the philosophical basis of Souriau's aesthetics is the demystified Kantianism we described at the outset, his immediate affinities within aesthetics are with other manifestations of the new age of industry and science. The central thesis that objective beauty depends on functional efficiency, and that the highest form of beauty belongs to the expression of the properties of structures and forces as analyzed and resynthesized by a clarifying intellect, is familiar to us from the more refined of the "functionalist" theories of modern architecture.[13] When we are not thinking carefully we tend to associate this functionalism with developments in Holland and Germany between about 1890 and 1930, but really it goes back much further. Odd as it seems when we consider the artifacts in which the functionalism was supposed to be embodied, the same set of ideas goes back to the organizers of the Great Exhibition in London in 1851, where Paxton's Crystal Palace itself manifested it in iron and glass.[14] The use of cast iron as a structural material was crucial, and both in theory and practice the architecture of iron was more at home in France than in any other country. Souriau quotes Eiffel, designer of the movement's most famous and most essentially French manifesto, on the dynamic significance of his monument. But the great original theorist of structuralism was Viollet-le-Duc: it is to his *Entretiens sur l'architecture* of 1872, with the stunning designs that illustrate them, as much as to any other single source, that historians trace the origins of the movement.[15] Note the date: 1872 was the year in which Muybridge first successfully photographed fast motion; Marey was already publishing, and his *La machine animale* was to appear in the following year.

If Souriau's book is allied to functionalism by its principal doctrines, its genre makes it an integral part of the heroic age of psychological aesthetics. Since aesthetics has to do with the perceivable as such, it is not surprising that the facts of aesthetic preference had been an object of investigation from the beginnings of experimental aesthetics. G. T. Fechner's *Vorschule des Ästhetik* (1876) was a landmark, and by the turn of the century a number of works analogous to Souriau's had appeared, purporting to establish the objective psychological bases of this or that aspect of aesthetic preference, of which Theodor Lipps's massive *Raumästhetik* (1897) is an outstanding example.[16] By 1910 it began to seem that aesthetics was established as a branch of objective psychology.[17] Souriau describes his own work as a byway in aesthetics, and in a way it was, but it was part of a network of byways that was beginning to establish a comprehensive means of mental travel.

The impetus of experimental aesthetics failed, and its results are mostly ignored. What happened to it? Partly, the easy work was soon done, and the more precise and detailed work, which continues to this day, presents immense difficulties to the investigator. Partly, the promise of the work depended on ignorance of the perverse intricacies of the central nervous system. One is taken aback by how quickly Souriau moves from facts about muscles to suppositions about the organism as a whole; and his account of vision concentrates, as psychologists since Descartes had done but as we can no longer do, on the behavior of the retina, as though a replica of the retinal image were somehow stamped somewhere in the cerebral cortex.[18] But what has done most to relegate the psychological aesthetics of that day to oblivion is the revival of linguistics and the development of semiotics under the influence of Saussure's *Cours de linguistique générale* (1916), and the associated "linguistic turn" in all schools of philosophy, which has been made habitual with us by today's concern with data processing.[19] The old psychological aesthetics purports to deal with appearances in abstraction from the systems of meanings to which they belong. Souriau's dictum that every animal is an artist is no longer acceptable, because the moving animal is not operating with a symbol system.

The scientific trends in psychology and movement analysis with which Souriau aligns himself were not, as we have seen, specifically French: the greatest name in contemporary psychology, and that which Souriau most often cites, is that of Wilhelm Wundt. But his book belongs to two traditions, in aesthetics and in general philosophy, that are distinctively French. In France more than elsewhere there persists a tradition of writing studies like that of Souriau, combining erudition with elegance and imagination, exploring the aesthetic significances of specific domains of experience. One thinks especially of Gaston Bachelard, though Bachelard does not share Souriau's objectivist ambitions; and we have recently seen a learned and impassioned volume on the aesthetics of perfume.[20] It is legitimate, I think, to associate the anthropological adventures of Claude Lévi-Strauss and the speculative structuralism of the late Roland Barthes with this genre of writing.[21]

On a deeper level, Souriau's book pertains to one of the most characteristic and persistent strains in French philosophy. We have already pointed to Condillac as providing the intellectual starting point for Rousseau's philosophy of education and hence, indirectly, for the cult of gymnastics that swept Europe in the nineteenth century. In a remarkable study published in 1938, Gabriel Madinier traces Condillac's heritage in a distinctive strain of French epistemology that runs through Maine de Biran and Ravaisson to Bergson, according to which the sense of the self is to be attributed to muscular effort, to the sense of effort resisted.[22] The theory that our awareness of the externality of the external world is derived from our experience of resisted effort is no monopoly of French thought. It is a commonplace of nineteenth-century empiricist psychology, and can be found in Alexander Bain (an author, incidentally, whom Souriau cites more than once).[23] But the line of thought Madinier traces through Maine de Biran is by no means empiricist, for the effort is identified as muscular effort, and the associated sense of self is a sense of the self as embodied. The foundation of epistemology on a sense of oneself as actually corporeal is surprisingly uncommon outside France, and remarkably pervasive inside; since Madinier wrote, it has become familiar to American readers through the work of Maurice Merleau-Ponty—and, surprisingly, in view of his reputation among philosophers, in that of Jean-Paul Sartre.[24] And it is clear that Souriau takes this point of view as his own. The reader who takes up a book on "the aesthetics of movement" might expect to read about the conditions in which we are pleased by the sight of things in motion. It comes as a surprise to find that we begin by considering the conditions in which we find beauty and take pleasure in the movements of our own bodies, and end by making that pleasure a fundamental factor in the appreciation of beauty in observed movements. But in using this approach Souriau has been true to one of the most characteristic standpoints of French philosophy.

It should by now be clear that Paul Souriau's *Aesthetics of Movement* can be located at the intersection of a number of the most vital tendencies in the thought of its place and time, even though most of those tendencies now belong to our formation rather than to the content of our consciousness. The nineteenth century was the century of revolution in all fields of thought and practice, the century in which our familiar world was made. We defend ourselves from it by derision, when we can, and it is hard for the layman like myself to get a clear and comprehensive picture of all the transformations that were taking place. That is not surprising, for everything was happening at once. But the result is that the foregoing remarks on the background and context of Souriau's work are to be taken as merely suggestive. They are offered in sincere and inadequate homage to a subtle mind and an endearing personality. What other professor of philosophy would appeal so confidently to his reader's experience of what it is like to rush down a wooded hillside at breakneck speed?

## Notes

1   Raymond Bayer, *Histoire de l'esthétique* (Paris: Armand Colin, 1961); *L'Esthétique mondiale au XX^e siècle* (Paris: Presses Universitaires de France, 1961). Bayer's reason for singling out *La beauté rationelle* may be no more than that its title suggests that it is the least specialized of Souriau's works.

2   Francis Hutcheson, *Inquiry Into the Originals of Our Ideals of Beauty and Virtue* (1725; 4th ed., London: D. Midwinter and others, 1738); Herbert Spencer, "Gracefulness" (1852), in his *Essays: Scientific, Political and Speculative* (London: Williams and Norgate, 1901).

3   The unsympathetic article on Cohen (1842–1918) by Julius Ebbinghaus in Paul Edwards's *Encyclopedia of Philosophy* (New York: Macmillan, 1967),

2:125–28, expatiates on the folly of the attempts, fashionable at the time, to achieve scientific objectivity in philosophy by psychologizing Kant. Cohen's neo-Kantianism was first presented in his *Kants Theorie der Erfahrung* (Berlin: Dümmler, 1871).

4  Ted Shawn, *Every Little Movement* (2d ed., 1963; reprint ed., New York: Dance Horizons, 1968), p. 61. My knowledge of Delsarte is almost all derived from Shawn: if he errs, I err.

5  C. W. Hackensmith, *History of Physical Education* (New York: Harper and Row, 1966), p. 135.

6  E. J. Marey, *La machine animale* (Paris: G. Baillière, 1873), translated as *Animal Mechanism* (New York: D. Appleton and Co., 1874). Notice how promptly the anonymous translation appeared.

7  J. Bell Pettigrew, *Animal Locomotion: Or Walking, Swimming and Flying, With a Dissertation on Aëronautics* (1873; 4th ed., London: Kegan Paul, Trench, Trübner and Co., 1891). "The observations and experiments recorded in the present volume date from 1864" (p. 15). Marey speaks of Pettigrew's work with supercilious derision (*Animal Mechanism*, pp. 210–11), which is understandable in view of the fact that Pettigrew had squabbled with him about who first published what, but unfortunate because he ludicrously misrepresents Pettigrew's argument. What was needed to settle the issue between them was, precisely, photographs of the sort that Muybridge was about to take, and it was in fact at Marey's request that Muybridge began to photograph birds in flight in 1878. See Anita Ventura Mozley's introduction to Eadweard Muybridge, *Complete Human and Animal Locomotion* (New York: Dover Publications, 1977), p. xxxii; the plates in question are nos. 755–71.

8  Mozley's introduction to *Complete Human and Animal Locomotion*, pp. xi–xxii.

9  Mozley quotes Muybridge as writing: "Artists' models are ignorant and not well bred. As a consequence their movements are not graceful, and it is essential for the thorough execution of my work to have models of a graceful bearing" (ibid., p. xxxi). Some of Muybridge's sequences involving nude women are distinctly arty: it is hard to believe that the starting position of plate 226, "Removing a water jar from shoulder to the ground and turning," is not directly derived from the pose of J. D. Ingres's *La Source*, famous since its completion in 1856 (see also plates 225, 235).

10  I rely here on Hackensmith, as cited in n. 5, and on Emett A. Rice, John L. Hutchinson, and Mabel Lee, *Brief History of Physical Education,* 5th ed. (New York: Ronald Press, 1969).

11  Here I rely on C. G. Renold's candid article contributed to the twelfth edition of *Encyclopaedia Britannica* (1920), 32:378–81. *Differential Piece Rate* does not figure in library catalogs. Taylor's standard work was *The Principles of Scientific Management* (New York: Harper and Brothers, 1911).

12  Jacques de Vaucanson (1709–1782) started the vogue for elaborate automata by works he exhibited just before 1740.

13  See, for instance, Walter Gropius, *The Scope of Total Architecture* (New York: Harper Brothers, 1955).

14  For the Great Exhibition, see Leonardo Benevolo, *History of Modern Architecture* (Cambridge, Mass.: MIT Press, 1971), chap. 6, with references to the work of Horace Cole; and, more generally, Siegfried Giedion, *Mechanization Takes Command* (New York: Oxford University Press, 1948). The discrepancy between theory and practice in design at the time of the exhibition is exemplified in Charles Locke Eastlake, *Hints on Household Taste in Furniture, Upholstery, and Other Details* (London: Longmans, Green and Co., 1868).

15  Eugène-Emmanuel Viollet-le-Duc, *Entretiens sur l'architecture* (Paris: A. Morel, 1863–1872). See Benevolo, *History of Modern Architecture*, p. 95.

16  G. T. Fechner, *Vorschule der Ästhetik* (Leipzig: Breitkopf und Härtel, 1876); Theodor Lipps, *Raumästhetik und geometrisch-optische Taüschungen* (Leipzig: J. A. Barth, 1897).

17  For a general work on aesthetics typical of this approach, see Max Dessoir, *Ästhetik und allgemeine Kunstwissenschaft* (Stuttgart: Ferdinand Enke Verlag, 1906). The second edition (1923) was translated by Stephen A. Emery as *Aesthetics and Theory of Art* (Detroit: Wayne State University Press, 1970).

18  See Nicholas Pastore, *Selective History of Theories of Visual Perception, 1650–1950* (New York: Oxford University Press, 1971); and, for the significance of the retinal image, Colin Murray Turbayne, *The Myth of Metaphor* (New Haven: Yale University Press, 1962).

19  Ferdinand de Saussure, *Cours de linguistique générale* (Lausanne: Payot,

1916), translated by Wade Baskin as *Course in General Linguistics* (New York: Philosophical Library, 1959).

20   Gaston Bachelard, *La psychanalyse du feu* (Paris: Gallimard, 1938), translated by Alan C. M. Ross as *The Psychoanalysis of Fire* (Boston: Beacon Press, 1964), and a number of other works in the same vein; on perfume, Edmond Roudnitska, *L'Esthétique en question* (Paris: Presses Universitaires de France, 1977), with a preface, incidentally, by Paul Souriau's famous son Etienne.

21   See especially Claude Lévi-Strauss, *La voie des masques* (Paris: Plon, 1979), translated by Sylvia Modelski as *The Way of the Masks* (Seattle: University of Washington Press, 1982), in which it is more than usually evident that what is presented as a scientific analysis of a set of symbolic equivalences is essentially the exploration of a range of sensibility.

22   Gabriel Madinier, *Conscience et mouvement* (1938; 2d ed., Louvain: Nauwelaerts, 1967).

23   Alexander Bain, *Senses and the Intellect* (London: Parker, 1855), p. 367. Bain here refers specifically to *muscular* effort—that is, his approach is naturalistic and not empiricist at heart.

24   Maurice Merleau-Ponty, *La structure du comportement* (Paris: Presses Universitaires de France, 1942), translated by Alden L. Fisher as *The Structure of Behavior* (Boston: Beacon Press, 1963); Jean-Paul Sartre, *L'Être et le néant* (Paris: Gallimard, 1943), translated by Hazel Barnes as *Being and Nothingness* (New York: Philosophical Library, 1956), pt. 3, chap. 2. The effect of Sartre's denial of a "transcendental ego" is to make corporeality a necessary aspect of our knowledge of the world as a world.

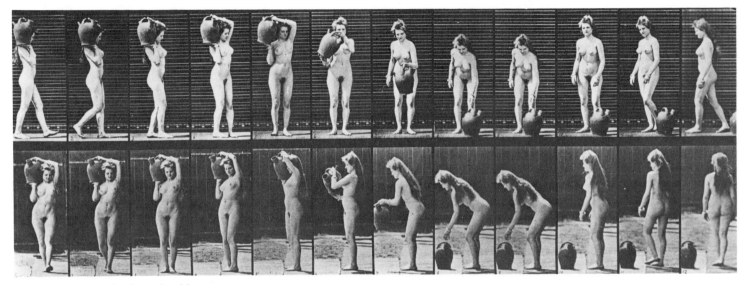

*Woman removing jar from shoulder*

## Translator's Introduction

In *The Aesthetics of Movement*, Paul Souriau proposes a theory of objective aesthetics. To those who would confine aesthetics to subjective judgments and purely affective impressions, he declared: "Physicists are not required to speak heatedly about heat."

Souriau sought to define the beauty of the arts by understanding them scientifically. In deciding to investigate movement, Souriau probably betrayed a personal predilection for the spectacle of bodies in motion. By offering an aesthetic methodology to an art that he felt was still "inferior"—he may have meant in its infancy—Souriau seems to have attempted to put movement on a level with the other arts.

Paul Souriau was a notable exponent of the French movement of aesthetics of the late nineteenth century. Continuing the line, his son Etienne (1892–1979) became professor of aesthetics at the Sorbonne and was founder of the Société française d'esthétique, as well as cofounder of the *Revue d'esthétique*.

Born in Douai in 1852, Paul Souriau taught philosophy at the lycées of Pau, then Angers. With his thesis on Invention, he obtained a doctorate in Lettres and was named professor at the University of Aix-en-Provence, then at Lille, and, finally, in 1893, at the University of Nancy, where he spent the greatest part of his career. Later, he became dean of the Faculté des Lettres and was correspondent of the Institut de France.

The body of his philosophical work includes: *Théorie de l'invention* (Paris: Hachette, 1881); *L'esthétique du mouve-ment* (Paris: Alcan, 1889); *La suggestion dans l'art* (Paris: Alcan, 1893); *L'imagination de l'artiste* (Paris: Hachette, 1901); *La beauté rationelle* (Paris: Alcan, 1904); *La rêverie esthétique* (Paris: Alcan, 1906); *Les conditions du bonheur* (Paris: Armand Colin, 1908); *L'esthétique de la lumière* (Paris: Hachette, 1913); *L'entraînement au courage* (Paris: Alcan, 1926).

As deputy mayor of Nancy he faced heavy responsibilities, especially during World War I. In his last years, he became professor emeritus and continued to write until his death in 1926. Beside his work on philosophical subjects, Paul Souriau wrote two plays concerned with social themes, *Le prévot de Bruges* and *Le mariage d'Élise, ou Les filles de fabrique,* and numerous books for children (*Le veilleur du lycée, Les crinières blanches, Les deux vagabonds, La plume noire*). Souriau was also an amateur artist. His letters were strewn with sketches of people and things, and the line drawings throughout the book are his own.

The photographs of Eadweard Muybridge, unique to this English-language edition, add a new dimension to the book. Muybridge was one of the pioneers—in France, Jules Marey, author of *Animal Mechanism*, was another—who effected a breakthrough after centuries of efforts by artists and scientists (since Leonardo) to visualize and represent the phases of movement that lie beyond human perception. Souriau, younger than Muybridge by some twenty years, was familiar with his work and cites him several times in the book.

Born Edward Muggeridge in England in 1830, by the 1860s Eadweard Muybridge was established in California as a well-known photographer. His experiments with the photography of movement began in 1872, when Leland Stanford, former governor of California, commissioned him to photograph his racehorse, Occident, to determine whether all four feet came off the ground at any point of his trot. This led to a collaboration between them at Stanford's Palo Alto estate, with Stanford providing the funds and Muybridge the technology. In order to take sequential action pictures, Muybridge used a battery of twenty-four cameras. The horse tripped a thread that triggered the shutters. Later, having broken with Stanford, Muybridge continued his work at the University of Pennsylvania. By 1885 he had accumulated some 100,000 photographs, not only of horses but also of domestic and wild animals, and, especially at Pennsylvania, of human beings in various activities.

Muybridge began lecturing in the United States, and later toured Europe, where he attracted great attention. To illustrate his lectures, he developed the zoopraxiscope that combined a projection lantern and rotating glass disks on which transparencies made from his sequential photographs were mounted, giving, when activated, the effect of movement. This was, in essence, one of the early motion-picture projectors. The eleven volumes of *Animal Locomotion* were published in 1887. They comprised 871 plates, each with twelve to thirty-six photographs. A less expensive selection appeared as *Animals in Motion* (1899) and *The Human Figure in Motion* (1901). Muybridge's photographs illustrate so vividly what Souriau put into words that one might think the two men had collaborated on this work. The photographs are reproduced by kind permission of Thomas J. Watson Library, the Metropolitan Museum of Art, New York City, and the Print Department, Smith College Museum of Art.

# Author's Introduction

In scientific research, the fastest way to reach one's goal is to take plenty of time. Aesthetics has long imagined it could solve the problems of beauty all at once, by a concentrated effort of thought. What has it accomplished? In what way have its dissertations on beauty served taste, not to mention art? By going too fast, it did not come one step nearer a solution.

A wild rose, the Cathedral of Notre-Dame, the Prelude of *Lohengrin* are beautiful things. But try to analyze such diverse objects until you have extracted the common element that must be there, since they awaken in you, no matter to what degree, an identical feeling of admiration. You cannot. That subtle essence of beauty that must permeate all beautiful objects escapes you and nobody has yet succeeded in isolating it. Is it even certain that there is such a thing as beauty per se, always identical to itself? Are we sure, for instance, that musical beauty has nothing in common with plastic beauty? It is possible that in aesthetics the various art forms constitute irreducible categories for which no common denominator can be found. But if, eventually, universal principles can be set forth, it will not be until exhaustive research into each art has been made. At this time, no treatise on general aesthetics can be written; we are still in the era of monographs.

Neither can we be too ambitious in this last area. Before we pry into the secret of nature's marvels or of art's masterpieces, we must first ask the most elementary questions. Rather than studying the sense of beauty in its highest forms, let us first investigate its simplest, earliest manifestations. There are many things in a Beethoven symphony; before explicating each one, tell me first why certain sounds give me pleasure, while others jar my ears. I would certainly like to know where the strange charm of this Veronese comes from; but I will never find out if I do not understand why green harmonizes well with red but very poorly with purple. These are not metaphysical questions, but questions of physics and physiology. We can no longer isolate ourselves; we must learn about the latest scientific research, accumulate detailed observations and, if possible, experiments. We will then solve the problem progressively and our speculations will rest on a solid base. This is what aestheticians are beginning to do.

These are the ideas that have guided me in the present book. I have chosen a very special subject that is usually touched on only briefly in works of aesthetics. It is unquestionable that under certain conditions the sight of bodies in motion gives us aesthetic pleasure; and we are not content with enjoying this kind of spectacle when nature chances to provide it; we also seek its display; we try to bring harmony and rhythm into our own movements. There is, therefore, a specific art whose objective is to give movement an aesthetic expression. Could not our judgments of taste, now abandoned to the whims of our feelings, be reduced to more fundamental principles? Can we not erect a methodology around this art, still inferior because it is quite empirical? I have, therefore, attempted to examine the subject again, in a scientific rather than a philosophical spirit. The question seemed basic enough at first, but, as I delved further into it, it became so complex that, after all is said and done, I have but skimmed the surface. One can draw many interesting parallels by applying the laws of motion to the arts of drawing, acting, dance, music, or even poetry, in which rhythm and, therefore, movement play such an important role. But I had to limit myself to laying a few footstones to the edifice.

The work has been divided into four parts. In the first, I have examined *the determination of movement*, that is, the physical and mental laws according to which we have a tendency to move one way rather than another. It is evidently the first question to address. When a man or any creature takes an attitude or makes any kind of movement, it is not usually to show himself off. Movements that are the substance of our judgments of taste are subject to these judgments only ultimately. It is logical, therefore, to study the movements themselves before seeking to understand their effect on the spectator. In fact, that is the only way to proceed. Before judging and especially correcting nature, we must learn to know it. It follows, therefore, that our aesthetics must be based on the knowledge of those movements that are the most natural to us.

Once that is done, we can study the conditions required for a movement to have an aesthetic value. To me, these number three: the mechanical beauty of movement, its expression, and the perceptible pleasure it gives. We will discuss them separately, beginning with that which offers the greatest objectivity, namely, *mechanical beauty,* or the exact adaptation of a movement to its end. The sight of a well-executed movement gives me real aesthetic pleasure, but it is intellectual, based on pure concepts; for we do not judge this movement by the effect it may have on our sensitivity, but for its intrinsic value, perceived by reason alone. In that connection, we will mention possible applications of our theory to the art of motion. Then, to provide an authentic example of judgments of taste founded on purely mechanical considerations, we will analyze the principle processes of animal locomotion.

There follows a discussion on *the expression of movement*. Here, we venture on less solid ground, for we have to find out to what extent we react to the emotions of a person executing a movement when we view it and what influence this empathy may have on our judgments. We will, therefore, consider the expression of ease in movement—namely, grace; the expression of force; and the expression of feelings. It is impossible to say whether or not judgments thus made have an objective or a subjective value. In fact, these judgments are relative and depend on what happens inside as well as outside us, since we try to envision, by the pleasure we experience in viewing a movement, the pleasure one has executing it. According to circumstances, these judgments will be more or less representative of reality. At times they have an almost scientific value and, at others, we have to acknowledge they are pure illusion. In any case, they are essentially distinct from those based on purely mechanical considerations and it is necessary to study them separately to determine, as well as possible, the principles underlying this special art. In this section, we will sometimes have to return to considerations discussed in Part 1, since we are examining the same things from a different point of view. In any case, the plan of our inquiry has to remain somewhat flexible. We cannot completely ignore, for instance, the effect that the viewing of movement has on a spectator, because the idea of what it looks like must have some influence on its execution. In such complex matters, one has a right to digress, though I have tried to follow my itinerary as nearly as I could.

Finally, we will examine *the perception of movement*, dwelling on visual perceptions that play the greater role in our judgments. Here we can consider a movement only by its appearance, as a more or less agreeable play of images and sensations;

we judge it solely by the superficial, momentary effect it has on our senses and imagination. It no longer has an objectivity. A perception pleases me, another does not, because that is the way my senses are organized. If they were organized differently, this entire aesthetics would have to be torn down and rebuilt. However, such as they are, these judgments have an influence on our taste. Whatever the value of appearances, one cannot deny the existence of a special art that proposes to produce those judgments.

Such is the plan to which I will try to adhere as closely as possible. My purpose is not to create a work of literary value or stray into subtle analyses of a debatable nature. I am concerned with substance far more than with form. My first aim is to determine which among our judgments of taste rest on a solid foundation; to pose the principles of aesthetics I would like to see established; and, above all, to show it is possible to found an art on a scientific, rational base. Beyond that, we have no choice but to enter those nebulous regions where taste considers things by their superficial appearance and our judgments are determined by nuances of feeling and impressions. If the reader hesitates to follow me through the minutiae of these analyses, little harm will come of it, for my work will be done.

# I   The Determination of Movement

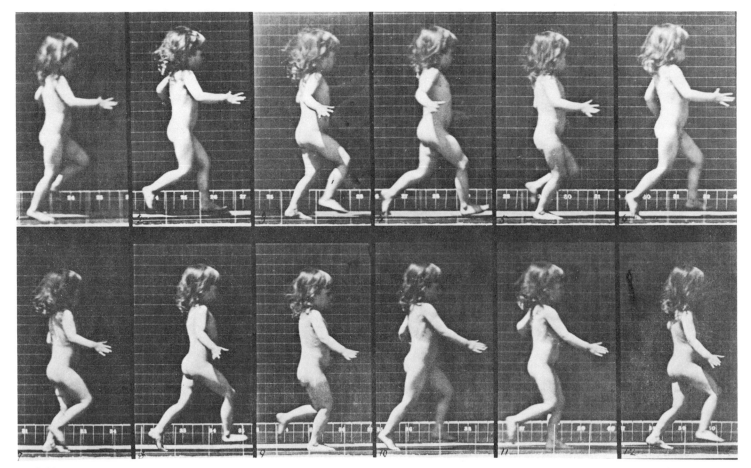

*Child running*

# 1   The Pleasure of Movement

It is evident that the movements of an animal are determined above all by its organic structure. Each of its limbs, according to the arrangement of the bones which support and the muscles which activate it, is capable of executing only a certain range of movements. And, according to its species, each animal is consigned to determined stances, gestures, gaits. Thus, anyone concerned, whether from an artistic or a scientific point of view, with the kinetics of the higher forms of life must start by considering the workings of the animal machine.

But anatomy indicates only the diverse kinds of movements we can execute. Alone, it cannot explain the play of life in creatures who feel, who think, who wish, who are not merely complying to mechanical agents. When one sees the way a watch is put together, one realizes at once how it works. A mechanic only needs to take an automaton apart to know what range of movements are available to it. But for the animal, mechanical factors are complicated by psychological determinants that can be just as constraining and certainly more delicate and of another order. These will be our main concern.

## The Physical Pleasure of Movement

Before it is a source of positive pleasure, our physical activity is stimulated by pain. It is always in some vague discomfort that one finds the explanation of these so-called spontaneous movements that are, in the child and the young animal, the first signs of vitality. Even those organs that function automatically and

whose workings seem wholly mechanical because they operate outside our awareness can have their local sensitivity, which determines the rhythm of their movements.

Against pain, movement is the best anesthetic. It dispels, at the moment they call themselves to our attention, even those small discomforts that accompany the normal functioning of our organs. When we make an energetic effort, we are, as long as it lasts, almost insensitive to pain. When we are standing still, a blow on the shoulder will hurt. In the throes of a game, the sharpest impact will hardly be felt. It is very likely that if we were to study our reactions to a given sensation while we were pressing on a dynamometer, the intensity of the perceptible reaction would be found to decrease in proportion to the pressure applied. We all know that an overacute sensation produces sharp muscular contractions resulting in convulsive movements. These movements are not an automatic response to the sensation. They are made not so much to dispel the cause of the hurt as to soften its effect. The convolutions of a worm that has been cut in two are of the same order as the howlings of a dog that has been hit.

But if the same discomfort is experienced frequently, the animal will notice that some of these disorganized movements contribute more than others to the relief of the pain, and it will come to prefer those movements. The reaction to a given pain by a given movement becomes a habit. In accordance with the general laws of evolution, a natural selection among reflex actions will establish itself and the useful ones will eventually predominate.

Beyond responding to pain, we move because we need to move. Every animal must consume each day a varying amount of energy to provide food for itself. The oyster clinging to its rock assimilates without effort, and passively so to speak, the vegetable residues that the wave brings. The slug, crawling slowly on its belly, eats with ease the leaves within its reach. The steer walks step by step through a field for hours at a time, grazing the grass it encounters. The wolf runs for miles every day looking for its prey. The swallow must fly unceasingly to obtain enough insects to satisfy its appetite. In addition to eating, animals also need to escape from their enemies and this requires an increase in activity. Each species, therefore, has a need to move every day to a greater or lesser degree and is organized toward that end.

If, as a result of changed circumstances, this activity becomes useless, the animal will nonetheless be compelled to move, since its physical constitution, adapted by heredity to the normal life of its species, cannot suddenly be bent to new living conditions. Organic functions continue to supply it with the same amount of energy and it must, in some way, use up this energy. Thus, the caged lion paces back and forth, the finch jumps from perch to perch. Thus also people who lead sedentary lives take pleasure in physical exercise. This need for movement is especially great in youth, because the young animal must practice all the movements it will have to execute later, as well as develop its muscles and joints. Every animal tends to expend a daily output of strength determined by the general needs of the species rather than by the chance needs of the individual.

But how is this output regulated? What makes us recognize that we need exercise? Something as indispensable to the good functioning of our organism cannot be the result of reasoning. It is evident that, in their activities, animals are not submitting themselves to a regimen, like the man who imposes on himself a daily walk ("une petite promenade hygiénique"). Though man's intelligence allows him to satisfy his physiological exigencies in a more rational way, it is not his intelligence that makes him aware of them. What would become of the most reasonable person if reason alone determined needs? It follows that one must be alerted to them by specific sensations.

Some get away cheaply with an explanation of the mechanism of physiological determinism by implying that we are directly conscious of our strength. If so, it would be very simple: when we are inactive, energy accumulates within us, resulting in a painful sensation of nervous tension which prompts us to use up the excess by some kind of activity. At first, this gives us some relief. Then, once our reserves are spent, we feel our strength failing and the need to rest returns. There is no harm in theorizing thus if we wish only to point out a relationship between our muscular sensations and the dynamic condition of our muscles. But we must avoid thinking we have here even the shadow of an explanation of what determines our movement needs.

What happens within us, during a period of rest, when our energy is accumulating? Our muscles are restored and are ready again to form new chemical combinations. But at no time are we conscious of the potential energy made available. We feel it no more than we do the potential heat in a piece of coal. The anticipatory feeling we have, which is taken for the consciousness of the energy we are about to expend in making a movement, is only a sensing of the effort that will accompany the muscular contraction. More than that: even at the instant the contraction occurs, we feel only the amount of tension in our muscles. This corresponds very little to the real amount of energy we expend. Indeed, if we merely flex our biceps we will be using as much energy as we would in lifting an object. To understand how we recognize our kinetic requirements, we must go beyond conventional rationales.

What do we feel when we have held still too long? Like appetite, the need to move is recognized by the effect of that need on our imagination. If we suddenly get hungry or thirsty, we do not think specifically: "How pleasant it would be to eat or drink!" but "How delicious a golden roast chicken or a foaming mug of beer would be!" Likewise, the youth cooped up indoors too long pictures himself playing tennis or canoeing, but he does not tell himself that it would be good for him to do his favorite sport. As this desire shapes itself, it becomes sharper and, if unrewarded, unbearable.

At the same time, physiological phenomena appear, increasing the discomfort. In the period of rest during which the muscle is being nourished and regenerated, the products of combustion, that is, the molecules that have formed stable combinations, are eliminated and replaced by fresh fuel, or unstable combinations. The muscle is then in what can be called a state of sensitivity. The least spark will cause an explosion, the slightest impression provoke violent reflexes. In this hypersensitive state, an effort is needed to control the spontaneous movements induced by the very idea of moving. Typical of this discomfort from enforced immobility is the schoolboy waiting for the end of the class. His back is aching, his legs feel heavy. When will the bell ring? He feels a compelling, increasing desire to jump from his seat. He wriggles, shuffles on the floor. A severe look from the teacher nails him to the seat. He sits still, but what torture!

Movement also gives positive physical pleasure. When we take part in an activity in which we put a lot of energy, all our functions are accelerated, our hearts beat faster, we breathe faster and deeper, and we get a general feeling of well-being. We are living more and feel happy to be alive.

Rapid movements even make us feel a kind of giddiness which has a fascination of its own. We abandon ourselves to the whirl of a waltz as we do to the swoop of a roller coaster. We follow the impetus and let ourselves go without restraint, with a certain disregard for ourselves. This is an essential element of the sensations we get from innumerable fast movements. They make us lose our self-control. Among children this need for fast motion is manifest at a very early age.

### The Psychological Pleasure of Movement

Just as it helps us escape physical pain, muscular activity can serve as an antidote for emotional distress. In grief, we cry out and thrash about. Even deep sorrow can be momentarily forgotten in physical acivity. When his mother was being buried, Byron had a servant bring him a pair of boxing gloves and began boxing with him as usual. But the servant noticed that he was hitting harder than his wont. Suddenly, Byron threw down his gloves and ran into his room. Who has not felt this need to shake off grief, to pace back and forth in order to forget an emotional hurt? Immobility tends to turn our minds upon ourselves and this very concentration increases our suffering. In action, we forget ourselves and think only of the goal we have set.

Exercise also gives us a positive satisfaction, notably in the feeling of achievement, which predominates. When I practice a movement or execute a feat with my body, I want to do it as well as I can. I even want to do it better than others. And when I

succeed, I have a feeling of pride. This drives me on with renewed ardor, sometimes to outstanding physical effort. Tell a
child to run as long as she can. She will soon stop, out of breath.
Give her competitors: the fear of being left behind will bring
out unexpected resources and keep her from feeling tired. She
will run to exhaustion. The emulation of competition has
pushed her to use every ounce of available energy. This rule is
known to all competitive runners, swimmers, and racers. One
never trains alone for activities involving speed. There have to
be at least two to create competition and mutual emulation.

Some have attempted—I do not know why—to establish
that play should be disinterested.[1] One might as well ignore the
meaning of speech. When we speak, we are always preoccupied
with communication. When we play, we are always preoccupied with the score. We may not be too demanding as to the
outcome; we may or may not question whether the effort is
worth it. But we do not want to exert our faculties in a void. We
set ourselves a goal. If I take a walk, I will say to myself that I
wish to go so far or to go here or there. If I play a game of skill,
I want to beat my opponent, or get a certain number of points,
or hit a given target. I am not, therefore, only seeking the pleasure of the activity. I wish to obtain a result that is agreeable
in itself. Games of chance would have no attraction if the playing were not more or less biased. We sometimes play for material or financial gain, most often for the honor of winning. But
is one really disinterested when working for the glory of the
thing? The hunter likes to hunt, not only for the pleasure of
walking through the fields after a hare, not only for the pleasure of bringing it home, but mostly for the proud joy of display-
ing his catch. The end, one might say, is evidently not worth the
trouble. But who cares? While I am doing my best to reach my

goal, I no longer measure its importance, I no longer think of
the reasons that first drew me to this trial. This is the goal I have
set for myself and I am going for it. If I think for a moment that
this goal is trivial, that is only a pretext, my ardor will cool.

It follows, therefore, that in any game or exercise, we always
make an effort to exaggerate the importance of our intention.
The player's hand trembles when he makes a decisive move in a
game of chess. A canoe navigates toward distant lands. A walk
in the forest becomes an exploration. In such ways, we satisfy
the spirit of adventure not completely stamped out by an overly
organized society.

It is, then, essential to the enjoyment of play that we build up
fantasies, that we imagine that this thing we are doing on a
small scale is being done on a larger one. We must substitute for
the trivial some larger motive for the activity in which we are
absorbed.

I may be deliberately deluding myself. I may only be half
fooled by the pretext I give myself. The fact remains that the
pleasure of activity for its own sake is not sufficient and that
I take interest in the game only to the degree that my pride is
involved. We congratulate ourselves for having bettered our
skill, we feel the urge to boast of our exploits. We would take
less pleasure in a game of skill if we did not realize and make
others realize after each game that we have become more dex-

---

1   See Immanuel Kant, *Critique of Aesthetic Judgment*, trans. James Meredith
(Oxford: Clarendon Press, 1911); Friedrich von Schiller, *Aesthetical Letters
and Essays* (Boston: Aldine, 1910); Herbert Spencer, *Principles of Psychology*
(New York: Appleton, 1861); Elie Rabier, *Leçons de philosophie* (Paris:
Hachette, 1903). Note that, throughout this book, reference sources have
been updated and, whenever possible, English language translations have been
substituted—Ed.

terous. Any activity in which we become past master has the danger of becoming tedious.

One can also observe in any physical activity a particular kind of pride, naïve and childish perhaps, yet all the deeper and more instinctive, in overcoming the forces of nature. Let nature but invite me to do something and I will refuse. Let it seem to forbid me and I will go ahead, from a spirit of contradiction or even rebellion. Thence the pleasure of climbing a slope, of pushing aside an obstacle, of clearing a ditch, of walking against a strong wind. On a sailboat, it is more fun to bear into the wind than to run with it, to run over the waves than to fly away from them.

But of all the forces of nature that we consider hostile and take pleasure in overcoming, gravity is the one that offers the most challenge and the one that we will fight in all our activities with the greatest obstinacy. Because of gravity, our bodies are a burden that nothing will relieve. In our fight against gravity, falling is a defeat; balance, a defense; the mere transference of weight is the beginning of liberation; ascension is a triumph. Why does one envy the bird its wings? Because, to us, flight seems the greatest victory over inertia and gravity, a real emancipation over matter. Man's very dreams reflect these aspirations constantly. What is the punishment of the wicked, of the impious, of Satan but the fall into the depths of the abyss? And what the reward of the elect but the glorious ascent into heaven?

Man thinks instinctively that, among the rules that govern him, the law of gravity, which weighs on the whole material world, is the most rigorous. If we have no power to swerve in the least from the direction in which the laws of mechanics take us, what does the freedom to which we aspire mean? We may be a mote in the universe, but at least we want this mote to have some independent movement, its own spontaneous and personal gravitation. Is this hope absurd? If man's movements are more complicated, are they freer than those of a grain of dust floating in a ray of sunshine? We have no answer to this, because the concept of freedom is one of the most hopeless in philosophy. Meanwhile, since doubt remains, we can take advantage of it and keep our illusions. Even if we are to be conquered by the blind forces of nature, it is already something to have struggled and fought. Such action has a value in itself that total fatalism cannot take away: it is a striving toward liberty and the beginning of psychological emancipation.

## 2   The Pain of Effort

The pleasure of movement, which prompts us to expend imme-diately all the energy we have available for that movement, is counterbalanced by the pain of effort.

To move a large stone, lift a finger, or execute any movement at all, we have to make an effort. Objectively, this effort con-sists in a certain expenditure of energy; subjectively, it is mani-fested in our consciousness by specific sensations, some of which are caused by the contact with the bodies on which we act, others by the contraction of our muscles, and yet others, by the volitional factor in the movement. We will study them in that order, which is the order in which we observe them, rather than how they occur.

It is extremely rare that movements should not be accompa-nied by some sensation of touch. When I walk, I feel the pres-sure of my foot on the ground, the binding of my shoe, the contact of my clothes. When I lift a weight, I feel its pressure on my hand and shoulder. Even when my movements do not put me in contact with any object, as for instance when I grimace, they still give me some epidermic sensations: I feel my skin stretching, relaxing, puckering. These contacts can be very strenuous, even painful, as in giving or receiving blows. I can see almost no instances when they can be agreeable in them-selves. Touch is above all a defensive sense, which serves to pre-serve us from harmful contacts. Its sensations are avoided rather than sought. Cast your mind on those objects that are deemed agreeable to the touch: it will be those with surfaces without asperities, that are smooth, elastic, in other words,

those that offer the least epidermic sensations.

Another class of sensations, usually less vivid but still easy to recognize, is those made by the contractions of our muscles: when we make an effort, we feel them swell, harden, vibrate. Physically, this contraction consists less in the muscle's short-ening than in its vibratory condition, for the strongest efforts are sometimes accompanied by the lengthening of the muscle. When the muscular fibers are contracted, waves of swelling travel at a regular pace from one extremity of the fiber to the other, following one another at a greater or lesser speed, ac-cording to the strength of the innervation. If we produce an iso-lated wave with the aid of electricity or some other local stimu-lant, we feel a jolt. But when the jolts succeed one another fast enough, we cease to be aware of them and we feel only a perma-nent sensation, though, in fact, the muscle maintains a percep-tible vibratory movement. To isolate this sensation from the preceding ones, one need only contract at the same time the antagonistic muscles in the arm or the fingers. There is then no exterior resistance, yet the sensation of effort is strongly in-creased. Some people, especially those whose muscular appa-ratus is not greatly developed, find it difficult to accomplish this experiment. They will then have to isolate the sensation of ef-fort through attention alone, by doing movements that de-mand a great deal of energy but avoid contact with overly hard objects.

Finally, under the heading of volition, I will assemble all the sensations that have to do with the cerebral work that necessar-ily precedes the execution of a volitional movement: an effort is needed for us to prepare a movement in our imagination, to determine us to execute it, and to maintain the muscle in con-traction. Physically, this effort corresponds to a certain expenditure of energy, for only the movement of a mass can have action on other masses. But physical effort, if never absent, can be infinitesimal. All that is needed, especially when the muscles are in a state of sensitivity, is an almost insignificant force of innervation to contract them. In this state, they can be compared to a pyramid poised on its tip, subject to falling on one side or the other at the least impulse; or to an unstable mixture of chlorine and hydrogen, whose balance will be instantly destroyed by the projection of a single ray of light. The mental effort that precedes our volitional movements is therefore in no way proportional to the force it costs us. Remember an occasion when you had to make a serious decision or mail a decisive letter and you will understand clearly the amount of effort required to contract a small muscle, far beyond the muscular contraction itself.

Looking over what I just said, you will perceive that each of the sensations examined was, in itself, of a more or less disagreeable character. It follows that effort, which is only the complex state of consciousness resulting from these various sensations, is in itself essentially disagreeable.

Furthermore, we have considered only movements that are of medium energy, isolated, and of short duration. If the efforts become greater, longer, or repetitive, the sensation will not only become more unpleasant, but it will be complicated by auxiliary sensations that will greatly exaggerate it, and mere discomfort may become actual pain.

Press your two fists together with all your strength: as the sensation of effort becomes painfully intense, you feel in your breathing a sensation of anguish and suffocation, because you are obliged to suspend the action of your lungs to take support on your thoracic cage. Any movement that forces us to make an effort in the lower torso or in the arms will cause this additional discomfort and I cannot think of a movement of any force that does not involve the whole body.

Another simple experiment will demonstrate what sensations will be produced by a prolonged contraction of the muscles. Let me extend my arm to the side as long as possible. First, I have only a slight sensation of effort, so generalized that I hardly know if it is agreeable or disagreeable; and it seems to me that I could stay in this position indefinitely. But after a while, waves of sensation pervade my arm, probably because I am studying its reactions and my various local efforts are magnified by the attention I am directing on them. Fatigue nears. Abnormal phenomena occur. First, my fingers become tense and I cannot keep them still without special concentration. My arm feels heavy and stiff, the joint locked. My shoulder and neck feel distended. Finally my arm begins to tremble. The muscular vibrations, no longer frequent enough to produce a permanent contraction, become perceptible; and the effort I must make to suppress these oscillations by contracting the antagonistic muscles only increases their rhythm. My arm drops and rises by fits and starts. It becomes unbearable. With a sigh of relief, I drop it. And for a few minutes more, it feels heavier than the other and numb.

When the muscle relaxes after a contraction, it repairs itself speedily. But if the contractions succeed one another at too short intervals, as in fast activities, or repeat one another too long, as in prolonged activities, the muscle will become tired and lose its ability to contract, until the least movement requires an excessive effort and becomes totally impossible. Even before muscle fatigue sets in, abnormal phenomena take place in our organism. The circulation quickens. The heart beats at an unusual speed. We feel our temples pulsing, our veins swelling, our lungs congesting. At the same time, our vasomotor nerves allow the capillary vessels to distend themselves, letting the blood rush through, our faces redden, and we perspire. But the most characteristic symptom as well as the most disagreeable one is what happens to our breathing. According to the observations of Lagrange, who has made an excellent analysis of all these phenomena, inhaling remains easy and deep, but exhaling becomes shorter, insufficient, giving the feeling of an unsatisfied need. This want of breath happens any time we expend too great an amount of energy in too short a time.[1]

We can therefore assert that effort always produces painful sensations and is the more painful as the expenditure of energy becomes greater. But there is not a movement that does not require some effort. Is it, then, always unpleasant to move? Does physical activity cause continuous discomfort, sometimes intense and sometimes dull, but never allowing a moment's respite? This would be a very pessimistic conclusion and in total contradiction to our statement about the pleasure of movement. Happily, both premises can be reconciled.

In the preceding chapter, we studied the benefits of movement. Muscular effort is its cost. If, in the final analysis, a movement brings us more pleasure than it costs in effort, we will find it, on the whole, agreeable.

The most agreeable movements are not, therefore, necessarily those that cost us the least effort but those that give us the most useful effect for the least effort. When we execute a given movement, we make a rapid calculation: we ask ourselves if it is worth the effort; and we only complain of the trouble we took if it is wasted.

It seems unpleasant to walk on soft, sinking sand, on ice, or on loose stones. Is it simply because we are forced to do something that is hard? No, for it would be much more tiring to climb a steep hill or to scale a rock, but that activity would not displease us. In those conditions, if walking is tiring, it is so morally rather than physically. We compare the efforts we make to those of the normal walk on solid ground, and we chafe at tiring ourselves with so little progress. Try to go a hundred yards by advancing three steps and retreating two, as some religious pilgrims are said to have done out of a spirit of penance: you will need a good dose of patience to finish. This is because, out of six steps you take, four are completely wasted; and that is exasperating. What is the meaning of Sisyphus's rock or the Danaïdes' jars full of holes if it is not that they represent the torture of wasted work?

On the other hand, there is delight when one can obtain more effective movement for the same amount of effort. That is what is fascinating about all gymnastic feats in which impetus is used to extend a movement with no extra effort.

Muscular effort is like money: we take pleasure in spending a lot on occasion, but for ordinary things we like to spend as little as possible. Thus are prodigality and economy reconciled. This analogy prevails even for certain whims: there are times when we like to throw money out of the window, out of bravado or in defiance of restrictions; in the same way, we sometimes like to waste our strength. And it is because we usually economize that we can allow ourselves occasional prodigalities.

Not only, then, can effort satisfy in spite of its painfulness,

1    Fernand Lagrange, *Physiology of Bodily Exercise* (New York: Appleton, 1890), p. 93.

but that same painfulness can itself be a source of satisfaction. That will be the pleasure of the least effort.

When a disagreeable sensation diminishes, our first reaction is to rejoice at this improvement: we forget the discomfort still present. To take an extreme example: when a man condemned to death sees his sentence commuted to life, he usually experiences an explosion of joy, when logically he should be only slightly less prostrate. If I have a violent toothache, the moment it abates, I feel a kind of hope which becomes happiness when it ceases altogether. Yet I no longer feel any sensation of any kind. It is therefore a totally mental pleasure, one of pure feeling.

It seems to me that the same thing pertains to effort. Muscular contractions in themselves never give actual pleasure; when the sensation of effort attenuates, however strenuous it may have been, it leads only to lessened discomfort; but the lessening of the raw sensation results in a distinct feeling of pleasure. It is the pleasure of diminishing movements, noted by Bain,[2] as well as the pleasure of alternate movements, in which the muscles rest by turns. If effort is agreeable at all, it is at the moment it ceases. Here are facts that tend to prove this. The delicious moment after a long, arduous ascent is when the summit is reached. The task you have imposed on yourself is over. With indescribable relief, you sit down, you eat, you drink, you look around. It is the expectation of this moment that sustained you during the climb and that is the one moment you will remember; you find it repays you amply for your fatigue. What is true of a long series of movements is as true of a simple one. The

pleasure of walking is mainly due to the periods of rest one takes. If there is any enjoyment, it is from the relaxing of the muscles, not from their contraction.

Are there cases when we seek effort for its own sake? That is possible: there are many cases where one likes to prick oneself, pinch oneself, hurt oneself! These are whims of the conscious mind. But surely these moments are exceptional, because underneath the unconscious is constantly endeavoring to avoid effort. I am quite sure that a careful search would always uncover something else, a pleasure unconnected with the effort, but provided by it. As complicated as the determinations of our consciousness are, they leave no room for such contradictions. The pleasure of pain is a pleasure bought by pain, or more simply an act, usually painful, which turns out to be peculiarly pleasant. Most often, however paradoxical this may seem, if we impose on ourselves an unpleasant sensation, it is in order to deliver ourselves from it. That is why, at the theater, one likes to be plunged into the most moving scenes in order to feel the relief of the happy ending. And, in music, the most irritating dissonances are sought for the harmony in which they are resolved.

This law of the least effort which appears to be based on laziness is, then, perfectly reconcilable with the pleasure of movement. In indolent, apathetic natures, it produces a tendency to inertia. Among most people, it is the best stimulant for activity.

In fact, most often it is not the immediate saving of effort that spares us the most fatigue; far from it. Take an example or two. It is the middle of the night. I am awakened by an unusual noise: the wind has risen and is banging the shutter against the wall. Another bang makes me impatient; will it continue long? Again! Really, this is unbearable! But I feel warm under my

2   Alexander Bain, *The Senses and the Intellect* (New York: Appleton, 1879), p. 86.

*Man starting a race*

bedclothes. It irks me to wake up fully and rise. Between these two evils, I choose the lesser one and arm myself with patience. Perhaps it will cease. Indeed, the noise stops. But here it is again! Exasperated, I leap out of bed, open the window, and secure the shutter. Frankly, would it not have been preferable to have done it right away? I had suspected I would have to go through with it. It would have cost me no more the first time than the last and I would have spared myself ten minutes of bad temper. There is also the story of the moneylender whose feudal lord called upon him to hand out a purseful of money or have six teeth pulled. Rather all his teeth out than give his purse! The operation begins. One tooth comes out, then another, and a third. At the fourth, he is writhing in pain. At the fifth, he gives his purse. Would he also not have been better off giving in at once? It is nearly always the same in the conduct of life. The lazy, who abandon themselves to the immediate least effort, lead the most tiring life of all and, in the end, give themselves much more trouble than do the energetic.

Energetic people do not let themselves go. They work, they fight. Because effort is unpleasant, they make the effort in order to liberate themselves from it. And they carry the effort to its maximum intensity in order to liberate themselves sooner.

In terms of physical movements, this explains to us the push off of the runner, the large wingbeats of the bird flying, the impetus of the horse taking off at a gallop to climb a slope. Ask a porter to carry a heavy trunk and he will accelerate his pace. When you go up several flights of stairs, you go faster as you feel yourself getting out of breath. When mountain climbers reach the summit, they never fail to end up in a run. For effort as for danger, there is such a thing as the *escape forward*.

Finally, the law of the least effort is also the best stimulant for mechanical ingenuity. It is because of this law that we instinctively attain perfection in movement. To move as much as possible with the least fatigue; to obtain the maximum result with the minimum effort; that is the fundamental law that regulates the development of all our activities, from the simplest locomotor movements to the most subtle manifestations of art.

Does this explain everything? By no means. To reduce the aesthetics of movement to this principle would be to establish an aesthetics of induction alone, which would go counter to my goal. I will, instead, return as much as possible to concrete reality. The only thing I wish to assert here is that it is the law of the least effort that plays the most considerable role in the determination of movement.

## 3  Laws of Attitude

It is easiest to study the laws of movement through the attitudes of our body, because motion is then arrested or sufficiently slowed down to permit accurate observation. That is, therefore, what we will examine first.

The attitude that demands the absolute least effort is that into which our limbs fall spontaneously when they are relaxed. What does this attitude consist of?

### The Law of Average Flexions

If all our muscles became completely flaccid as soon as innervation ceased, the problem would be simplified: abandoned to itself, the body would obey only the law of gravity; it would collapse like a puppet or an articulated skeleton. Its attitude, every time, would be that of a fall.

But this only happens exceptionally, as, for example, when after a violent exercise one drops into an armchair or sprawls onto the floor in a state of collapse. Though they imply effort, such attitudes hardly give the impression of ease. In fact, they are somewhat painful to observe, because they imply exhaustion.

In its normal state, a muscle preserves a certain tone, even when volitional innervation is totally absent; when limp, it stays in a semicontraction; so that if it is in a lengthened state when the effort ceases, it will tend to return to its initial position with a force proportionate to the length of the stretch, almost as if its fibers had the elasticity of a rubber band. Setting aside for a moment the effects of gravity, consider, for instance, the principal muscles of the arm. Suppose my arm is fully extended: at this point, the biceps is stretched to its full length and the triceps fully contracted. If I let my arm go, will it stay in this position? It will not, for the biceps, being completely distended, will tend strongly to return to its normal position; while the triceps, far from opposing it with an equivalent effort, will tend to lengthen in order to return to its normal contraction which had been considerably exceeded. The arm will therefore shorten until the spontaneous efforts of these two antagonistic muscles counterbalance one another exactly.

The antagonistic muscles, which are activated in the alternate movements of our limbs, are not opposed to one another symmetrically enough for us to determine a priori this position of equilibrium. However ingenious its combinations, the animal machine is far from being a masterpiece of mechanical simplicity: it was evidently not made all of a piece, but by successive touchings-up and often by the use of organs originally designed for a different purpose. Though the most complicated movements, such as the rotations of the eye in the socket or of the humerus in the hip joint, could have been obtained by the action of three bundles of muscular fibers, it so happens that the simplest movements always put into play a somewhat complicated apparatus.

But if the position of equilibrium of the limbs cannot be determined a priori, we can determine it empirically and accurately enough by noting that it must be equidistant from the farthest points the limb reaches in its largest oscillations. One can then, step by step, by working on each articulation successively, determine the attitude of least effort of any limb. In point of fact, it is the position our limbs take when we float in a bathtub. Armchairs designed to give us this position will be, for that reason, more comfortable than others.

When the eye is at rest, we look straight in front of us, a little below the horizon. This has been called the primary position of the eye. This concept is important in the study of physiological optics. Each limb also has its primary position, to which it returns as soon as it becomes limp. This fact is of some importance in the aesthetics of attitudes.

When we want to rest or sleep, we try to get as close as possible to this position. Reclining in bed, we might take pleasure in stretching our arms or legs for a moment, but they will soon fold up of their own accord under the influence of antagonistic muscular forces that tend to balance one another.

In the standing position, this action will be less evident, because gravity intervenes and helps to determine our attitude. When I am standing, one of my legs at least must be straight in order to support the mass of my body; and my arms, which of their own would tend to bend in half, hang down, carried by their own weight. But in people who have very developed musculature, the specific activity of the muscles will outweigh that of gravity. The professional gymnast always holds his forearm slightly upward, in the manner of a schoolchild carrying a dictionary; the mountaineer always has his legs slightly bent. In most quadrupeds, the back legs, which are more strongly muscled, maintain their primary position at rest, because their various joints are kept inflected by the permanent contraction of their muscles, whereas the front legs, which are frailer, have to stretch more in order to support the weight of the body.

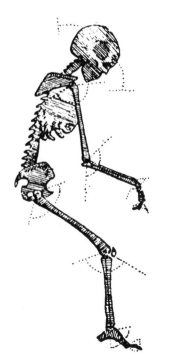

*Figure 1*

### The Law of Stability

If our only preoccupation were to make our attitudes feel as comfortable as possible, we would always tend to the attitude of absolute least effort, in which each of our members is in its primary position. In practice, our attitudes adapt themselves to the specific action we are about to do, and thence their variety.

But this adaptation of the body to action still leaves a certain freedom in the choice of attitudes. And it is within this limitation that the law of the least effort must find its application. By studying a few of the attitudes we take the most naturally, we shall see that we instinctively combine them in such a way as to obtain the greatest ease compatible with their end.

A man is taking a walk, cane in hand, and stops to contemplate the view. This attitude of pause (fig. 2) would be tiring if it lasted, because it keeps the limbs stiff and requires some effort of balance. If our walker wishes to prolong his contemplation, he will have to settle into a more comfortable position. The first thing he does is to put all his weight on one leg which he straightens, raising the hip on that side. Suppose he takes support on his left leg. From this one action will naturally result accessory movements which will fully determine the attitude. The right hip being lowered, the right leg has to bend or be placed slightly forward. The spine curves laterally, causing the shoulders to place themselves in opposition to the hips. Automatically, the left hand comes to rest on the hip and the right arm straightens and leans on the cane which serves as a prop. So, little by little, the body finds itself in the attitude pictured here (fig. 3). It goes without saying that this attitude is determined by convenience alone and is in no way inevitable. Other attitudes might be just as convenient. The least effort in posture is a problem complex enough to allow several parallel solutions. But, certainly, this is the attitude most frequently adopted. I am only describing it to provide a concrete example for the general remarks that follow.

We have noticed at the outset that instinctive motion of the cane trying to find a point of support on the ground. Its purpose is evidently to give the body more stability by buttressing it. In the first posture, the man is held erect only by the contraction of his muscles, which demands a certain effort. In the second posture, the body has a wide base of support; the muscles can relax a little, he will not fall. It is therefore an attitude of least effort,

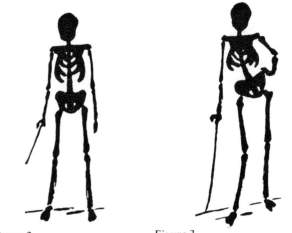

*Figure 2*          *Figure 3*

in which the economy of muscular energy is obtained by multiplying the points of support. The more tired one becomes, the more points of support will be needed. The next stage would be to sit, with the weight on one's hands, the next to lie down on one's side with the weight on one elbow, or seek some object to grab or on which to lean or rest the elbows.

By multiplying the points of support, we get a feeling of security that allows the total relaxation of inactive muscles. When they are in an unstable balance, all our muscles are on the alert, ready to contract to ward off a fall; no muscle dares relax. Whereas, when they are in a secure balance, they let go; this results in a further economy of muscular energy. That relaxation, which occurs according to a certain rhythm, is very pleasant.

This creates a problem for artists who are working with models. How can they keep the model in a position of unstable balance for a long enough time, when normally the pose cannot be sustained for more than a few seconds? If she is given no support, she will tire. If she is given one, she will rest and will furnish only the slight play of muscles required by her stable balance.

Second in importance to the leaning on the cane in the typical posture above is the extension of the leg and arm. It enables the body to obtain its balance at much less expense. For if the leg on which I am leaning is bent, the resistance will be provided by the muscles, which entails work. But if I hold it straight and even a little hyperextended, my muscles can relax completely. My body is resting on a solid support that holds it up without any effort. The muscular relaxation is so complete that a light blow on the back of my thigh will be enough to unsnap my knee and almost make me fall.

In all attitudes of least effort, we find these rigid supports used to substitute the passive resistance of the limbs for the active resistance of the muscles. Such stances also enable the limbs to find a support within the body itself when they cannot find one on the outside. With the leg extended, the arm can rest on the hip as it would on an armchair. Sitting at a table, we lean on an elbow, resting our head on our hand; lacking a table, we rest our elbows on our knees.

Another frequently used way to consolidate our body frame in certain postures is through ligaments or tendons. We can cross our arms, which is like making a knot. We can join our hands by intermingling the fingers, which forms a coupling with a very strong mortice; or we can grasp our knee or the nape of our neck with our hands. The joining together of the limbs forms a homogeneous, compact mass which supports itself.

We find analogous movements among most animals who need periods of rest. A curious example, which is like a grotesque exaggeration of this procedure, can be found among quadrumanes: when the spider monkey prepares for sleep, it wraps its long thin arms around its body and surrounds the whole with its tail, giving the appearance of a package tied tightly with string.

In any attitude that has to be held for some time, our body tends to get into a position that assures us of the most stable balance with the least effort.

*The Law of Asymmetry*

Let us return one last time to our illustrated attitude and analyze the way the efforts are distributed. The unevenness of this distribution is striking: whereas some muscles are strongly contracted, others are absolutely relaxed. The pressures are not distributed any more evenly: almost the entire weight of the body rests on the sole of the left foot, which should be crushed by it; and the extra weight is carried by the right hand alone.

A variety of examples will show this is not in any way accidental. Let us study the posture depicted in a picture gallery. We find an identical opposition in the placement of similar limbs, the same unevenness in the distribution of effort and resistance. When one leg is extended, the other is flexed; when one arm is stretched, the other is bent. Furthermore, to avoid any touch of symmetry, the movements of the arm and of the leg on each side are usually in opposition, so that any correlation must be sought along the diagonals. Let us allow that the artists placed their models in such a way as to vary their poses for artistic reasons. We cannot say, however, that these attitudes are artificial; on the contrary, they look quite natural and give us an impression of ease.

We leave the museum and look around us. Here are two people in conversation on the sidewalk; a soldier reading a poster; a stroller leaning against the railing of a bridge; a hackney horse waiting at a stop, with the driver asleep in his seat; a concierge in front of her lodge, broom in hand; a laborer smoking his pipe. All these attitudes in which art evidently has no part and which have been taken with no regard for elegance are dissymmetrical.

Now we only have to ascertain that this dissymmetry is not accidental. For one might believe that it is by chance only that each of these people has fallen into a specific attitude, and that, because there is a greater chance for this attitude to occur, it is therefore the most frequent. For since our movements are alternate and give our limbs a dissymmetrical position, especially in their extreme phases, it would be natural to believe that, when we pause, we will find ourselves inevitably in a dissymmetrical position. But if this were the case, the dissymmetry would be particularly evident in the early moments of the attitude, when the influence of the movement that led us into it is felt the most; and it would somewhat lessen with time. But observation indicates that the contrary is true. Most often, one might even say almost always, we will stop in a square, symmetrical position, because the effort to stop demands an equal effort in all the limbs. Observe for example a horse stopping, a runner reaching his goal, a stroller sitting on a bench or lying on the grass. It is only the next moment, when we get into a permanent position and settle down, that the dissymmetry appears and is gradually more emphasized. It follows that dissymmetry is being sought intentionally for the ease it provides and because it en-ables the limbs that are not working at maintaining a balance to return to their primary position.

We prefer to wear out one part of our body twice as much in order to give the other part a complete rest. At first sight, it is hard to see what we gain by it. It would even seem that discomfort and effort, being distributed on a lesser number of points, would be felt more. But where painful sensations are concerned, the most unbearable one is continuity. No matter if pain increases in this area, as long as it ceases there! One could also invoke a psychophysical law, according to which sensations increase in an arithmetical progression while irritation grows in a geometrical one. However debatable the strictness of this formula may be, it is nonetheless certain that a doubled pressure will not give us exactly twice as strong a feeling of being crushed; so that by completely unloading a part of the body in order to load another, we not only displace the discomfort; in effect we diminish it.

Need we say that, in practice, we do not bother with such calculations? We do not weigh the pros and cons before settling into an attitude; we get into it without thinking, by a simple reflex action. In the most symmetrical position, an effort cannot be equally divided between similar limbs. The fact is that the limbs that are the most uncomfortable seek relief and, by an automatic movement of self-gratification, shift the entire weight onto the opposite limbs, leaving them to fend as they can. And it is no less a fact that, as a result of these instinctive movements, there is real economy. Had it been detrimental, this instinct would not have maintained itself.

*The Law of Alternation*

A muscle suffers more from a weak contraction when it is continuous than from a strong contraction when it is followed by a complete relaxation. It is difficult to hold the arm up horizontally for ten minutes, but nothing is easier than to raise it and lower it regularly within the same period, though it does require more energy. In order to maintain an attitude longer, it would therefore be advantageous to oscillate between two positions as dissimilar as possible which, by putting into play totally different muscles, would permit each one to first contract and then relax.

This program, which sounds complicated in theory, is in practice realized naturally. The alternation of attitudes is an immediate consequence of their asymmetry.

We have said that when we have stayed in one position for some time, we feel the need to change it. If in this first position, the efforts were about evenly distributed between similar limbs, it would be quite difficult for us to take or imagine a completely different pose. Consider for instance the attitude in our figure 2. The two arms are extended: one could, I suppose, bend them. But the legs are also stiffened: how can one flex them both? There seems no other solution but to sit. In figure 3, on the contrary, the problem presents no difficulty. Because this position is totally asymmetrical, nothing is easier for me than to reverse it totally; I need only take the position that is exactly symmetrical to it. Follow this movement in your imagination; the similar limbs being always disposed opposite one another, it is clear that every time an attitude is reversed, the pose will be completely different from the previous one.

We find an example of these complete reversals of attitude when a man or an animal stretches after a long rest to remove the stiffness from the body. Attitude dances, which are still seen in the theater but which are regrettably no longer shown in dance spectacles, are very graceful and give an impression of perfect ease by the alternation of symmetrical poses.

This change occurs naturally, almost on its own. The same reason that made us shift the weight of our body onto certain muscles will make us reverse it again, as soon as the new working muscles are tired.

The story is told of a carnival man at a country fair who exhibited a troup of turkeys dancing on a metal plate. His secret consisted of heating the plate from below: the poor turkeys would lift one foot and then the other to avoid being burnt. We do the same when carrying too hot an object, like roasted chestnuts, which we throw from hand to hand; or when we are carrying a very heavy load, like a large suitcase which cuts into our hand: every once in a while, we change sides. It is the same, after a while, for the growing discomfort of a position. In any attitude held for some time, the oscillations we make between two symmetrical positions will establish a kind of rhythm. And the more dissymmetrical each attitude is, the more effort we will be spared.

It is true that, in practice, it is impossible to obtain exact dissymmetry. In any position, the muscles that are working the least still have something to do: they cannot rest completely while waiting for their turn. The most comfortable attitude must finally become tiring, at which point we have to resort to more drastic measures and change it. Since general fatigue augments constantly, it will become increasingly difficult to find a pose that can be sustained any length of time. We try all positions and find them equally painful, until, little by little, fatigue and sleepiness bring us invincibly to the position of the least effort.

A good illustration can be found in the attitudes of travelers in a night train. They first look at one another, seeking elegant resting positions. Gradually fatigue takes over and gracefulness disappears. You see them propping themselves into a corner, leaning on the armrest, stretching their legs, sprawling on the seat, straightening up again with a groan, until sleep overcomes them. And the pale dawn falls on them, sleeping in all sorts of odd positions.

# 4   Natural Rhythm of Movements

## Rhythm in Nature

Rhythm consists in the recurrence of the same phenomenon at regular intervals. There is a rhythm in the ringing of a church bell, in the impacts of a wave against a cliff, in the twinkling of the stars, in the beats of the heart. There is no rhythm in the swinging of a poplar that occasionally bends in the wind, because the movements are not regular enough; none either in a waterfall, in the flight of a bullet, or in the gyration of a top, because they are not periodic.

Rhythmic movements are very frequent in nature. Herbert Spencer devotes an entire chapter of *First Principles* to enumerating them:

When the pennant of a vessel lying becalmed first shows the coming breeze, it does so by gentle undulations that travel from its fixed to its free end. Presently the sails begin to flap; and their blows against the mast increase rapidly as the breeze rises. Even when, being fully bellied out, they are in great part steadied by the strain on the yards and cordage, their free edges tremble with each stronger gust. And should there come a gale, the jar that is felt on laying hold of the shrouds shows that the rigging vibrates; while the rush and whistle of the wind prove that in it, also, rapid undulations are generated.[1]

Reading this chapter, one is inevitably led to concur with the author that rhythm is the fundamental law of all mechanical movement.

1   Herbert Spencer, *First Principles* (New York: De Witt Revolving Fund, 1958), p. 254.

The hypothesis is indeed very plausible. In nature, there is no such thing as a continuous linear movement. When a molecule of matter receives an impulse that tends to send it in a straight line into space, it will be limited in its course by either the forces of cohesion or the forces of gravitation that connect it to the molecules from which it is receding, or by the inertia of the molecules it encounters and against which it rebounds. Its linear movement is thus soon modified either to a limited oscillation (such as the oscillations of a clock, the vibrations of an elastic body, the trajectory of the stars), or to a wave that spreads from molecule to molecule, imparting a regular movement to each one—a pendular movement for linear waves such as sound, a circular movement for transversal waves such as disturbed water or light. The tendency of natural phenomena to acquire a rhythmic pattern is also explained by the fact that the effects of a constant force are, in most cases, intermittent. For example, a wave beating regularly against a cliff produces periodic collapses of the cliff. The bow of a violin passing over a string first carries the string along with it, then drops it to catch it again in the opposite direction. When I blow into a reed instrument, at first the increasing pressure of my breath pushes the reed away from its position; then a whiff of air escapes, the pressure immediately goes down in the pipe and the reed returns to its position of balance; then, the mechanical system having returned to its original state, the same cycle of motions will necessarily recur with perfect regularity. All these examples have an identical explanation: the desired phenomenon, necessitating a certain amount of energy, occurs only intermittently, when the source of energy that produces it has expended a sufficient amount of force; and this expenditure having been constant, the intermittences must be regular; that is to say, the phenomenon must have a rhythmic pattern.

But if we can break down the most irregular-seeming movement into a certain number of simple rhythmic movements, one has to recognize that the majority of natural phenomena, as they appear to us, have no perceptible rhythm. The belief in the universal rhythm is the result rather of scientific induction than of immediate observation; nothing would be easier than to make a list longer even than Spencer's to prove that the law of natural movements is incoherence. To his twenty pages of rhythmic movements, we would assemble a volume of those that are not. This is because the most simple phenomenon is still of infinite complexity; even if each of the forces that comes into play in producing the phenomenon tends to give it a rhythmic pattern, the result of all these combined forces will always be a more or less irregular movement.

Imagine two metronomes, one set to beat four times a second, the other five. Here are two very simple, perfectly rhythmic movements. Now have them beat together in the next room; you will hear a series of sounds that will follow one another at sometimes greater, sometimes smaller intervals, and you will be incapable, even in your imagination, of recognizing the two component rhythms. To preserve the idea of rhythm, not only would each of the two movements have to be very regular, but there would also have to be some simple relationship between them, such as two beats to one. This concurrence cannot happen by chance and must be expressly set by the experimenter.

It is only in the physics laboratory that it is easy to find examples of perfect rhythm. In nature, the physical movements in which the law of rhythm is best observed happen to be those that escape immediate perception, either by their slowness, as in astronomical motions, or by their rapidity, as in sound and light waves. Our senses will show us little else but imperfect rhythms; and, however frequent they are, we will still have to look for them. If there is a tendency to overstate their frequency, it is because they attract our attention more than the others. Thus there is a belief that very brightly colored flowers predominate in nature, because they attract all our attention. In fact, the bright ones are the exception.

It is precisely because it is exceptional that rhythm attracts us so. When we discover an order within the incoherence of natural phenomena, we are happily surprised. The rhythm in physical movements is like a geometric figure among haphazard lines. If, on the contrary, our eyes were to find regular figures everywhere, then irregularity would please us and regularity would seem insipid.

## Rhythm in Muscular Movements

Though exceptional in nature, rhythm is the constant law of muscular movements.

This tendency to periodicity is evidently not the effect of the will, which operates only occasionally and when it has a specific reason to intervene: it is intermittent. Whenever it enters as a factor in muscular contractions, it is a disturbing element. It determines the beginning and the end of a series, interrupts it when necessary, but does not maintain its periodicity. For instance, our eyelids blink fairly regularly, our chest rises and sinks in an even movement, outside our consciousness. If we do focus on it, our blinking will occur only with a special effort and will become irregular, even as we try to maintain its rhythm. The physiologist who wishes to measure the quantity of air that his lungs normally exhale is obliged to take no account of the early results of his experiment, but to continue it for some time, until his breathing becomes unconscious and mechanical again: only then will its normal rhythm return.

The difficulty we have in regulating these automatic movements is understandable, when one realizes that the mind of itself has no notion of duration. How can we measure it? By the repetition of a same phenomenon, taken as unit and deemed to be perfectly regular.[2] But ideas and sensations, being subjective phenomena, are far too variable to be used as a unit of time. We must therefore turn to a more objective measure; and the most practical of all, one we always have at our disposal, is the duration of a muscular contraction. If, for example, we want to count seconds, we utter a certain number of sounds, or beat a measure, or think of a rhythmic movement that we know from experience takes that amount of time. Therefore, rather than regulate the rhythm of these movements, the mind has to use them as a chronometer to get the notion of time, which means that these movements must have a regulator that is distinct from the will.

## Physiological Causes

The rhythmicity of these movements is due first of all to causes of a physiological nature which we shall classify in three groups: the law of compensation, the tendency to repetition, and the effects of habit.

2    See Antoine Cournot, *An Essay on the Foundations of our Knowledge*, trans. Merritt H. Moore (New York: Liberal Arts Press, 1956).

*1. The law of compensation*    Any contracting muscle that requires a certain expenditure of energy will soon be exhausted: we are warned by a feeling of fatigue that induces us to stop the contraction for a while. This sensation of fatigue, by recurring periodically, regulates the rhythm of our contractions outside our awareness, by a simple reflex action, exactly as the periodic sensation of asphyxiation regulates our breathing.

One conceives that the more energetic the muscle contraction has been, the longer the recuperative rest must be to enable it to contract again; and this leads us to think that there must be a fixed relationship between the energy of rhythmic movements and their frequency. If I execute only movements in which the expended force is insignificant, such as those of a pianist running her fingers over the keyboard, or of a telegraph operator clicking away at his Morse machine, these movements can follow one another at an extremely rapid rhythm. But the movements of an oarsman rowing upstream or of a gardener digging with a shovel are of necessity spaced much further apart. In fact, it takes usually more time to execute an energetic effort, because, most often, the only way to use more force in a movement is to make it larger. If I want to hit very hard with a hammer, I will have to raise my arm as high as I can. In a physical exercise in which one must expend, according to the occasion, a differing amount of energy, it is curious to see how these variations in the effort entail a corresponding variation in the speed of the rhythm. Each of us, for instance, has a normal gait into which we fall automatically when walking on flat terrain; but if the road slopes down, our step will inevitably accelerate; if we reach a rise, it will slow down of itself, and the more so as the road becomes steeper. In all these examples, one sees that the natural speed of a rhythm is in reverse proportion to the work that each movement costs.

To highlight this law of compensation, we have assumed so far that the total output of energy was always about the same. To put the facts in their full complexity, one must also take into account the accidental stimulations or the intentional efforts that can increase, at a given moment, the intensity of the innervation. We then see that the speed of rhythmic movements must vary in direct proportion to this intensity. When I am doing a mechanical job, any sudden emotion will be translated into a sudden acceleration of the rhythm of my movements; even my heart beats faster and I get out of breath. Or, if my movements keep at a constant speed, their energy increases. Or again, which happens most frequently, my movements increase both in strength and speed. A swimmer gets frightened when he feels grass brushing against his leg and starts immediately to strike the water frantically. In music, it is rare for a crescendo not to be accompanied by an acceleration. But these variations in the intensity of innervation do not escape the law of rhythm. Any extreme stimulation will be followed by a compensatory period of calm, which, in turn, will give way to a new fit of activity. Imagine that in a series of efforts I am making, one of them happens to be a little more energetic than the others; the dynamic balance is broken: the effort following that one will have to fall below the average in intensity and that will permit the next one to rise above it again. This alternation of strong and weak beats, which is like a rhythm within a rhythm, is so natural that we find it everywhere, in music and poetry, as well as in muscular movements. There has even been an attempt to consider it as *the* essential phenomenon of rhythm, which is an exaggeration. In music, for instance, the rhythm with one beat is much more frequently used than one thinks.

*Man throwing a stone*

2. *The tendency to repetition*   Even when we intend to make only one movement, we usually have a tendency to precede and follow it with complementary movements, more or less conscious, which are like the preparation and the echo of the principal effort. It is very rare that movements in which we want to put a certain energy do not form in this way a real rhythmic phrase.

Consider a man getting ready to leap, throw a stone, or wield an axe, in other words, to make some decisive movement. You will see that he always starts with preparatory movements of an increasingly greater scope and speed. These movements are doubly useful. First they are like a study, a rehearsal of the final movement: at the moment when he executes the desired movement by a sudden muscular release, he no longer has time for reflection; he must therefore combine in advance the play of his muscles, by trying it out at a slower pace; then he must rehearse the rapid motion to make sure that all is in order, that he has gotten hold of the movement and that nothing will be in the way when he has to execute it. Secondly, a violent movement is not only a feat of skill but also of strength. And to use all one's strength, some preparation is necessary. A muscle from which one suddenly expects a great effort is unprepared and functions poorly. Take a jump on both feet: you will bounce a certain distance; try again: you will surely go a little farther. In a feat of strength, one usually succeeds better the second time: the muscles must have time to get rid of their stiffness and warm up.[3] That is the function of preparatory movements.

Let us apply this to different rhythms. When I knock at a

3   See Fernand Lagrange, *Physiology of Bodily Exercise* (New York: Appleton, 1891), p. 39.

door, I do not knock just once, but two or three times. A call that does not have at least two syllables, the first serving as preparation, cannot be made with enough force. The child learning to talk uses only the accentuated syllable of a word and repeats it in order to stress the sound.

In a tune with a well-marked rhythm, the notes that must be accented are almost always preceded by faster and weaker notes, apparently for pure pleasure, but they are actually indispensable in preparing the attack of the principal sound. If you look through musical scores, you will see that, whenever the tunes are strongly accented, the musical phrase starts on the upbeat of a measure; in other words, the first strong sound is preceded by preparatory notes that facilitate its emission.

If we cannot attack energetic movements all at once, neither can we interrupt them suddenly. It is an almost universal law that all large movements are followed immediately by a small movement which is like its echo. The hairdresser cutting her client's hair makes an extra click of the scissors every time she takes a clip; the blacksmith hammering on a horseshoe follows every blow on the iron with a small blow on the anvil; if you hit a table three times with your fist, you will hardly be able to refrain from hitting it a fourth time. The fact is easy to explain. It is difficult to interrupt suddenly a rhythmic movement that is becoming automatic. By virtue of the habit acquired and the force incurred, the movement continues a little after the decision to stop it. And the elasticity of bodies almost always causes them to rebound after a violent impact.

This all contributes, then, to making the echoing movements, which reinforce the principal movement in a well-marked rhythm, more natural. In general, the echoing movements are fewer than the preparatory ones, so that in the natural rhythmic phrase, the strong beat is usually situated toward the end. Significant examples of this structure of the rhythmic phrase are found in Beethoven's sonatas, where the rhythmic movement is so well marked. A typical form he seems to favor is made up of four preparatory notes, an accent, and one echoing note. It is purely by convention that in our musical notation the strong beat has been placed at the beginning of a measure.

3. *Effects of habit*   The fact of having executed a movement several times in a row is reason enough to continue it, so much so that to make it cease suddenly a special motivation is needed and an effort has to be made to stop. Cross your legs and give the upper one a pendular movement. After a certain number of swings, this movement will become so mechanical that it will continue on its own: you are surprised to observe your leg still in motion, quite unintentionally.

How can we explain this tendency, which is the essential ingredient of habit? On this point, we are reduced to mere conjecture; all explanations so far proposed tend to be metaphors rather than real explanations. But the fact is undeniable: any rhythmic movement becomes automatic, and the more uniform it is to start with, the faster it becomes automatic.

We should note, however, that when we repeat a movement several times in a row, we have a slight tendency to repeat it faster than originally. To demonstrate this clearly, let us turn again to music, where the variations of motor rhythm are the most perceptible.

In a work that has several movements, the last movements are almost always in a faster rhythm than the first; and within each movement, the rhythm accelerates in the final measures; when it does slow down, it is an exception and to produce a special effect. When a song has several verses, the second verse will take perceptibly less time to sing than the first. Give a pianist or a violinist the timing of a piece with a metronome, then ask her to play and see what will happen: in the first measures, the player heeds the regular clicking in her ear and is mindful of keeping time. But little by little, her attention is withdrawn from the metronome as an insignificant sound and she concentrates entirely on the sounds she herself is producing; in fact, there always comes a moment when the score itself indicates a rhythmic change, a held note or a ritardando, which establishes a change between the rhythm of the metronome and that of the piece; the concurrence observed in the beginning inevitably becomes lost. From there on, the player, freed from this obstacle, abandoned to her own inspiration, will not fail to accelerate the movement. This tendency, operating constantly and at each repeat, often causes orchestras and opera choruses to perform at a greater speed than that indicated for the piece by the composer, to the extent that, if special attention is not paid, music pieces would end by being completely distorted.

Is this phenomenon at odds with the effects one would expect habit to have? On the contrary, it is precisely through habit that these effects can be explained.

Any rhythmic movement, from the very fact that it becomes a habit, is executed with increasing facility. If one were satisfied to consume the same amount of energy constantly, this decrease of resistance would in itself produce an increase in speed. But the movements themselves become more energetic. The muscles, gradually warming up, are apt to contract with greater force. The mind indulges in that intoxication of speed we have mentioned and the acceleration becomes irresistible.

*Mechanical Causes*

To these physiological reasons are added others of a purely mechanical nature.

Because muscles are connected to the bones by fixed attachments, our limbs can only move by oscillation and not through complete revolution, as the wheels of a steam engine do. Most of the articulations are hinged rather than ball-and-socket joints and their ligaments are very tight, which permits only oscillations of an elementary kind, that is, simple alternated movements. Where does the regularity of this alternation come from? For the movement of my legs, it comes only from the inertia of my own body, which, once it is given a certain impulse, continues to move of its own in a uniform motion. When I walk or run, once my legs have thrust my body forward, they must inevitably follow: I therefore cannot help moving them at a certain rhythm. I can only slow down or accelerate progressively, for the body mass, acting like a flywheel, resists both an abrupt stop and a sudden acceleration.

One must also take into account the mass of the locomotor organs, which regulate their oscillations. When I swing my arm forward once, it will, of its own accord, make several swings of equal duration, though of diminishing size. Each of my limbs has its own rhythm. Though not identical with a pendulum whose speed of oscillation increases according to the square root of its length, locomotor organs behave approximately in the same way. Certainly, the variations of speed occur in the same direction, the shorter limbs having the faster swings. This law of rhythm is verified in the beats of bird wings. According to Marey, the buzzard gives 3 wing beats per second, the owl 5, the pigeon 8, the sparrow 13. For the insects, the speed increases at a much faster rate: the dragonfly gives 28 vibrations, the wasp 110, the bee 190, the bumblebee 240, the common fly 330.[4] In such circumstances, it is evident that the rhythm of movements is not regulated by the will; the animal cannot produce each oscillation by a specific effort, nor can it be clearly conscious of it.

It goes without saying that this law of rhythmic movements is not rigid in any way: our limbs remain subject to the influence of the will, which can make their oscillations more or less rapid by varying the tension of the muscles. But this constant causality, which incites us to choose one rhythm rather than another, always acts in the same direction: it cannot fail, therefore, to come through in the end, in spite of changes of mind.

Accordingly, it is an irrefutable fact that short people have more vivacity in their movements than tall ones. This proportion is maintained in the various animal species. Among mammals, compare the elephant, the horse, the dog, the rat; among birds, the vulture, the hawk, the titmouse, the hummingbird; the same goes for reptiles, fish, and insects. In animals of the same class, agility increases regularly as size diminishes. Does this mean that small animals have more muscular energy than large ones? Not in the least. If their movements are quicker, they are also smaller, so their total displacement is no greater. Their muscles do not seem to work at a greater pressure nor is the work supplied for each pound of animal more considerable. In fact, from this point of view, small animals would be at a disadvantage in comparison with larger ones. If they cover the distance of their own length more times in one second, in

4   Jules Marey, *Animal Mechanism: A Treatise on Terrestrial and Aerial Locomotion* (New York: Appleton, 1874), pp. 228, 185.

that same second they will not have traveled so far; if they jump higher in proportion to their size, in fact they will not rise as high. What is, then, the reason for this greater agility? Animals, of course, are not seeking to compensate for the smaller scope of their movements by greater speed, as if they all had to displace themselves at a uniform rate. They only seek to move as fast and as easily as possible. But their limbs tend to take a certain rhythm, proportionate to their size; and this constant causality always ends by regulating their speed.

### Harmony of Body Rhythms

When several parts of our organism get into motion at once, will they function independently from one another, as if they were isolated? That is impossible. The different pieces that compose the animal machine are too interdependent not to always exert an influence on one another.

Let us consider, for instance, the rhythmic movements of circulation, respiration, and locomotion. The beats of the heart, the contractions of the diaphragm, and the flexions of the leg are doubtless not directly connected; but there is between them a certain harmony, essential to the good functioning of the organs. For instance, if I move faster, my heart must send more blood to my muscles to restore them and my breathing must accelerate to activate the combustion that produces force. That is why each organ has been conditioned to modifying its action to fall in line with the others. At this moment, for instance, I am sitting still; my pulse is going at about sixty beats per minute; if I breathe faster, my pulse will rise to seventy-two; if I breathe slower, it eventually drops to fifty-five and becomes weaker. If I now alter my muscular motions by rising and doing a few vigorous movements, my pulse accelerates and beats more strongly and my breath becomes labored; these three kinds of movement are related in such a way that, when one is altered intentionally, the other two alter accordingly, if not in the same proportion, at least in the same direction.

Due to this overall interaction, each of our movements must have a repercussion through our whole body, modifying the play of all the other organs. Some of them also have a special interdependence: a synergy of the muscles according to which the movement of one mechanically involves that of the others, such as the general contraction caused by effort; a synergy of the nerves, which produces symmetrical movements in organs whose muscular structure may be totally independent. Sometimes this interdependence is constitutional, as in the movements of the eyes; in other cases, it can be produced just by habit. For example, it is difficult to move the left hand back and forth in one place while moving the right one perpendicularly to it, or to make a capital D with one hand while a foot moves in a circle. These are both easy movements; there seems no reason not to be able to do them together. But the muscles absolutely refuse to do it. In general, "any one organ, however small, when made to move quickly, imparts its pace to all the other moving organs."[5]

This harmony of muscular movements has become so natural to us that our will is powerless to disturb it.

It is impossible to focus on several things at the same time. When I execute several movements simultaneously, I can only observe one of them; and the others, abandoned to my reflexes,

5   Alexander Bain, *The Senses and the Intellect* (New York: Appleton, 1879), p. 87.

will take the same rhythm spontaneously, or at least a rhythm that combines with the first in the simplest relationship.

When we are not observing our respiration, it regulates itself to the heart beats in a one to four ratio. For instance, if our pulse is sixty-four, we breathe sixteen times. If we start to walk, the rhythm of our steps will prevail over that of the heart and it is with this new rhythm that our breathing will enter into a simple relationship: we usually take one complete breath for every four steps. And there will even be a tendency to accent this breathing in four efforts, two inhalings, two exhalings, to make the rhythmic harmony more perfect. In cold, damp weather, when the breath is condensed into a mist, it is easy to verify this law by observing passers-by: when they are walking at an average speed, they let out their breath every four steps, with the regularity of a running locomotive. If they hasten their step, their breath will be visible every two steps, always adjusting to the walk in a simple relationship. Making identical observations from passing horses and dogs, I have observed that their respiration is as regularly rhythmical as our own, if their pace is sustained.

In movements that require a great deal of work, like those of a digger filling a cart, of a gardener pulling a pail of water from a well, or of the blacksmith beating on the anvil, the effort makes them hold back their breathing periodically, so that the rhythm of one must coincide with that of the other.

Make your right hand go back and forth, like a conductor. The left, which you are not watching, will move at the same rhythm, in a parallel action if you let your shoulders swing, and symmetrically if your bust is motionless. Make the right hand move faster: the left follows. Shift your attention from right to left: now it is the right hand which will have reflex movements;

and the harmony will always be maintained between these two movements, with immovable regularity. Let us try to disturb it by a special effort of double attention. I will watch both my hands at once, endeavoring to make one go faster than the other: I soon notice that it will go exactly twice as fast as the other. This is easy to ascertain, by taking a pencil in each hand and registering these oscillations on a sheet of paper. Increase the difference: it will become one to four; so that the motions of the faster hand are always multiples of the motions of the slower one.

It would be much more difficult to set their rhythm in a two to three relationship. Under the conditions of the preceding experience, it is quite impossible. It can be done by beating with the pencils on the paper; and then, only by counting out a measure of six beats, the unit of which will serve as a common measurement to both, and by counting very slowly. As soon as the movement goes faster and therefore becomes mechanical, this artificial rhythm disappears and falls back to one of the preceding ones. In some piano pieces, the left hand must play two notes for three in the right; one knows how difficult this is for a beginner. And these two independent series meet at fixed intervals, close enough to permit one to keep the feeling of the rhythm by singling out their concurrence. It would be absolutely impossible to execute together two rhythmic movements that did not have a simple relationship between them. Try, for instance, to shake evenly the right hand *a little* faster than the left; your muscles will refuse to do it, because their two rhythms have no common measurement.

In the ordinary walk, it is the arms that establish the beat, because they swing freely and have a greater tendency to take their own rhythm. Testing this myself, I found that my arms make about eighty-five swings per minute, which is my most leisurely pace, and my legs, barely seventy-two. If I accelerate my walk, it is my arms that have to follow my legs; and, instinctively, they will bend a little to keep up with the rhythm. On running, they bend even more against the chest.

The various organic rhythms have therefore a tendency to coordinate, independent of our will, according to a simple and regular rhythm to which they return when we make them deviate from it. But far from trying to counter this tendency, we usually take pleasure in favoring it as much as possible and in bringing the various organic rhythms to as simple as possible a common denominator.

Have a metronome beat at an average speed, in front of several people, for example at seventy beats per minute; then ask these people to consider this rhythm. Some will find it a little slow, others a little fast: we could say it is a question of temperament. But ask each person to determine, by trial and error, the rhythm that suits him or her the best, then count each pulse: you will find that chosen rhythm and pulse will coincide practically exactly. This is because the beats of our heart give our whole body rhythmical vibrations that we feel unconsciously; and when the sonorous rhythm that hits our ear is not in tune with this interior rhythm, we have a feeling of discordance; and we try to get rid of this feeling by re-establishing a common rhythm.

That is probably the reason for our attraction to rhythm, which is one of the most remarkable effects of music. When a band is passing by, I am not content to listen to the sounds as they are emitted. I sing along with it, or I make rhythmic sounds in my throat which, by virtue of the law of harmony, will also regulate the cadence of my step. If the rhythm of the passing band happens to almost correspond with my stride, I cannot help falling in step with it. It would take a special effort to walk faster than that tune or even to establish between the two rhythms a difference of phrasing. I make my accents coincide exactly with theirs. Once this concurrence is established, my step will accelerate or decelerate along with the tune. It is the same in dancing: once the dancers have gotten the rhythm, they are carried away by it; if the orchestra slows down or goes faster, they will do the same, not with the intention of keeping in time but because the cadence carries them along irresistibly.

# II  Mechanical Beauty

*Two men fencing*

# 5  General Principles

## *Purpose of This Study*

In any physical exercise, even when it seems that only strength is required, skill is also needed. Horse trainers know that no energetic work can be obtained from an animal that has a badly shaped or underdeveloped skull. Given equal vigor, the more intelligent or specially gifted person will be able to develop more strength than the weak-minded one. Whether lifting a case, doing carpentry, executing a feat of balance, jumping, or swimming, there is one way of proceeding that is more dexterous than the others. A practiced workman will furnish more useful work than an apprentice. With some intelligent thinking, a moving man will displace a piece of furniture that a very strong but inexpert man can barely set in motion. A person starting gymnastics will very soon observe she is improving surprisingly rapidly: is it her strength that has increased so fast? Actually, the increase of muscular energy is obtained slowly, by continuous practice. But what she is doing is utilizing her existing strength more efficiently.

Nevertheless, there is no validity in the frequent belief that it is not necessary to know the laws of mechanics to move or to hold one's balance and that theoretical knowledge is no longer useful at the moment of execution. Doubtless, at the moment one executes the movements required by an exercise, its execution has to be mechanical and the muscles already trained for the complicated actions demanded of them. If I have to ponder about the gesture I am about to make, I will do it badly, because the very fact that I am pondering proves that I am not quite sure

how to go about it. But, if I have no time for reasoning, does it follow that my reason has nothing to do with it? Far from it. On the contrary, because the action must happen quickly, I need all my presence of mind and faculties of invention to overcome accidental obstacles and deal with the unexpected, like the squirrel whose bounces from branch to branch are a perpetual improvisation. Gabriel Séailles has shown how much creative imagination there is in dance and fencing, how much mechanical genius there is in well-regulated movements.[1] All of us have had occasion to be surprised at the way we have, under the whip of necessity, solved practical problems that would have seemed insurmountable had there been time for thought. Have you never, for instance, been propelled onto a steep slope and had to descend it at full speed, choosing at one glance the most solid support, bouncing, jumping, sliding, grabbing at branches? Once at the bottom, you cannot understand why you did not fall a thousand times.

If reasoning is of no use in the execution of movement, it plays an essential role in preparing for it.

We learn to move from experience, that is, by trying things out first and reasoning about them afterward. Even to combine the simplest movements such as walking, jumping, climbing, some premeditation is necessary. A thoughtful child, aware of his surroundings, will succeed faster and better than another. If the locomotor movements of some animals are, from the start, well adapted to their end, it is because each of them inherits, in the shape of instinct, the total experience of the species; yet it is very rare, at least in superior species, that an

---

1  Gabriel Séailles, *Essai sur le génie dans l'art* (Paris:     1911), pp. 138, 139.

animal does not have to implement that instinct with some personal apprenticing.

I will go further: if experience suffices to handle the daily movements of locomotion reasonably well, theory and planning are far from useless when one comes to sports and gymnastics that are the artistic element of movement aesthetics. A teacher of gymnastics, of riding, of fencing who knows physiology and mechanics will train his or her students in a sounder method; if they understand the why of a movement, they will progress much more rapidly.

Finally, with the use of theory, new methods of locomotion will be devised with far superior results than the natural ones. In a study on swimming, James Pettigrew shows the inconveniences of the breast stroke in which the arms move forward while the lower legs kick. He notes: "The body is impelled by a series of jerks, the swimming mass getting up and losing momentum between the strokes. To remedy these defects, scientific swimmers have of late years adopted quite another method. Instead of working arms and legs together, they move first the arm and leg of one side of the body, and then the arm and leg of the opposite side . . . an arrangement calculated greatly to reduce the amount of friction experienced in forward motion."[2]

A scientific method is also being developed for speed walking. Daryl Philip, in an article on "Pedestrianism in England," describes a method used to obtain the maximum speed in walking.[3] The leg advances with as little flexion as possible and with no weight on the big toe, but only on the heels, a procedure that strikes me as very artificial looking. Likewise, a method of

breathing has been devised for the singer. It is evident, then, that to obtain better results, one has to re-examine procedures and establish which muscular practices will give the maximum work with the minimum effort. As a result, new methods will sometimes replace the instinctual ones.

The reasoned study of locomotion has another theoretical advantage, that of correcting our judgment on the beauty of movement.

Movement already has a certain amount of beauty when it is rhythmic, because rhythm is a law, a definite form, something intelligible. But this beauty is not the one we admire the most, for, though it speaks to the intelligence, one does not sense in it the action of intelligence. True kinetic beauty is provided by the evident finality of a movement. Any movement we execute intentionally is a problem to be resolved: there is a goal to reach, and it must be reached in the simplest way possible. For instance, if, in the gesture of seizing an object, the hand reaches toward it in a groping way (or too slowly or too fast), it has evidently not made the most intelligent use of strength; but if the hand reaches toward the object with precision and assurance, its movements are perfectly adapted to the desired goal and the gesture will be beautiful.

Let us consider a more complicated movement, such as those of a gymnast walking on a balance beam. If he is a novice, his gestures will be abrupt, jerky, more harmful than helpful and will be uncomfortable to watch. But why, precisely, do they displease us? Is it because they lack ease and imply an effort? It is rather because they are gauche, clumsy, unintelligent. On the contrary, the practiced equilibrist who does immediately what

2   James Bell Pettigrew, *Animal Locomotion* (London: Kegan Paul, Trench, Trübner & Co., 1891), p. 84.

3   *Le Temps*, August 22, 1888.

is needed to regain his balance gives us the spectacle of a difficult problem instantly and most elegantly resolved. We will analyze this problem in the next chapter.

The question of the aesthetics of movement thus posed can be resolved in a scientific way. Certainly, gracefulness is a seductive thing. But is it not also very relative, often illusory? How do we judge it? By the vague feeling of sympathy awakened in us at the evident ease in motion; by these instinctive predilections that one rightly says cannot be discussed for want of common principles to give the discussion a solid base. But, in judging the beauty of a movement, its aptness, its adaptation to the intended goal, I can reason from principles. When I say: this is a movement well executed, that is a clumsy gesture, I am stating a truth as objective, as independent of my tastes and personal feelings, and as absolute as when I prove the exactitude of a physics experiment.

We will therefore examine a few precise examples in order to establish how elementary principles of mechanics can be applied to the art of movement and to enable us to reason about it. For the question of art, we will look for solutions of several problems in gymnastics. For the question of taste, we will analyze the principal modes of animal locomotion. There may be some temerity in getting into these complex questions that are still under study and new in certain aspects; errors of fact or of reasoning are possible, even probable. It would indeed be far more prudent and philosophical to discourse on the essence of the beautiful or on predetermined aesthetic judgments: in such matters, you can reason to your heart's content, no one can prove you wrong. But, in the end, one has to come to details. What would be thought of the aesthetician who would formulate the laws of sculpture as follows: "To make a beautiful statue, inspire yourself from good models; give your work the proportions indicated by good taste; and watch especially that no detail should harm the whole!" That is correct, but not practical. Go and use your chisels with such advice!

All the critics who are concerned with movement aesthetics agree that the most beautiful movements are those where force is best utilized. They will say for example that a graceful skater is the one whose every movement is adapted to skating with nothing counteracting her acquired speed. No doubt. But if I skate, what I would really like to know is what attitude gives me the most balance, what movement the most speed. If I observe the clumsy actions of a skater, it will not satisfy me to hear she is using her strength poorly. What I want to know to enlighten my judgment and shape my taste is how she fails the laws of mechanics, and, if her foot is wrongly placed, how she should place it. If one does not go as deep into it as that, the general principles have no meaning at all. We will therefore attempt to apply our principles to facts. At least our method has one advantage: if we err, we will be discovered.

In training for an exercise, once we have found the most efficient programming of movement, all we have to do is execute it in a way that economizes our efforts the most. Here we must respond to an objection that readers will surely make. When we spoke of the determination of our movements, we saw that they obey the law of the least effort. It would seem, therefore, that the best thing to do is to rely on nature. Doubtless, the law of the least effort, acting constantly upon us, will not fail after a while to get us into the most advantageous rhythm. But let us not forget that we are dealing here with unaccustomed movements, for which our body has not yet acquired a habit; and it so happens that we are seeking an intelligent method to spare ourselves those more or less painful gropings and fruitless efforts that we inflict on ourselves when we learn by repetition. We must therefore find out, through reasoning, which method will impose itself sooner or later and try to conform to it from the start. We can then establish general principles applicable to all body exercises.

### Moderation of Pace

First of all, volition has to come into play to moderate the pace of rhythmic movements. For the speed of movements, not mentioned up to now, is a very important element to consider in terms of economy of effort. It is usually neglected in abstract mechanics, where it is always assumed that the work of a force is simply its intensity multiplied by the distance to its point of application. In reality, it is impossible to abstract the duration of an effort in this way: the real work of a motor in motion is not only a function of space but also of time.

When the muscular contractions are very slow, the muscle has to stay tense too long and tires from its own internal work. This is because we must use up energy to keep the muscle in contraction. Since these elementary waves, accumulating into a full contraction, last only as long as it takes them to travel from one end of the muscle to the other, we must renew them all the time; and this demands an expenditure of energy proportionate to the length of the contraction. Therefore, given equal external work, a very slow movement requires more force than a faster one. The muscular machinery is like a hydraulic wheel with leaking buckets. Such a machine would gain by functioning rapidly. There are also accessory causes of fatigue that produce a constant loss of force in any physical activity. In walking, for instance, beyond the effort of propulsion that depends only on the distance covered, we must also consider the effort necessary to stand and keep one's balance, which increases with time. Allowing that in the normal walk, these two efforts are equivalent, it follows that for a given distance, if one walks half as fast, one's fatigue will increase by exactly a third. In a general way, one may be sure that a movement that is too slow consumes a certain amount of energy needlessly.

But this is not the danger to be feared. We have indeed noted this curious tendency of rhythmic movements to accelerate rather than decelerate. This tendency is most noticeable when several people work together at the same activity. They emulate one another. Each tries to take the lead to show that he works better than the others. In all exercises or manual work that require rhythmic movement, swimming, canoeing, running, climbing, handling a saw or a plane, beginners make the error of going too fast. From the point of view of economy, there is no greater mistake. Exaggerated speed produces a real waste of forces as much for the external work of the muscles as for their internal work.

Suppose a cart is being loaded with sand: by virtue of a well-known principle in mechanics, in order not to waste force, each shovelful has to be lifted from the ground without jerks and deposited in the cart without undue haste. It is evident that an abrupt jolt would unnecessarily consume energy in unproductive muscular vibrations, and that any active force that the spadeful of sand might have retained when falling into the cart will have been obtained at the expense of the worker. But to get this result, it is indispensable to put a rhythm in one's movements, which cannot be done by rushing.

If, instead, we wish to put into motion the mass of our body itself, overly rapid movements will have the same disadvantage. In the first place, they cause physiological irregularities that exhaust us by forcing our pace. If, for instance, I have to go a distance of two miles, it will take me forty minutes at a good normal pace. If I hurry, I can do it in thirty-five minutes. But, without gaining much time, I will have spent much more force in convulsive contractions of the arms and legs, in precipitous breathing, in faster heart beats, in perspiration. Second, when we move rapidly, we cannot pass from one movement to another with the roundness and the sinuous, varied inflections that are characteristic of calm, leisurely movements. We observe, for example, that the more our movements are rectilinear, the more abrupt they are. A woman who is doing her hair puts her hand to her head leisurely; instinctively her hand will make a large rounded gesture. But if she is in a rush to remove a pin that is pricking her, her hand will rise quickly in a straight line. The reason is evident. The way our limbs are articulated, their extremities must move along somewhat complex curves. To raise a hand to her head, the woman must lift her wrist, her forearm, and her arm. From the natural composition of these rotatory movements, which do not all take place in the same plane, a sinuous path of a complicated formula will result. But it would be almost impossible to do this same gesture fast: to do so, she would have to resist the centrifugal force which would tend to chase the hand away from her body. She does not even think of it: she is in a hurry, her hand goes straight to its goal and even goes beyond, carried by its momentum, then comes back to it. It is the same for all rapid movements: of necessity, the limb is suddenly carried forward and reaches the end of its journey at a noticeable speed that must be abruptly stopped or even reversed by an effort of the antagonistic muscles.

In rhythm movements, it will always, therefore, be an advantage to limit oneself to a moderate speed. The limbs do not gather momentum in vain; they are given just the necessary speed to effectuate a portion of their oscillation. Like a steam engine in which the steam ceases to enter the cylinder before the piston has ended its course, the innervation of a muscle ceases before it has finished its contraction and the mere relaxing of the fibers carries the limb gently to its journey's end. As to finding this happy medium, it is clearly enough indicated by the natural rhythm of the organic functions and the pendular oscillations of the limbs.

### Regularity of the Rhythm

Automatism has great advantages for economy.[4] When I watch my gestures, all my muscles are held in a semicontraction, that is, in a state of vibration, ready for any command: this exhausts them rapidly. In executing a volitional movement, there is always a certain waste of energy. The principle of the least effort, we have said, belongs to the instinct rather than to the will. The less we are conscious of it, the more it manifests itself. Mechanical movements will therefore be simpler than the others: any sign of elegance or embellishment is inevitably eliminated. (Compare, for instance, ordinary handwriting to penmanship.)

4  Extra details of great interest may be found in Fernand Lagrange, *Physiology of Bodily Exercise* (New York: Appleton, 1890), pt. 6, chap. 6.

In any case, automatic movements spare us the work caused by attention itself that, in volitional movements, is added to the work of the muscles. When one is very used to an exercise, one no longer has to worry about the result itself. See for example what happens in speech and singing. The child makes a visible effort to try to articulate; later, he will only need to think of the sound of the word for its articulation to follow. A soprano in her early studies knows the exact sound she wants to produce, but she has to grope for it and seek the right throat position; she does not know how to place her voice; for the practiced singer, on the contrary, the very idea of the sound, the sight of the note immediately produces its emission.

Automatic movements also have the great advantage of removing the sensation of fatigue itself. In many cases, the sparing of energy they provide is more apparent than real, since the muscle gets tired as a result of the work it is required to do; but, psychologically, this appearance is everything; for nothing is more painful to me than the fatigue I feel. Let us consider, for example, the walk. I feel an effort as soon as I take a few steps or when I start to walk faster, that is, generally speaking, at the moment I make my body accelerate; but, if I just continue the movement I started, I lose consciousness of the work my muscles are doing. If, after a steep climb, you reach a flatter section, without realizing it you continue to make energetic movements and it almost seems that you are propelled into a descent. I remember once trying to convince a cyclist that it was pure illusion when he insisted in all seriousness that his marvelous instrument would work of its own when it reached a lesser slope. New words that you articulate very carefully tire the throat and feel rough on the tongue; the same words pronounced with only the ideas they express in mind seem much smoother. One tires fairly rapidly of playing scales and fingering exercises on the piano, but music pieces can be played for hours with no lassitude.

This effect is further intensified when awareness is eliminated. I am told of a retarded woman who turns the pump wheel in a public bath from morning to night without feeling tired. This reminds me of a hen with both cerebral hemispheres removed, who for hours kept pushing a pendulum away that kept returning to hit it. This is because the sensation of effort, like all sensations, presupposes a certain recapitulation of the memory. When I am in continuous pain, I do not only suffer from my current pain but also from yesterday's and tomorrow's. Without memory and without imagination, pain is almost infinitesimal. Leibnitz said with justification that animals can only have very slim pleasures and pains. It is the same for the feeble-minded and the retarded. And it is the same for us all when we execute reflex movements. They are doubtless not completely unconscious, because we must at least feel in a muted way the sensation that provokes them and because we are nearly always aware of the movement we have made; but the degree of consciousness they require is at the most what one would expect from an animal of the lower species. Conversely, it is impossible to pay attention to the execution of volitional movements without paying attention at the same time to the sensations that accompany them and exaggerating them accordingly. Therefore, if we want to economize our forces, we must try to always give our movements a perfect, almost mechanical regularity.

It may be interesting to see these physiological and mechanical considerations applied to the art of poetry. Where does this need to put a rhythm to human words originate? How, especially, does one explain that all nations seem to have conspired to give their verses just about the same maximum length? I think that the most satisfying explanation of this curious fact is the one proposed by Becq de Fouquières.

Many a poetry reader may imagine that he is allowed to breathe when and how he likes when he is reciting verse. This is an error. Besides the logical breaks of thought where we must pause to take a big breath in order to rest from the effect of recitation, the output must be regulated so that each unit of muscular force which determines the breath flow produces a unit of work which is the verse. Never could a Greek bard, without succumbing to fatigue and exhausting the attention of his listeners, have managed to recite one or more of Homer's Cantos at a time, if his output had not been regulated like a waterfall or a steam jet. The poet may be compared to the blacksmith whose breath follows the rhythm of the blows he gives on the iron placed on his anvil. Just as the blacksmith's regular muscular motion is translated into sounds that follow one another regularly, so is the poet's respiratory rhythm translated into an acoustical rhythm.[5]

## Muscular Synergy

To lift a ten pound weight with my index finger, I must make an energetic effort. With my arm, it is easy. Easier still with my leg, which barely feels the overload. It is not because the weight itself is felt to be gradually less heavy, for experience has taught me to take these differences into account and to interpret them fairly correctly. It is because my sensations themselves are less painful. Spread over a larger number of muscular fibers, the ef-

fort becomes less acute and is no more than a large diffuse sensation that I endure with ease.

It may be objected that since the contraction of one muscle necessitates a certain effort in itself, independent of any exterior work, this spreading of the work over a large number of muscles can provide no economy. This is true, but only if the muscles function in emptiness, that is, without encountering any perceptible outside resistance: in that case, it is evident that, because the effort is proportionate to the mass of contracting fibers, it will be to our interest to contract as few as possible; and this explains why, according to the law of Wundt,[6] all eye movements are done in a way that implies the simplest innervation. This also explains why, when movements demand only skill and precision (like writing or playing the piano or the violin), it is recommended that the beginner give up those contortions, shoulder lunges, and swayings of the body which needlessly complicate his movements. But as soon as strength is needed, muscular synergy is required to avoid fatigue. To lift a heavy weight or overcome a great resistance, the internal work is almost nonexistent compared to the external work. The effort of the contraction is much greater than the effort of innervation, so that on the whole there is economy in increasing the latter to decrease the former.

In this way we will not only spare ourselves the painful sensation of effort, but will be able to actually develop more energy. Since force is engendered by the muscles, not transmitted to them, and since each muscle only disposes of a limited supply of energy regardless of the effort of the innervation, it fol-

---

5   Louis Becq de Fouquières, *Traité général de versification française* (Paris: Charpentier, 1879), p. 16.

6   Wilhelm Max Wundt, *Éléments de psychologie-physiologique*, French ed., 2:87.

lows that to impart to a movement all the energy available, we must activate the greatest possible mass of motor fibers at the same time.

Look at a stonecutter hammering the stone with small rhythmic blows: you cannot quite tell whether his effort is in the arms or in the hips. This spreading of the effort over the mass of the body enables him to work all day without excess fatigue and to furnish, even with rather weak muscles, a considerable work output. If we just place our hand on a heavy rock to try to displace it, the effort is still localized in the arm, and the stone resists. But if we make a greater effort by calling on extra muscles, press our shoulder, our hips, our legs into the rock, all the muscles that can, directly or indirectly, contribute to the impulsion come into play.

When you throw a stone or give a vigorous blow of the fist, it is as much with the legs as with the arms. When you jump from both feet or when, in fencing, you rise from a deep lunge, you work as much with the arms as with the legs. The *ronds de bras* of a ballerina, apparently only designed to give her leaps more elegance, really serve to make her whole upper body contribute to her balance and progression. In the sport of the *savate,* so graceful to watch, there is not a muscle in the body that does not participate.

In the plain walk, the movement of the limbs specially designed for locomotion are always aided by complementary movements of the arms, head, or spine, designed to spread the effort of propulsion over a greater number of muscles. These complementary movements which are found among almost all animals are what gives each individual his or her characteristic gait, like the stork which pushes its beak forward with each step.

But to prevent these various muscular actions from opposing one another, it is indispensable to have them enter into a common rhythm. This is what is meant by muscular synergy.

Two carpenters carry a large beam on their shoulders: if their walk is not synchronized, they will pull against each other, which will soon oblige them to get back together. Three blacksmiths beating together on the anvil must beat in turn in a predetermined order or risk hitting one another's hammers. Oarsmen who do not observe a perfect, unified rhythm will inevitably entangle their oars.

As long as several people are working together, they must combine their movements in order to hinder one another as little as possible. This is also true for the collaboration of our muscles in a single movement. If each of our limbs followed its own rhythm, our activities would become incoherent: sometimes the movements would neutralize one another, sometimes add to one another, and this would cause tugs and jerks, which not only would be unpleasant from the point of view of muscular sensation, but also very unfortunate for the output of work. When on the contrary our various partial movements enter into a common rhythm, the play of each of our members is easier, our muscles work together and can combine their actions in the most advantageous way.

In all movements of some complexity, the muscles must work at the desired movement, not simultaneously, but one after the other; and the efficiency of the result depends on the rhythm at which one has been able to set this series of partial efforts; they have to combine in such a way that each muscle comes into play only at the favorable moment. This is what you might call successive synergy. It is hard at first, but once this rhythm becomes a habit, the procedure seems quite natural. In

*Men at anvil*

order, for instance, to execute a pull up on the rings, one has to have strong arms. But that is not enough, especially at the moment when the elbows have to bend outwards; observe the trained gymnast and you will notice that he overcomes the critical moment with an imperceptible swinging motion, complementing his arm effort by one in his hips. As long as he has not discovered this muscular trick, he can be as vigorous as can be but he will not succeed, though it seems so simple once learned.

Suppose you are asked if you are capable of climbing a vertical ladder with one arm. Knowing that the traction on one arm has always been considered an exceptional feat even among professional gymnasts, you will have to admit that it is absolutely impossible for you, however confident you are of your strength. If you try, however, you will find that by applying muscular synergy intelligently, nothing is easier. Once your hand clutches a rung, if you bend your legs abruptly while arching your back, you will raise your center of gravity by the single action of the large muscles, and your arm then can reach rapidly to grab the rung above. If you fail the first time, it is for lack of know-how rather than strength. In this case, the muscular trick consists in reversing the usual rhythm of the leap. In the jump on two feet, the different muscles of the body enter into action successively, starting from the top. In the ladder exercise, they act in the reverse: they go into play successively, starting from the bottom. Reasoning bears this out. In the jump on two feet, your point of support is below you. If you begin to give an impulse from the legs, you have to lift the whole mass of your body with the first effort; whereas if you start with the arms and continue through the hips, ending with the legs, each of the muscles will be acting only upon a mass that has already received a certain amount of acceleration; so your whole body

will release itself progressively, like the spiral coil that one releases after pressing it down on the floor. To bounce from rung to rung up the ladder, evidently these movements must follow each other in the reverse order, since the point of support is above. On the face of it, there is no reason why this jump by traction should not bring one's center of gravity as high as the jump by pushing; one can rise quite easily to a height of twenty-five or thirty centimeters which corresponds to the average jump on two feet, measured, it goes without saying, by the actual elevation of the center of gravity.

Let us analyze in detail one last example of this muscular synergy. This is particularly instructive, because it shows the proportion of skill and even the cunning needed for efforts that seem, on the surface, to require only brute force.

The problem is to lift a heavy barbell off the ground and to hold it at arms' length above the head. It seems that there is only one way to go about this: bend, seize the weight, and stretch the arms. But that would be very tiring. Now look at the trained weight lifter: first he bends, lifts the barbell with the right arm while leaning on his knee with the left; then with a motion of the legs and hips, he projects the mass of the barbell and holds it with his bent arm to the height of his shoulders; next, with a thrust of his shoulder, he throws it a little higher; then he stoops and twists his body under it to be in a position to stretch his arm; finally, proudly, he rises. And we see this feat of strength executed almost without effort. I have purposely emphasized the phases of the movements as if there were pauses in between, in order to analyze them more effectively. In reality, a gymnast tries to minimize and blend them together as much as possible, in order to lessen the effort by taking advantage of the momentum of the mass he is lifting, as well as to conceal the

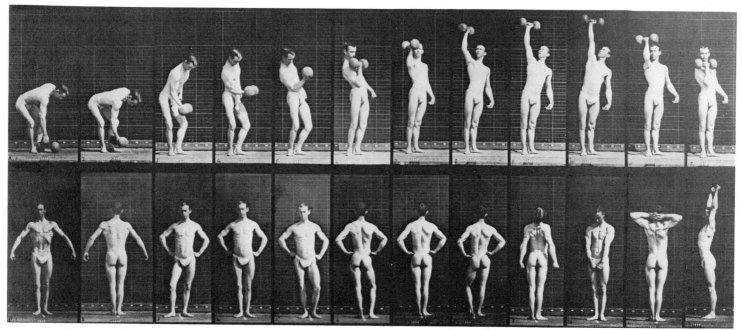

*Man lifting dumbbell and flexing muscles*

process. The great preoccupation of bystanders watching the performance of the strong man on a street corner is to see if, by any chance, he is not an impostor. So our gymnast will attempt to execute his trick as smoothly as possible and to lift his barbell, in appearance at least, in one single motion.

# 6    Applications to Balance and Locomotion

Before examining specific examples, I would like to draw the reader's attention to two principles, simple enough in theory, but in practice usually neglected. We will refer to them again when we deal with animal locomotion.

The first principle is: to displace a mass, a point of support is necessary. Elementary mechanics, which mentions only the point of application of forces, is so abstract that it can make us overlook or misinterpret this essential truth. One must be aware that a mechanical force can only act upon a mass by bringing it closer to or farther from another mass. As a result, the action of a force is always divided between its point of application and its point of support. When I jump, the effort I make to leave the ground tends to push it away from me with a force exactly equivalent. This is always the case, whether the point of support is firm or mobile, hard or elastic.

The second principle, as simple and as often ignored in practice as the first, relates to the direction of the forces: the action of mechanical forces is always directed along the line that joins their point of application to their point of support. For example, when a coiled spring pushes two masses away from each other, it will always, whatever its shape, give them a rectilinear motion. This principle explains the convention of representing simple forces by straight lines, though the forces themselves evidently cannot be conceived as linear; but this way of representing them corresponds properly to the direction they give to the masses upon which they act. Let us examine a few applications. When I stamp on the ground, my leg is like a spring that has its point of application at my body's center of gravity and its point of support on the ground. If I draw a line between these two points, I will call it my line of force. Theory indicates and experience proves that I can only give an impulse in this direction. If I am standing, for example, my line of force is vertical and I can only execute a vertical jump. To jump forward, I must first drop my weight or put one foot back, which comes to the same thing, in order to make my line of force oblique to the ground. We will see that in nearly every problem of gymnastics, the difficulty first encountered is caused by groping for this line of force until the desired resistance is felt, instead of examining how the problem can be solved through theory.

If you keep these principles in mind, you will be less likely to ignore good mechanical sense, both in the theory and in the practice of body exercises.

## Problems of Balance

### 1. Equilibrium of a bicycle

How can you balance on two wheels placed in front of one another in a horizontal plane? It seems as difficult as walking a tight rope. You can succeed in ten minutes, however, as long as you have an intelligent instructor to tell you what movements to execute. Strangely enough, few people who practice this exercise are capable of showing a novice how to keep his or her balance; they do the right movements instinctively, without knowing why or even what they are doing exactly, and this proves once more the usefulness of theory to a teacher of gymnastics.

The program for this exercise is simple. When you feel yourself falling to one side, you should turn the wheel sharply to that direction. The centrifugal force then carries you to the other side and you will find your balance again. After this movement is executed a number of times, it becomes so mechanical that you could not fall even if you wanted to.

### 2. Equilibrium on the balance beam

The theory of balancing on the balance beam is more difficult to analyze and much more delicate to apply.

A gymnast is practicing the walk on the balance beam for the first time. This presents him with a set of conditions different from his normal walk where he needs to place his foot on the side he is falling to regain his equilibrium. Now, his supporting base being linear, his balance is only secure against a forward or backward fall; the danger is in falling to the side. This is not precisely an unstable position but it is a critical one; that is, even if his body has no immediate tendency to fall, the slightest impulse will induce a fall. Look now at our novice acrobat. He takes a few steps, feels he is losing his balance, and stops to regain it. From then on, he is lost. With a comic desperation, he fights against gravity that is pulling him down, he wriggles and throws his arms from side to side. Finally he falls. What mistakes has he made and what should he have done to regain the perpendicular?

The moment he felt himself falling to one side, he instinctively tried to throw himself to the other side, but to do this, he needed a lateral point of support. It is evident that all the contortions in the world would not have changed the direction in which gravity was beginning to draw him.

In the midst of his incoherent gestures and the pendulum movements of his arms, one could still guess at his intention to carry a portion of his weight to the other side of the beam. This was indeed a step toward the correct solution. For under such circumstances, since his arms are the only part of his body that he can maneuver freely, one can predict that it is by using them as movable counterweights that he will have to try to regain his equilibrium. (If it is a question of holding completely still, the simplest way is to take one's whole weight on one foot and use the free leg as counterweight. That is what juggler equilibrists do. In such cases, the balance is perfect.)

But there must be a right way to use this counterweight. Suppose I am falling to the left and extend my right arm. What have I gained? Nothing. For, in order to extend my arm this way, I have to take support on my own body and push it away in the very direction it was already falling. Should I then extend my left arm to the left? Temporarily it might help; but once the effect of the reaction has helped me straighten up for a moment, my arm, having reached the end of its movement, will recover any momentum it has given my body. In effect, the position of my center of gravity will not be modified by any movement in which my body gets a point of support on itself, and I will continue to fall exactly as if I had not moved. Since my only exterior support is on this bar, it is on it that I must make an effort to straighten up.

Once this is understood, the solution to the problem begins to emerge. Let us draw from the gymnast's hands two perpendicular lines to the bar, lines $D$ and $G$. These are the lines of force along which his arms must move in order to obtain a useful result. Suppose he is falling to the right: he will raise his left arm along the line $G$, bringing it for instance from $a$ to $b$. If you study the illustration (fig. 4) you will see that as the mass of the arm rises, it goes to the left and acts as a counterweight, exactly as if it had gone from $a$ to $b'$. But although the movement from $a$ to $b'$ would have produced a backward motion of the body,

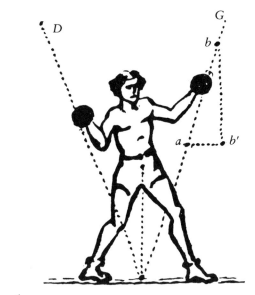

*Figure 4*

the movement from $a$ to $b$ does not, because the mass of the arm is only moving away in a perpendicular line to the bar which is its real support. The center of gravity of the body is therefore correctly carried over to the left. If he does this movement fast enough, he can use not only the dead weight of his arm but also its active force to straighten himself.

If he feels he has gone beyond his goal, he will lower his left arm, still along the line $G$, and raise his right one along the line $D$. Thanks to such oscillations, he gains absolute control of his balance with a minimum of displacement.

You may experiment with this in a more practical way, by holding a chair or a large book in each hand and placing your feet simply one before the other. You will observe that any arm extensions you make to the right or the left are immaterial to the maintenance or loss of your balance, but if you move them along the directions we have indicated, that is, along the perpendiculars to the base of support, you will realize that you are displacing your center of gravity in one direction or another at will.

It is true that these pendular arm movements may be insufficient to regain your balance, if you start them too late; in this case, you will fall whatever you do, having exceeded the limit of deviation that can be corrected, or what we might call the maneuverable zone of equilibrium. In order to extend this zone, acrobats on the tight rope use a balancing pole. Then there is no problem of balance. The construction lines on figure 4 also indicate how to maneuver weights. As to the body twists, though it is theoretically possible to discover some usefulness to them, it is best to resort to them as little as possible; they have the disadvantage of disturbing the balance by making us lose that delicate sense of weight that presupposes absolute calm and composure.

In conclusion, it would be useful to discover what has to be done to maintain oneself in these unstable positions with the least work possible. For there may still be a specific way of executing the above maneuver.

We know that for an object to be in a stable balance, it must not only have no tendency to move away from its position; it must also tend to return to it on its own when slightly displaced.

The condition needed for such balance is evidently that it cannot be displaced from its position without its center of gravity being raised. In other words, in its stable position it should have its center of gravity placed as low as possible in relation to any future position it can be given. A large pot placed on its three legs, a trapeze suspended to its two rings, a marble at the bottom of a hollow dish are all examples that answer the above condition. In order to displace these objects from their stable positions, one would have to accomplish some work.

In contrast, let us consider an object placed in an unstable balance, such as a pyramid poised on its point: its center of gravity is at maximum height compared to any new position it may be in. When an object placed in an unstable position begins to fall, it tends to move farther and farther away from its present position by reason of its weight. But it is impossible for the object not to start falling, even supposing it is perfectly balanced at the start: for all outside forces that affect it would have to counterbalance one another exactly, which is infinitely improbable. Consequently, it will fall and work will have to be done to return it to its original position. In other words, an object can be maintained for some time in a position of unstable balance only with a certain expenditure of energy.

How can we reduce this work to the minimum?

If objects fell at a constant speed, one could let the fall continue as long as one wished: what would be lost? Consider, for instance, a clock weight descending with perfect regularity; it would not matter whether one wound it up every day or every hour or every minute: the work needed to return it to its position would always be proportionate to the time elapsed. But a free fall, in which objects fall at a uniformly accelerated speed is different: it is to one's advantage to let the fall continue for as short a time as possible because, if a given amount of work is needed to raise it again every second (since the space traveled is proportional to the square of the time of the displacement), it will take four times as much work to raise it every other second. The ideal would be to raise it every instant, opposing an antagonistic effort to each infinitesimal descent of the center of gravity: one could thus maintain it in balance without any work, during a given time.

Practically speaking, this is manifestly impossible. For one can only perceive the fall of an object when it has reached a certain point; once perceived, more time is needed for this sensation to produce the required muscular reaction; finally, it is impossible to measure this reaction precisely enough to return the object to its exact position of balance without going beyond it. In fact, an object we are trying to maintain in an unstable balance always takes an up-and-down rhythmic movement. It falls to one side, we push it back to the other, and so on. Try as we may, it is impossible to maintain it absolutely still.

Why even try? The effort to maintain the object's balance is tiring, not so much because of the physical energy expended as because of the attention required. So that, though it is mechanically speaking economical to limit the oscillations as much as possible, it is mentally advantageous to allow them a certain amplitude. Since it is impossible to prevent them, one might as well let them get big enough to be really perceptible. When we practice a balancing trick for the first time, we apply ourselves first to obtaining absolute immobility: and we are at once on the alert, wondering on which side the fall will occur; when it does happen, it will of course take us by surprise and we can only correct it with a violent motion that will throw us to the opposite side. I have remarked that, on the contrary, trained acrobats forestall the action of gravity by losing their balance purposely in order to regain it more easily; it is evident that one can correct more easily a volitional oscillation measured in ad-

vance than an accidental one. The equilibrist preparing to walk a slack rope no sooner places his foot down than he automatically begins those rhythmic movements of the arms to which he would sooner or later have to resort to regain his balance.

In pursuing these studies, it would be interesting to analyze, from a mechanical viewpoint, each new balancing trick that circus acrobats are continuously creating. The Japanese have made marvelous discoveries in this area and are especially remarkable for the perfect ease with which they execute their astonishing exercises. But we must forego such analyses, however instructive they may be, as they would be too lengthy.

## Problems of Locomotion

*1. Skating*   Skating is certainly one of the most graceful and original exercises devised by man. A beginner venturing on the ice for the first time feels very anxious. In vain do her feet seek a point of support on this slippery surface that seems to be stealing from under her. Then, somewhat emboldened, she will try to advance by making the usual motions of the walk: inevitably she falls.

The reason is that, in spite of the apparent analogy between walking and skating, the conditions of balance and propulsion are radically different.

In order to start walking, the pedestrian drops his weight forward, taking support from the foot left behind; if he wishes to stop, he will do the reverse, inclining his body backward and making an effort on the foot he has brought forward. He is always, therefore, taking his support either in front of or behind him.

But when you look at the blade of a skate, you understand

immediately that it offers no resistance to sliding in the direction of its length and that, consequently, it can offer no support in that direction. The novice skater who, out of habit, keeps seeking support behind her to push herself forward, or in front of her to stop, will necessarily fall forward or backward. Experienced skaters themselves never fail to commit this error when they practice leaping over an obstacle.

On the other hand, the blade is constructed in such a way as to bite into the ice with its edge, which prevents it from sliding to the side. Only a transversal push will offer the skater a solid support. This leads us to formulate the simple rule that governs the balance and the propulsion of the skater: the push off must be perpendicular to the line traced by the skate.

Once this principle is established, practice has to follow. If you slide forward on one foot, whatever your speed, you must hold your body erect so that the projection of your center of gravity falls exactly in the middle of your skate. The tendency of beginners to put their bodies forward must be resisted, for the slight friction of the ice, not yet mentioned for the sake of simplicity, would already have made you tip in that direction. To trace a circle, you will lean toward the center, in order to resist the centrifugal force which tends to fling you away from the circle. Practice will teach you the required angle of inclination.

To get into motion, you place your feet at right angles, then transfer your weight from one foot to the other. This is the initial push off, which is easy to do correctly, by bearing down fully on the edge of the skate and shifting to the side, without lifting the heel. It is only after gaining some speed that problems begin, because you become less conscious of what you are doing. The thing to understand is that, even when going full

speed, the foot with which you shove to accelerate must execute exactly the same maneuver as at the start: avoid seeking support behind you and put your weight squarely to the side, in a direction exactly perpendicular to the line traced on the ice by the supporting skate.

Let us suppose that you are sliding on the left skate at a speed $v$ and that you are carrying to the right the projection of your center of gravity at a speed $v'$: the line V which is the diagonal of the parallelogram formed by $v$ and $v'$ indicates the resultant of these two speeds: this is the direction in which you must place your right foot on the ice for your next slide.

By shifting continuously from foot to foot, you would, if the ice were perfectly slippery, be accelerating with each new effort and therefore acquire an unlimited speed. But since the sliding of your skate always requires a certain amount of work which is proportional to the space you travel, the distance you can reach as a result of a given effort is limited. Add to that the resistance of the air which increases rapidly with the speed of

*Figure 5*

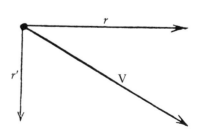

travel. After a while, your speed will become regular, for the new efforts you make will be just sufficient to maintain it.

In the action described above, the entire weight of the body shifts alternately from one foot to the other. One can, if one wishes, skate with both feet on the ice: one will be tracing a double sinuous line instead of a series of oblique ones. In this new action, used especially when skating backwards, it is, at first, hard to understand how the propulsion is obtained. The skater advances with no apparent effort, with only a slight motion of the hips. In reality, the skate is pushed off according to the same principles as before; but the weight is not completely transferred from one foot to the other, allowing each foot to rest a little all the time. That is why, though this action is perhaps more elegant than the preceding one, it cannot produce the same speed.

Is it possible to skate with one leg? Is there a skater who has not tried? I have never seen it done myself and I believe the feat is considered impossible. It could be executed, however, by replacing the shove of the skate described above by a jump to the side. Why could one not also gather speed by skating on one foot? The maneuver would consist in shifting one's center of gravity alternately to the right, then to the left of the sinuous line traced by the skates, by executing a series of jumps to one side then to the other, linked by a slide; the difficulty would not be to give oneself these impulses, but to regain one's balance after the impulse is given. Theoretically, the feat is not impossible; it is up to expert skaters to make the attempt.

What happens, finally, when I wish to leap over an obstacle? This is when it is most essential to determine my line of force correctly: the reaction must be abrupt, energetic, and any false maneuver would expose me to a serious fall. From the analyses above, we conclude that it is absolutely impossible to jump forward as I do on solid ground; for I would have to find a support behind me. Two solutions remain: either to leap over the obstacle sideways; or to approach the obstacle at great speed and execute a vertical jump at the last moment, which, combined with the horizontal impulse, will give me exactly the desired trajectory.

2. *The trapeze*   The movements of the trapeze, by their elegance and aerial character, hold a place of their own among acrobatic feats. But the main reason for analyzing the movements on the trapeze is that it may later shed some light on the still obscure theory of flight.

The simplest and best known of such movements is that of the swing. Almost everyone has practiced this exercise. But one may not always realize its mechanical theory nor the actual movements one executes in order to obtain swings of increasing size.

Suppose you are motionless, with your feet on the board and your hands grabbing the ropes. In which direction can you move your center of gravity? Twist anyway you please, you will be unable to displace it forward or backward, because of the lack of support. The only thing you can do is lower or raise it in relation to the seat, in other words, to bring it closer or farther from the point of suspension. Even if you were in full flight, the conditions would be the same; your efforts will always be directed perpendicularly to the surface of the seat which serves as your point of support, because that is the only direction in which you will find some resistance. Therefore, the correct maneuver is simply to keep the body always erect on the board, with your knees flexed in descent and straightened in ascent. Clearly, the result will be to amplify the swings you would be making without this action. When you reach the bottom of the journey at a certain horizontal speed which would already tend to make you rise to a certain height, the effort you make to raise your center of gravity in relation to the seat will add to this horizontal component a vertical one that will carry you even higher.

Naturally, it is in the first period of the ascent that the effort is the most effective and must be the most energetic. Past a certain degree of inclination, it would only tend to fling you back.

One can easily ascertain that this simple maneuver produces the desired effect by operating in the same way on a pendulum. Figure 6 indicates well enough how the experiment works. Under such conditions, it is evident that one can only apply simple tractions on the swinging weight. Consider the momentum of the swing as illustrated on the figure. While the weight recedes from me, carried by its own momentum at a tangential force $f$, I pull on the cord with a central force $f'$. The two forces, perpendicular to one another and acting upon the weight simultaneously, will result in the force $F$. Its speed will therefore increase in the ratio of $f$ to $F$ and its active force in the ratio of $f^2$ to $F^2$. The slight paradox in this experiment is that the direction of my effort on the weight, which carries it high and forward, would appear to carry it high and backward. One is also surprised when executing this experiment at the vigor of the effort that can be applied to this mobile mass, once it has gathered enough momentum. The larger the swings, the more resistance it offers. In the end, by pulling on the cord with all one's might, one can swing the weight at a prodigious speed.

It is from this simple swinging motion that most movements in aerial acrobatics derive. These exercises are of such variety that one might think they involve different procedures of impulsion. Grasping the horizontal bar with both hands, the gymnast swings higher and higher until he makes a full turn around the bar. On the rings, he swings by raising his bent legs above his head and then throwing them forward. On the trapeze, he gets himself going by sliding down to his knees and righting himself again; or, with his hands on the bar, he pushes himself forward by giving his body a swinging motion that he combines with that of the trapeze. The procedure is always the same: in every case, the impetus is given by raising the center of gravity in the ascent and lowering it in the descent. Any movement that tended to throw only part of the body backward or forward would be completely lost and would bring only confusion to the useful movement. The fact that in all these exercises the total body is used for the propulsion is due to the law

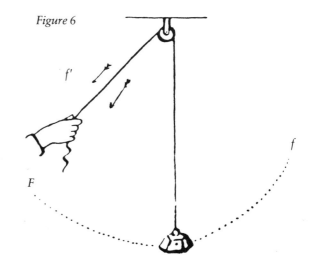

Figure 6

of synergy and to the need for having the greatest possible number of muscles contributing to the effort. But these partial efforts finally converge into the central effort of traction; at least, it is only when that happens that the swing can be done all at once in the most economical, effective, and graceful way.

In this necessarily summary study, I have only considered the simplest movements practiced in gymnastics. The circus offers opportunities to study many complications and refinements, especially on the flying trapeze. The sight of acrobats flying from trapeze to trapeze, floating for a few moments in the air as if in flight, combining their swings, moving together or apart in a play of muscles whose secret the eye cannot detect, is a spectacle of great aesthetic value, more thrilling to watch than any other.

# 7   Terrestrial Locomotion

Let us now examine how our colleagues, the animals, have solved the problem of locomotion. To this end, our most valuable tool will be direct observation.

In view of the infinite variety of locomotor instruments among animals, we will have to limit our study to the most typical and frequently used procedures, disregarding the singularities or simple variations of nature. We will discuss terrestrial, aquatic, and aerial locomotion.

The procedures used by animals to move on the ground can be reduced to two kinds: *reptation,* in which the movement involves the whole body, and what I call, for want of a better word, *articulated locomotion,* which is activated by specialized organs.

## Reptation

Reptation is the mode of locomotion generally used by animals of the lower species. Its characteristic is that it places the animal in contact with the ground for almost the entire length of its body so that it can only advance by dragging itself with a varying amount of friction.

If you picture the crawling animal as formed by a continuous line of solid dots, you can see that these dots may execute two kinds of movements. The first is a longitudinal motion by which they move toward and away from one another, so that the body of the animal shortens and lengthens without losing its straight line. This is the vermicular motion. The second is a transversal oscillating motion by which the line of the body is inflected first to one side, then to the other. This is called the undulatory motion. In fact, all crawling animals are both elastic and flexible; their body can always stretch as well as curve a certain amount. But some types are more prone to one type of movement than another.

*1. Vermicular motion*   Consider an earthworm resting on the ground. Its body is in the primary position, that is in a half-contraction; all its rings are still capable of stretching and shrinking further. It now begins to move (fig. 7).

In order to do so, it first advances its head by stretching its forward rings; this progressive motion continues until the portion carried forward is heavy enough. The animal then pauses and, partly pushing, partly pulling them, drives its posterior rings forward. Finally, nothing remains but its stretched tail, which it withdraws. It has now made one step. Then the same movements start all over at a very regular rhythm.

This method of locomotion, which seems rather complicated, in reality works very simply. All the rings are successively executing the same movement. First they stretch, then swell as they shrink. Nothing prevents them from sending a second or third wave before the first one reaches the extremity of the body, but no speed would be gained in so doing. If the waves were more numerous, they would also be shorter, because the animal, having its entire length in contact with the ground, can only carry forward a limited number of rings at a time. The part of the body that slides on the ground must always be lighter than the part that serves as support. Whether the movement is executed with one wave or several, the proportion of sliding and supporting parts remains the same. The only difference

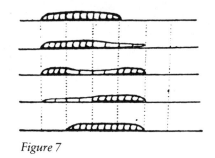

*Figure 7*

will be that in one case the steps will be long and slow and in the other, shorter and more frequent. The worm prefers to take large steps.

In the above description, the animal advances in the opposite direction to the wave it is transmitting; this is necessary because the initial movement is an elongation. Suppose, on the other hand, that it initiates the motion with a contraction, that is, by withdrawing one of its extremities. It will then advance by the other extremity and the muscular wave will move from tail to head. This is the case with slugs, snails, and probably all gasteropods. When you watch one of these animals crawling on the ground, you see it moving in one piece, with no partial movement visible, leaving a sticky trail. How does it propel itself?

Put it on a piece of glass and look underneath (fig. 8). You will see a series of light spots appearing near the tail, moving in a line toward the head where they get lost one by one. If I touch the animal's eyes, it will stop in surprise and the movement of the spots is interrupted. Then, gradually reassured, it starts creeping again and the motion of the spots resumes. These observations indicate that the creeping sole of the snail is tra-

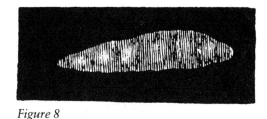

*Figure 8*

versed from tip to tip by a series of muscular waves. The lighter spots probably are due to the stretching of the fibers which makes them more diaphanous. Once the wave reaches the head, it is released and the animal advances at this end as much as it had retracted at the other. Here, as in the first example, the speed of the progression is proportional to the frequency and amplitude of the steps.

*2. Undulatory motion* The undulatory motion will be apparent in animals that are more flexible than extensible. Numerous animals move this way. Even when they have specialized locomotor organisms, they have recourse to undulatory movements to aid them in swimming or walking. These movements therefore deserve our special attention, not only because they are beautiful to watch but because they are used so frequently. Once we have grasped them in their complexity, the other systems become clear. The effort we must make to do so will be rewarded by the aesthetic pleasure they give.

Try to imagine an undulatory movement and you will see at once a sinuous line inflected several times on each side of an axis. You will find it more difficult to visualize the progression of these sinuosities. Now draw a sinuous line on the ground and picture a serpent advancing along that line (fig. 9). In your imagination, as the snake follows the line in a uniform motion, its body undulates regularly from head to tail. Now that the relationship of waves and body is clear, we can eliminate the idea of progression and picture the snake executing the same undulations without displacing itself. A more visual representation can be obtained by shaking a long cord at one end, producing undulations on the ground.

The undulatory movement implies a superior organization to that needed for vermicular motion. An animal that is absolutely filiform or formed by a single bundle of muscular fibers might move in a vermicular motion but in order to obtain an undulatory movement, there must be at least two juxtaposed muscular bundles, capable of contracting independently from one another.

Take a paper ribbon and wet it on one side. The wet surface stretches, the other contracts, and the ribbon rolls up on the drier side. Wet it half on one side, half on the other and it will twist in the shape of an S. If you wet a long ribbon alternately on each side, it will form a series of regular waves. Now we understand easily the mechanism of the undulatory motion in crawling animals. Suppose we have a diagram of an animal formed by two muscular bundles, A and B (fig. 10). Suppose each bundle executes a vermicular motion, with A contracting while B stretches. A series of transversal waves will run through

*Figure 9*

the entire body of the animal, succeeding one another at a rhythm all the more regular that, once initiated, each wave tends to transmit itself through the body on its own. In the same way, when you hold the end of a cord and give it a simple up and down motion, the wave is propagated through the entire cord.

In a more complex animal, such as the snake, formed by a series of vertebrae linked by a great number of criss-crossed muscular fibers, the undulation will always be obtained by the same procedure, that is, by the alternating of two vermicular movements spreading from fiber to fiber. How can these movements be utilized for progression? First, the wave can be transmitted either from tail to head, in the direction of the progression, or from head to tail, in the opposite direction. But one will observe that the undulation is always from head to tail. Theoretically, there could be a forward progression with a back to front horizontal wave. The conditions would be similar to those of vermicular reptation. Some ringed animals may crawl that way. But it would be a most ineffectual kind of locomotion, for it would further delay the inherent slowness of the motion caused by ground friction. Moreover, it would only be possible on a perfectly smooth surface. On a soaked, sandy, or grassy terrain (and even more in water), the wave would be rendered useless by resistance and the animal would retreat instead of advancing. Rather than progressing in spite of this resistance, it is much more advantageous to use the resistance as a point of support. That is what the snake, which undulates from head to tail, does. Any resistance that interferes with the transmission of the wave is utilized to carry its body forward. The animal will advance, whatever surface it is placed on, as long as it is not polished like glass, which is exceptional. Plunged in water, it will swim. This method of progression by retrogressive waves lends itself to very diverse conditions of living.

Let us now try to comprehend its mechanism. As the animal undulates, all the parts of its body move at the same time, in a somewhat complicated maneuver. They have two relative movements: first, a transversal oscillation, that carries them alternately to right and left of the axis of the body; and second, a rectilinear oscillation, that makes them in turn advance and retreat and that can be represented by the projection of the actual movement on a line parallel to the body axis. But we can ignore the transversal movements which do not affect progression; all we need say about them is that they must compensate one another so that the total of the parts going from right to left is equal at all times to those going from left to right. It is in the rectilinear movements of the different parts of the body that we shall find the explanation for progression.

In any kind of reptation, a portion of the body must serve as support to push the other part forward and some points must retreat or at least remain stationary while the others advance. The question is to find out which of them push and which are being pushed. Watch closely a captive snake crawling on the floor of its cage and observe that the movement is not the same in all parts of the body; the points situated in the median part of the waves, where the body axis crosses them, are retreating. On

*Figure 10*

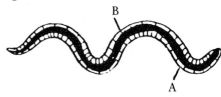

the contrary, to the right and to the left, the movement at the crest of the waves goes from back to front, forming on both sides of the central current a double countercurrent.

From this observation, we conclude that the crawling serpent takes its support on the median part of its waves, in order to push forward its lateral parts.

We would achieve the same result if we followed the trajectory of a given point of the body. Suppose we choose a point on the crest of the wave, on the animal's left. We will see this point advancing first very rapidly, going diagonally to the right. Then its speed slows down as it nears the line of the axis. For a moment it recedes; then it starts advancing again, with an increasing speed that reaches its maximum at the moment it is carried on the top of a new wave, to the right of the animal.

At first, we don't see why the animal advances in such a way. Is it because in its median parts it drags its body on the ground transversely, while in its lateral parts it glides lengthwise? But the friction of a linear body on a flat surface is sensibly the same, whether it slides transversely or longitudinally. There-

*Figure 11*

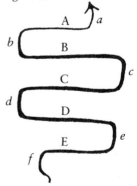

fore progression will only be possible on one condition, and that is if the waves have considerable width and little length. Let us consider, for greater simplicity, a diagram of a reptile, undulating from head to tail in rectangular waves (fig. 11). The effort that tends to push the transversal lines ABCDE backward must necessarily take its support on the longitudinal lines *abcdef;* if therefore the waves were longer than wide, the animal would retreat; if length and width were the same, it would undulate in place. In order to be pushed forward with enough strength, the animal has to fold itself over in wide undulations.

*3. Improved reptation*   On the whole, in all the above systems of locomotion, the expended force is poorly used; for the animal progresses only by describing a very sinuous path, covering a lot of ground without advancing much, and losing a great deal of energy by useless friction. This mode of locomotion, necessarily very slow, is painful to watch.

As a result, crawling creatures have found a way to vary and perfect the system. In order to diminish the friction, they make sure they always lift a little above the ground the part of the body that is being pushed forward; and at the same time, they press harder onto the part that serves as support.

The earthworm is careful to lift its head as it moves forward. The caterpillars that creep in a vermicular motion from tail to head have adopted a mechanically effective method. They lift their tail, curve it back, and put the tip down on the ground. They have thus shortened themselves by a certain amount, which is the length of their step. After that, they need only to relay this vertical wave toward the head and flatten it out and the step is done. This system is mechanically very advantageous. For, once the wave is formed, only an infinitesimal effort is

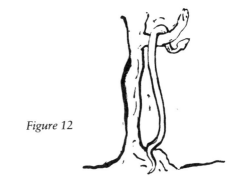

*Figure 12*

needed to transmit it forward, as each ring rises off the ground and sets itself down again with no perceptible friction.

But of all the creeping animals, those that take the best advantage of reptation are indisputably the serpents. Their methods are infinitely varied. Their mode of locomotion has something paradoxical about it. Lying full length on the ground, they stretch themselves and shift a loop to the side, using it as a support to carry themselves forward. Sometimes they can be seen hooking themselves onto the branch of a tree by their front rings and climbing mysteriously, the shorter part descending as the longer part rises (fig. 12). I have spent hours in the zoo, seeking the law that governs these strange evolutions. I finally observed that they are obtained by the progression of a wave moving from head to tail. In other words, these various methods are only variations of typical reptation.

Having observed them only fleetingly, I cannot tell how our garter snakes can move so rapidly by creeping on a flat surface. Most likely they set down on the ground only the median part of their waves, where the motor effort is concentrated, lifting the crests slightly to lessen friction. But again, this is only conjecture.

Snakes with slow paces and somewhat soft bodies must preferably adopt the transversal reptation of which the Algerian horned viper gives us a typical example. This is a very ingenious mode of locomotion. When a horned viper creeps over the sand in its cage, you will see a kind of undulating package rolling from one side to the other, always displacing itself along a line perpendicular to its body axis. And it is indeed by rolling that the animal advances. Figure 13 will explain this movement better than words.

The parts indicated by a thick line stay on the ground during the undulation, the thinner parts are those that are lifted slightly to travel, and the broken line shows the new position the waves take. In this system, the work yield is at its maximum, because the point of support of the effort is fixed and the loss of energy from friction is zero. In fact, this result is obtained very simply. In order to transform longitudinal reptation into transversal reptation, or the glide into a roll, the animal need only lift slightly the part of the wave where the movement takes place in the direction it wishes to go.

*Figure 13*

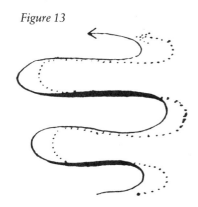

*Articulated Locomotion*

Simple reptation implies an organism that has very little differentiation, in which all parts of the body are equally affected by the act of locomotion. It can only be employed by animals of the lower species. With those higher on the animal scale, we see the appearance of special organs that concentrate the motor effort on a limited part of the body. This is what we call *articulated locomotion*. Does this specialization necessarily mean mechanical progress? Not always, for we have shown that among creeping animals, locomotion can occur under almost perfect conditions. But this differentiation is indispensable if the animal is to acquire more varied aptitudes and superior faculties. One could therefore say that the progress is a mental rather than a mechanical one.

To judge the value of this mode of locomotion, it is important first to understand its operation. This is much more difficult than it might appear. In order to know how an animal walks or runs, we must first analyze the mechanism of its motion. The movements are always so complicated and so fast that they can only be grasped once their laws are understood.

If you skim over the multitude of terrestrial animals, you will at once be struck by the diversity of their organs of locomotion. A few primates, a number of rodents, and all the birds travel by means of their back legs; a prodigious number of animals belonging to the most diverse species walk on four feet. Most insects walk on six. Among many anthropods, there is almost no limit to the multiformity of locomotor organs. The variety of gaits is just as great. Some animals advance in bounds, others in continuous progression; some are organized to climb; and in

each species, the paces can be further diversified, almost indefinitely, according to circumstances.

Since we cannot examine them all, we will restrict ourselves to a description of the gaits of the quadruped. These gaits seem to have solved the problem of terrestrial locomotion with the most elegance. We will study them in the horse where they are exhibited in their most typical form.

The horse has three characteristic paces: the walk, the trot, and the gallop.

*1. The walk*   In the walk, the horse puts each foot down on the ground in succession. To realize how this pace is set, you must observe it from the start and at its slowest. Watch a horse browsing in a meadow. Poised at first squarely on its four feet, it shifts a little forward by the action of its hind quarters. Then, at some point, the balance is lost and it brings its foreleg forward, the left one, say; then, almost at once, the right posterior leg advances. A pause. Then the horse advances its right foreleg, then the left back one. The reason is one of balance. As it moves its left front and right back legs, the other two members give it a solid base with their diagonal support.

To accelerate its walk, the horse will skip the intermediary pause; it will not even wait for one foot to have accomplished its movement before moving the other. But the beats of the four feet will always follow the same order: left back, right front, right back, left front.

This typical gait may be altered in many ways. The horse's beats succeed one another at equal intervals but other quadrupeds may exhibit a less regular rhythm. We can indeed find no specific reason why the beats of the hind legs should follow those of the forelegs in such a way as to fall exactly in between.

*Horse walking*

*Horse trotting*

When we observe the walks of a number of quadrupeds, we realize that they are governed by one rule only; they must lift their forepaw shortly before it is chased away by the hindpaw that takes its place.

*2. The trot*   The characteristic of the trot is that the beats of the posterior legs coincide exactly with those of the anterior ones, so that we only hear two sounds instead of the four in the walk. The transition from the walk to the trot is obtained, as Jules Marey has ascertained with the help of registering apparatus, by accelerating the movements of the hindquarters which catch up with the front legs in a few strides. The two beats of this gait can be analyzed in the following manner: on the first beat, the horse moves its left front and right back legs forward; on the second beat, its right front and left back.

This simplification of rhythm is due to lateral flexions of the spine that force the shoulders and haunches to move in opposite directions. This is for the same reason that, when walking rapidly, the arms of a human swing in opposition to the legs.

In the horse, the trot is a high, rapid pace: the rebounds are strong enough for the animal to lost contact with the ground and find itself elevated in the air for a moment after each stride. I do not know why some people think the trot is an artificial step. On the contrary, this oppositional movement of the shoulders and haunches is so natural that it can certainly be found among most quadrupeds, both on earth and in the water, at least as a pace with a component of effort.

*3. The gallop*   The gallop has endless variations. The hunting gallop of the horse, or canter, is a three-beat gait; its racing gallop a four-beat one. A steer will not gallop like a roebuck, nor a terrier like a greyhound. To find one's way among this multiplicity of gaits in order to develop a law, we must not pay attention to the rhythm of the beats, which is precisely the variable element. We have to find out how the pace is established. Watch a harnessed horse being put to a trot. From time to time, it will try to gallop and it is easy to see what it does then: it attempts to bounce forward by hitting the ground with both back feet at the same time. This is the characteristic effort in the gallop. By giving us the justification for this gait, the horse is also telling us its law.

Scan a book of instantaneous photographs of galloping quadrupeds.[1] You will ascertain that the two back legs always have a common moment of support. If they step on the ground one after another as in the canter or almost simultaneously as in the gallop, whether they make one sound or two, these are only modifications of detail; the essential thing is the pendular movement of the hind legs, that kind of kick that takes them back, then forward, together.

Usually, the forehand executes approximately the same movements, but the limbs are just a little less unified, both coming and going. This is understandable if you remember that the anterior quarters serve more to maintain the body in balance than to give an impulse. Observe that a horse starting to gallop is still trotting with the forelegs when the hind legs are preparing to jump. The animal finds it advantageous to maintain this successive support on its front legs as long as possible, which protects it from excessive reactions.

1   See especially Eadweard Muybridge's album of photographs, *Animals in Motion* (New York: Dover, 1957), showing the gallop of horses, dogs, cats, and a number of wild animals—Ed.

As to the different kinds of gallop, they are obtained by a difference of interval between the front and backquarters. In the canter, the forehand will sound the beat at the same time that the back legs sound their second one and the result is a three-beat rhythm. The supports succeed one another in the following manner: supposing the horse gallops on the right side, consider the moment it hits the ground again after a first leap. It will place the left posterior foot on the ground; then, both the right posterior and left anterior, then the right anterior.

In the gallop, the two back feet, hitting the ground almost simultaneously, will have finished their two beats before the forehand begins and we hear a four-beat rhythm. In very fast running, such as that of the hare, it is likely that the movements of the front paws are exactly in opposition to those of the hindquarters, with the front legs going back as the back legs forward. In the light of the law of synergy, it is impossible for the spine not to participate in the impulse, by bending and stretching: these motions are perfectly visible in animals with long supple bodies.[2]

2   See Muybridge's photographs of the galloping greyhound (pl. 120 and 121) and galloping cat (pl. 127), ibid.

In the final analysis, what is the value of these different modes of animal locomotion from the mechanical viewpoint? As varied as these procedures are, we can greatly simplify our search by observing that many of them differ only in form; in the end, they are equivalent in their work yield. Thus, whether the muscles are inserted in the bones in one way or another, whether the limbs are long or short, it can have a great deal of importance according to the animal's need for force or speed, but it changes nothing in the final yield of energy. The way an animal combines its gaits is important for the rhythm of the balance, but is unimportant from the mechanical point of view. By gradual reductions, all the modes of locomotion can be brought down to two typical procedures: the walk and the spring. Both differ essentially from reptation as the mass of the body, lifted above the ground by the motor limbs, displaces itself without friction. And the specific difference between them is that, in the walk, the animal never leaves the ground totally, but is always supported on at least one limb; whereas in the spring, the animal is in the air for a certain amount of time with no contact on the ground.

The walk is, by far, the gait in which muscular energy is best utilized. Once the animal has taken the first impulse, it has almost no further work of strength to accomplish, only work of speed. Once the body mass is pushed forward it continues to progress by virtue of the acquired force; if the animal tires, it is rather from following this force than from pushing it; the only energy it expends is to overcome the internal friction of its articulations and restore to its limbs the active force they lose when they move backward. Since this internal work is no greater than in any other kind of locomotion and the external

*Horse galloping*

work is reduced to its simplest manifestation, we can see how economical such a gait is.

Let us now examine what happens in the spring. Here there is probably less internal work, since the number of movements needed to cover a given space is diminished. But the external work of the muscles, which is needed for the displacement of the body mass, is much greater. At each spring, the animal must propel itself forward and into the air: to the effort necessary to obtain a horizontal propulsion, which is the only useful one, is added the effort of ascending, which is a pure loss. If the muscles had perfect elasticity, the animal could rebound from the ground by a simple reaction and there would be only an initial expenditure of force. But whatever the natural elasticity of the muscles—and even admitting that in jumping animals such as the kangaroo or the sparrow it is greater than for other species—it will never suffice to propel the animal as high as the first time. The ascending effort must therefore start over and over again.

From these considerations, it follows that the spring can only be, so to speak, an accidental gait. If the animal has to give itself a considerable acceleration, such as the grasshopper escaping from our hand, or the cat trying to reach the top of a wall, or the tiger leaping onto its prey, it cannot help springing. If at a given moment it needs to pick up great speed at any cost, it will then again have to move by jumping. For since it cannot accelerate or lengthen its stride indefinitely, because the pendular movement of the limbs is limited in speed and length, it will have only one way to accelerate its progression: that is to spring from one foot to the other, trying to go as far as possible. Such paces require a great expenditure of energy and cannot be maintained too long. But at that moment it is not a question of aiming for economy. Is it a matter of traveling a great distance or covering a given space at leisure? Then the animal must attempt to avoid all vertical oscillations or at least to reduce as much as possible the moments in the air. The most advantageous gait will be the walk or the lowest, flattest, least accentuated run.

This observation already permits us a glimpse at the conclusion we will reach later, which is that in certain cases, the most graceful movements are far from being those in which force is best utilized.

The different methods of aquatic locomotion may be classified into three groups: natation by undulation, by oscillation, and by propulsion. These terms, chosen somewhat arbitrarily, will become clearer as they are analyzed.


*Undulation.*

The characteristic feature of this procedure is that the propulsion is continuous, with no dead spot in its motion. In this respect, undulation resembles terrestrial reptation to such an extent that it might be called aquatic reptation.

I will mention vermicular motion in swimming only for the record, as it does not seem to have any real effect. If you throw an earthworm or a slug into the water, it will continue its usual movements, but to no avail, as it cannot displace itself because it lacks enough friction to support it. Yet the water molecules closest to the surface are in a peculiar state of cohesion that acts like an elastic pellicle. In absolutely calm water, it would therefore theoretically be possible to advance on this surface by friction. Some mollusks are seen crawling on the ceiling of ponds with their motor soles skyward, but this mode of locomotion (which is desperately slow) can only be very exceptional.

The true undulatory motion, on the contrary, has much more efficient results and is better suited to aquatic than to terrestrial locomotion. One can therefore assume that it was first developed for swimming rather than for displacement on the ground.

Consider an aquatic animal swimming by undulating from head to tail with all the strength it has. Young eels, which trace undulations of admirable regularity, are excellent subjects of observation. I stop one with a piece of wood. It now undulates in place, pushing behind it, in a continuous motion, the total mass of water intercepted between its undulations. (For a given length, the rounder the undulations and the flatter the body, the greater that displaced mass of water will be.) To produce such an effort, the animal must necessarily have a point of support. At this moment, it is supplied by my piece of wood. If I withdraw the wood, the eel is immediately thrust forward, with a reaction exactly equivalent to the force it was applying on the water; at the same time, the undulations increase in speed as a result of the reduction of resistance. After a while, it moves at a constant speed. At that moment, the dynamic balance is restored. The resistance that the molecules of water oppose to it by their friction and inertia is exactly equal to the effort it applies on them by its undulations.

This method of progression allows great speed with little expenditure of energy. Its cross section being of almost negligible size, the animal displaces forward only an insignificant mass of water; and we know, on the other hand, that a smooth surface glides on the water with minimal friction; therefore, the animal's progression will be determined by the least thrust of its retrogressive undulations. The work yield is thus very satisfactory, especially at fast speeds. For, if the effort must always be divided between the point of application and the point of support of the force, the work is spread between these two points proportionately to its displacement. But while the progression of the animal is very rapid, its retrogressive waves, which are acting upon relatively heavy masses of water, impart little speed on them and there is almost no drift. Nearly all the expended energy is therefore used for progression.

In this system, the evolution toward the specialization of functions occurs in two ways, by the development of the fins and by the specific attribution of the posterior part of the body to undulatory movements.

In order for an animal that swims by undulation to find enough resistance in the water, it is important that it be as flat and ribbonlike as possible, because convex surfaces give too easily when an effort is applied to them. On the other hand, such a structure is not only unfavorable to the development of interior organs but incompatible with great muscular vigor. The proof is that flat fish are always poor swimmers and that, conversely, all fish that need a great deal of force and velocity have their muscles disposed in compact masses. The ideal, then, is for the surfaces with which the animal beats the water to be as flat as possible and at the same time for the general shape of its body to be nearly cylindrical. This apparently difficult problem has been perfectly resolved by the development of an unbroken fin, a kind of membranous crest, sustained, when necessary, by rigid ribbings, which rises on the body of the animal perpendicularly to the plane of undulation. This structure is cleverly built to resist lateral thrusts and to give in to longitudinal ones, so that it increases the reactive force of the undulations without in the least impairing the progress of the animal.

With this basic principle, the configuration of the fins can be infinitely varied. One fin can be scalloped, subdivided into several median fins; or it can be reduced to two narrow crests, a dorsal and a caudal one; it can even have developed only at the tip of the tail; and thus we have, by imperceptible stages, approached the second method of aquatic locomotion to be studied.

Among a great number of animals belonging to very different species, the undulations are restricted to the posterior part of the body. For the salamander, the tadpole, the crocodile, the water rat, the otter, for instance, these undulations are produced very simply. All the organ has to do is to start a pendular movement; the resistance of the water does the rest, transforming the oscillation into an undulation. Indeed, if you picture the animal displacing itself in the water by giving its tail a simple pendular movement analogous to that of a vibrating rod, you will realize that the tail does not need to bend completely to one side or the other. Each oscillation that starts at its base determines only the formation of a wave that is immediately chased backward by the opposite oscillation. Hence the organ is crossed from one end to the other by a series of retrogressive waves.

What we have said of aquatic reptation indicates the mechanical value of such a procedure: it makes excellent use of the expended energy, provided the waves are rapid enough. It is an excellent propulsor and if the mass of the body that it puts into motion is not overly heavy and its shape is slender enough, the speed obtained may be considerable.

## Oscillation

In this system, the tail, which is the propelling organ, is activated by an alternative movement, oscillating from one side of the body axis to the other.

When observing the oscillations of the tail of a fish, one is tempted to compare them to the rudder of a ship. But reason proves and experience confirms that it is not by such a simple movement that it moves forward. Place yourself at the back of a rowboat and give the rudder a back and forth movement as vigorous as you wish. You will hardly advance, even if you take care to pull the bar vigorously and push it back gently. The reason is that if the rudder, in its backward motion, tends to push the boat foward, it tends to pull it back when it goes forward. These two equivalent and antagonistic efforts compensate for one another more or less and the boat stays almost motionless.

It would be more correct to compare the tail movements to that of a scull. Study a mariner in the act of sculling. You will notice that he not only gives his scull a back and forth movement but that at each stroke he slants the plane of the motive surface with a slight twist of his wrist, so that it always hits the water obliquely. As a result, the effort he exercises on his oar is composed of two thrusts: a lateral one which tends to make the boat turn slightly, and a longitudinal one which tends to push it forward. The lateral thrusts nullify one another and it is the longitudinal thrusts that alone have an effect and move the bark forward.

Figure 14, in which I have represented the path of the oar on the surface of the water by a broken line and the slanting of its plane by diagonal lines, will make the maneuver sufficiently clear. This is exactly the way a fish must move its tail, by virtue of its structure. And it is the only way it can produce an effort that is effective. As the tail wriggles from right to left of the line of its axis, the caudal fin, under the pressure of the water it beats, bends into the wanted oblique. All the animal has to do is give it the back and forth momentum; the slanting of the plane

*Figure 14*

happens automatically. The same explanation applies to the procedure of swimming by vibrating cilia, a common practice among a great number of animals of the lower order.

One last problem is left. If the caudal fin always presents itself to the water in the most advantageous position, does not the action of the tail counteract the movement? In each of the tail's oscillations, there is a serviceable phase when it beats the water from front to back and a disserviceable phase when it goes the other way. But in the first phase, it presents to the water a convex surface that has little resistance. In the second phase, on the contrary, it beats the water with its concave, biting surface. In other words, the tail's action might seem much more detrimental than useful to the animal's progress.

That would indeed be the case if the animal proceeded by simple alternative curvatures of the body line, similar to those of a flexible wand being bent in one direction or another. But observation proves that it only proceeds this way exceptionally; for instance when, surprised in its rest by an unusual noise, it rushes suddenly forward. In that situation it does first start to bend over and then springs back like a bow and bolts forward until its momentum is used up. Observe it, on the contrary, in a continuous swimming pattern. You will see that it describes in the water a sinuous path and that consequently it advances by undulating from head to tail, taking the successive shapes shown in figure 15. It is even more evident when you see it swim against a rapid current by undulating in place. In such a movement, you see very clearly the motive waves traveling from head to tail, hitting the water from front to back in the serviceable direction.

All we have said of the swimming of the fish applies as well to swimming mammals, such as otters, seals, porpoises, and whales which move by imprinting vertical oscillations to the back paws or caudal fins; and it is very likely that each one must have a body limber enough to undulate as the tail oscillates, in order to slink into the water with that sinuous motion which eludes resistance as well. If there are aquatic animals that move by a simple oscillation of the tail, without the help of undulatory movements, the most one could say is that they have a very inconvenient mode of locomotion.

As we have described it, the process of swimming by oscillation of the fin combined with an undulation of the body gives excellent results. And it is the one we see employed by all strong swimmers of the rivers and oceans. If there is a considerable waste of energy at the start, when the animal takes off by throwing eddies of water behind it and bending over deeply, once it is on its way it needs little force to maintain its impetus: the tail finds an almost solid support in the always renewed masses of water to which it has no time to impart much active

Figure 15

force. Meanwhile, the undulations of the body gradually lengthen and its path noticeably approaches the straight line, so that most of its expended energy is utilized for progression.

One characteristic of this mode of locomotion is that it is not reversible. By just moving its tail, a fish can only swim forward and so evolves on a horizontal plane alone. The variation of evolutions it does need, however, is obtained by modifying the plane of the lateral fins, which it does at will. It also utilizes these fins to come to a stop.

*Propulsion*

In this system, the animal pushes behind it the masses of water on which it takes its support, by a motion comparable to that of the oar. The only difference is that after the oarsman plunges the oar into the water to give it an impulse, he pulls it out of the water as he brings it close to him, whereas the motive organ of aquatic animals stays continuously immersed in its back and forth motion. It must therefore be built or maneuvered in such a way as to offer more resistance on the going than on the return.

This can be obtained by a change of speed, a modification of shape, or a change of plane.

The resistance that water offers to the movement of floating bodies is greater as they displace themselves faster. Though the law of this progression has not yet been determined exactly, experience has shown that the water resistance seems to be proportional to the square of the speed. As a result, the animal that swims by alternative movements can only progress if the backward movement of its members in their useful phase is much more rapid than in their forward, disserviceable phase. It is also helpful if the back and forth motion is discontinuous. For, after having thrust itself forward by a sudden shove, the animal continues to progress by letting its paddles drag behind it, until its initial momentum is used up: only then will it bring them in to give another thrust. That is how it will get a maximum yield for a given expenditure of energy.

We also know that the resistance of the water to the displacement of bodies differs widely according to their shape. At equal speed and size, a convex surface will encounter much less resistance than a concave one. Therefore, if the paddles of the animal are spoonshaped in such a way as to hit the water with their concave area when it pushes them back, and to present only a convex surface when it brings them forward, the difference in resistance will work for the forward progression.

Among most animals that swim by this rowing action, the digits are connected by a flexible membrane, which are more developed in species that are better adapted to aquatic life, such as the frog, the swan, and the beaver. This mode of construction is still more advantageous than the preceding one: the palm opens up into a pocket when the animal thrusts its legs back; it closes again when it brings them forward; the resistance differential between the two beats of the movement is thus as great as possible.

Finally, when the paddle is flat and rigid, as are the paws of water turtles and the limbs of most cetaceans, the animal must maneuver them so as to hit the water with the broad part of the backward-thrusting paddle and to present only the narrow blade when it brings the paddle forward. It is exactly the same movement that is given to the oars of the racing yawls.

This mode of progression is quite advantageous for quick acceleration, but it is not suitable to fast, continuous swimming and is, after all, inferior to oscillation. As ingenious as the construction and maneuvering of these paddles are, they have an intrinsic weakness that remains in spite of the various correctives we have described: the animal can only advance in jerks. The whole phase of the return of the paddle is lost for progression and it even retards it. We therefore only see it utilized by amphibious animals or those recently adapted to aquatic life. The paddle is an organ originally made only for terrestrial locomotion, which later happened to be used in swimming. It often has to serve both uses, which prevents it from being perfectly adapted to either.

There are a number of similarities between flight and natation. We must, however, resist the temptation to draw a parallel between the two systems. Air, which is light and elastic, behaves quite differently from water under the impact of motive organs. Even though the equipment used for aerial locomotion might be, structurally, very analogous to that used for aquatic locomotion, each has to be maneuvered differently to be effective. To examine the theory of flight, we must, therefore, start from the beginning and avoid parallel analyses which would sacrifice the truth.

The different procedures used for aerial locomotion can be reduced to three types: vibrating flight, flight by propulsion, and gliding flight.

## Vibrating Flight

In this procedure, used mostly by insects, the wings execute an extremely rapid to-and-fro motion and their action is about equally effective in both phases of the movement. As a result, the effort of propulsion can be considered continuous.

If we examine closely the membranous wing of a fly, a wasp, a bumblebee, a dragonfly, or a hawk moth, we see that it is almost always constructed the same way. In its anterior part, the membrane is thicker and supported by rigid ribbings that resist any lengthwise flexion. In its posterior part, the membrane is thinner; the ribbings are lacking or are very slender and are inserted diagonally on the principal ribbings.

By virtue of this structure, when the wing begins to vibrate, the part that is thin and fragile will bend under the pressure of the air it beats. It thus automatically slants its plane in the same way as we noted in the maneuver of the scull. The animal just has to raise or lower its wing by contracting the two antagonistic muscles alternately and the wing takes the angle needed to chase the air perpendicularly to the plane in which it oscillates.

Let us suppose that the insect vibrates its wings in a horizontal plane, as the fly does, for example, when it hovers. This movement will chase the air downward, so that, by reaction, the body will be lifted. If this push is equivalent to the action of gravity, the animal will hover in place. If the push is stronger, the fly will rise vertically.

To convert this ascending motion to a horizontal one, the insect will have only to incline the plane of oscillation of its wings until the force of its propulsion, compounded with the action of gravity, gives it the desired resistance. If, for instance, we represent by $p$ the action of gravity on the insect and by $f$ the force of its vertical ascension (fig. 16), we see that, in order to displace itself horizontally, it must point its flight in the direction $f'$, which will give it the resultant direction F. The diagonal line AB, perpendicular to $f'$, shows how much the insect is required to incline the plane of oscillation of its wings in relation to the horizon in order to move horizontally along the direction F.

How does the insect manage to make its wings oscillate at will in one plane or another? It is possible that it controls their action enough to place them in any direction it pleases. But it is more likely that the wings function always in the same way and that the insect modifies their angle by swaying its body. In order to do that, it only has to shorten or bend its abdomen,

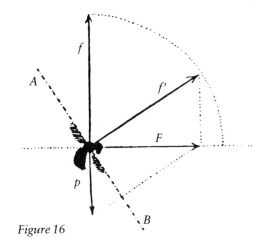

*Figure 16*

which it utilizes as a mobile counterweight. Finally, the changes of direction can be obtained by beating one of the wings more strongly than the other. Then the animal revolves on the wing which has the weaker oscillation and will turn around.

I have assumed until now that the wings of the insect are perfectly flat and that it has only two. These conditions are indeed sufficient for flight. But this typical construction can be modified in several ways. The wings of certain insects are concave, in order to act more strongly in the descent than in the ascent. This modification is observed more particularly among the heavier ones which have to make a greater effort to maintain themselves in the air. Others have two pairs of wings instead of one. These are usually the larger insects. One conceives that the very simple apparatus we have described would become too fragile or too difficult to maneuver if it were to be executed on a larger scale, just as the rigging suitable for a small boat is no

longer appropriate for large ships and must be replaced by a more complicated system of sails.

Let us now evaluate this locomotor equipment from the mechanical point of view. It is certainly the one that allows the greatest ease in its evolutions and can be maneuvered the most spontaneously. The wing of the insect functions instinctively without supervision, like a tiny propeller continuously turning at great speed. On the other hand, in its action, there is inevitably a great deal of lost work. To maintain itself in the air, the insect must continuously resist gravity by counteracting it with an effort to ascend. Though we have not yet learned to calculate it, the sum of energy expended must be considerable. And such a tiny creature could not fulfill the task unless its muscular vigor were not relatively much greater and its vital activity more intense than that of other animals. Its propelling system is admirable for its simplicity and efficiency. But it is perhaps the least economical of all.

This indicates that we were on the wrong track in our attempt to build a flying machine that would lift a man in the air by the single action of a propeller. We were taking as our model the propeller used by insects, which is the least suitable to our size and weight and to the mechanical power we dispose of. One can use a propeller activated by a machine to push a dirigible. But it would be a grave miscalculation to ask that it maintain in the air an object *heavier than air*.

### Flight by Propulsion

In the flight by propulsion, or rowing action, the wing acts intermittently, pushing the air back with a sharp thrust in the downbeat. It is the usual flight pattern of medium-sized birds.

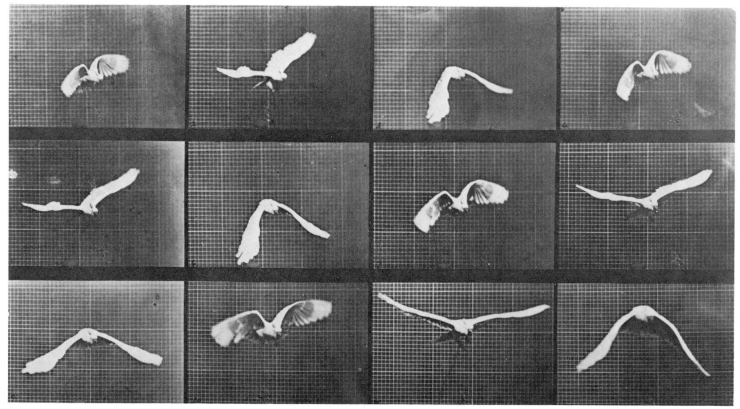

*Flying cockatoo*

We could easily determine a priori in which direction a bird must push the air in order to move horizontally and what must be the intensity of its effort, given its specific weight and speed, by means of a construction similar to the one we made for the insect. Without going into details, we realize that the air must be pushed obliquely, downward, and backward. That is the only way the wing beat can produce for the bird the vertical component it needs to ascend again and the horizontal component that will propel it forward.

But what is the mechanism involved? The bird in full flight executes such complicated and rapid movements that the eye can barely catch them and it is impossible to analyze them with precision. It is to be hoped, however, that with the help of the instantaneous photographs and precise methods of investigation that J. Marey has initiated, we will soon have in hand the necessary data. Until then, all we can do is propose a few hypotheses.

Let us not forget that a priori reasonings are always conditional. The theory can indicate to us what should happen if the bird flies a certain way. It will even allow us to assert that it flies one way rather than another, supposing animals are always using their locomotor organs to the best advantage. But, in fact, how does it fly? At this point, the solution can come only from observation.

The first idea that presents itself when we try to imagine the mechanism of flight is that the wing must beat in the direction in which it pushes the air. That is indeed how the wing would give the most powerful and direct reaction. But this would require excessively quick beats to sustain the bird in full flight. Imagine for instance a homing pigeon flying at the speed of about fifteen meters per second. To advance by propulsion, it would have to give its wings an even greater speed in the upbeat. The mechanism could not withstand it.

Direct observations, and especially the study of instantaneous photographs,[1] show that the wings of the bird in flight almost always move down and forward, that is, perpendicularly to the direction in which we said the air must be pushed. Under such conditions, it is evident that they must beat the air obliquely, taking the same position as the insect's wings in their downward phase.

If you wave a fan in front of a lit candle, you will verify that a beat made this way has the wanted effect. This experience is interesting for another reason. It proves that air, which is a light, elastic fluid, does not behave like water, which is a dense, incompressible one, but according to a much more complicated law. Wave a fan before a circle of lit candles: those in front of which the fan passes in the first phase of its oscillation barely tremble. Their flames just bend in one direction, then the other. Then the action gets stronger and the candles go out suddenly as if the air were directly pushed only at that moment.

This system of flight has a great advantage over the preceding one. It is that, whatever the speed of its translateral movement, the bird need only move its wings at a uniform and quite moderate speed. Once it has accelerated a certain amount, it just has to beat the air a little flatter; in other words, it must bring the plane of the wings nearer to the horizontal, in order to exercise the same effort on the air without increasing the frequency of its beats. Finally, the lifting of the wings can be done passively, just by using the resistance of the air to which it presents the inclined angle of a kite.

1   See those published by Jules Marey in the *Revue Scientifique* 2 (1886):675, and *La Nature,* December 3, 1887.

The laws of resistance of the air are still so imperfectly known that it is impossible to say precisely how much force is developed at each wing beat. It is certain that though the muscles of the bird are not capable of furnishing a greater effort than those of a mammal at any given moment, they can furnish considerably more work over a period of time. A man needs almost a quarter of an hour to elevate his own weight a hundred meters high. Yet he supports himself on ground that is resistant. A swallow, which supports itself only on air, takes less than two minutes.

As for the utilization of the expended energy, flight by propulsion should be placed between vibrating and gliding flight. For if the bird's wings act upon the air exactly in the same way as the insect's in its descending period, one can suppose that at the end of this period and during the total ascent, it acts rather like a kite, that is, according to the principles of the gliding flight.

## Gliding Flight

The characteristic of this kind of locomotion is that the animal glides on the air keeping its wings stretched and still.

Picture a gliding bird, an eagle, for instance, dropping, with stretched wings, from the height of a steep rock. If its wings are stretched horizontally, they serve it only as a parachute. Instead of falling to the ground in a few seconds, at a uniformly accelerated speed, it will drop slowly at a constant speed. Suppose, on the contrary, that at the instant it falls, it sways its body forward in such a way as to make the angle of its wings slant slightly in relation to the horizon. The effect obtained will be different. It will descend obliquely toward the ground, as if sliding down an inclined slope, and will be able to cover a considerable distance in the air. Furthermore, when it has acquired in this way a certain translateral speed, it can use this speed to climb back to a certain height. In order to do that, it just has to make its body sway in the opposite direction, usually by a movement of the tail, and to present its wings to the air in the position of a kite. A while ago it was using its height to give itself speed. Now it is using its speed to give itself a force of ascension. That is the movement that in falconry was called the *resource* or *reclimb*. Suppose the animal has a speed of 9.80 meters per second. It is the speed it would have acquired by falling from 4.90 meters high. And it is also at this height that the live force acquired in its fall will make it reascend, at least if we take no account of the slowdown due to air resistance.

These two typical movements, oblique descent and reascent, can be modified or combined in an infinite number of ways. Sometimes the animal descends in a spiral, sometimes it will dip straight down to the ground to give itself a lot of impetus all at once; or it will alternate descent and ascent, swaying in the air with incomparable ease. If its initial height is considerable enough, these various evolutions will last for several minutes. But eventually it will have to descend to the ground, for however wide the surface of its wings, it will not provide the bird with a perfectly resistant point of support: as it glides in the air, it also sinks. One must also take into account friction and the resistance it must overcome, which consume part of its energy and are pure loss. The ascents will therefore never be equal to the falls. In these perpetual conversions from height to speed, from virtual power to live force, which constitute gliding, there will be some waste every time. When, from waste to waste, the animal has spent all its disposable energy, it will find itself on the ground.

If, therefore, gliding birds maintain themselves indefinitely in the air, it is because they do not always let themselves slide passively, but accomplish a positive work from time to time to regain height. Thus the swallow, the martin, the jackdaw, the hawk, after gliding for some time, lift themselves with great wing beats. Among most sparrows, at least when they fly at leisure, the gliding and the rowing alternate according to a regular rhythm, which gives them their characteristic flight pattern. What do they gain by adopting this gait? We know from our own experience that violent efforts followed by a complete rest are less tiring than smaller efforts that are continuous. It is possible that the wings of these birds function well only at high speeds, so that it is advantageous to them, when they move at moderate speeds, to proceed as they do.

All this is easily understood. But here is a difficulty. Many reliable observers assert that such gliding birds as the albatross and the frigate bird can stay in the air for whole hours without a single wingbeat. One often sees birds of prey climbing toward the sky in a spiral, their wings stretched out. Can gliding, then, be used for an active, continuous flight? With a simple plane surface constantly supported by the air, could the bird not only maintain itself indefinitely, but even accelerate?

That is mechanically possible. The bird would only have to execute a swaying movement in the air. We have seen how, when swinging on the trapeze, a man gives himself the needed impulse by a thrust directed perpendicularly to the surface of the seat, at the moment of ascension. We have also seen how slightly one has to move one's center of gravity in this direction to give oneself considerable acceleration. But this oscillation that the seat executes by taking its support on the ropes from which it hangs can be reproduced identically by the wings of the bird by using the air for support. If the bird starts a more or less regular swaying motion and at each ascent lifts itself a little on its wings, that simple effort, obtained by a displacement of the body so slow, so continuous that it can escape observation, will give it a powerful impulse. It will thus regain the height which its passive reascent made it lose at each oscillation and will be able to maintain itself in the air indefinitely.

By augmenting its effort, it will even be able to obtain oscillations of an increasing magnitude which it will utilize either to rise even higher or to acquire a greater horizontal speed. In the latter case, once it gets to the highest point of its oscillation, instead of turning around to descend the aerial slope it has just climbed, it will go over its crest in virtue of the speed it has acquired and will let itself glide down the other slope.

Is this, in fact, what happens? The only way to determine it would be to take a number of instantaneous photographs of a bird in flight, in order to follow it in its diverse evolutions, and then to study the photographs carefully. If one recognizes that the movement of the wings is such that, first, they always lean on the air perpendicularly to their surface; second, their lowering coincides with the ascent of the bird; and third, as they lower, they tend to chase the air down and forward; then it will become evident that the bird moves according to our hypothesis, that is, by a simple swaying movement.

In any case, this procedure of aerial locomotion would not only be theoretically possible, but more advantageous than the other. This is a strong presumption in favor of our hypothesis, because the animals are generally well served by their locomotor instincts. It is indeed in this flight pattern that the wings find the most resistant support in the air, since they are leaning on it perpendicularly to their surface; and it is also the pattern in which effort is the most efficient since it happens progressively, without jerks and fits and starts.

Venturing in the domain of applications, I will add that it would be the kind of flight that would be the easiest to reproduce artificially. All the theoreticians who have been concerned with the problem of flight have surely been haunted by the desire to reach a practical solution. "The history of artificial progression," says J. Bell Pettigrew, "indorses the belief that the fields etherean will one day be traversed by a machine designed by human ingenuity and constructed by human skill. . . . Of the many mechanical problems before the world at present, perhaps there is none greater than that of aerial navigation. Past failures are not to be regarded as harbingers of future defeats, for it is only within the last few years that the subject of artificial flight has been taken up in a true scientific spirit."[2] For his part, J. Marey says: "The reproduction of the mechanism of flight now occupies the minds of many experimenters, and we hesitate not to own that we have been sustained in this laborious analysis of the different acts of the flight of the bird by the assured hope of being able to imitate, more or less perfectly, this admirable type of aerial locomotion. . . . We hope to have proved to the reader that nothing is impossible in the analysis of the movements connected with the flight of the bird: he will no doubt be willing to allow that mechanism can always reproduce a movement, the nature of which has been clearly defined."[3]

2    James Bell Pettigrew, *Animal Locomotion* (London: Kegan Paul, Trench, Trübner & Co., 1891), p. 258.

3    Jules Marey, *Animal Mechanism, A Treatise on Terrestrial and Aerial*

When we already have at our disposal balloons that are nearly dirigible, it would, doubtless, be wiser and more practical to apply ourselves to perfecting this system rather than venture into the unknown and try to construct a flying machine. But it may be in our interest to invent one, when all is said and done; and it does not seem to me that this problem is insurmountable. An apparatus that allows man to glide will be constructed whenever one wishes. Its structure could be of the simplest. No mechanism, no propeller, no beating wings: a simple perfected parachute, a large plane surface constructed a little like a kite would suffice for passive gliding. Suspended to this motor surface or mounted on it, one would only have to carry one's center of gravity forward or backward, to the right or the left, in order to reproduce the swaying movements by which the gliding bird obtains its various evolutions. As to active gliding, it can be obtained, as we have shown, by a simple swinging movement. Only one thing can be questioned: it is whether a man would have sufficient muscular strength to regain at each oscillation the entire height inevitably lost in passive reascent. In a steady workout, a man of medium strength can hardly lift his own weight more than twenty cm a second. In order for him to sustain himself in the air for some time, it would be necessary for his gliding apparatus not to descend any faster. Since the surface of the wings can be increased and, therefore, the speed of the fall slowed down almost indefinitely, the problem is evidently not unfeasible. To convince partisans of aviation of their folly, it has been said that it would be impossible for man to manipulate immense wings. But this presents no difficulty in our system. Nothing would be easier than to maneuver wings

*Locomotion* (New York: Appleton, 1874), p. 277.

ten meters wide, or twenty meters square if necessary, since it would only be a question, after all, of raising or lowering one's center of gravity in relation to them. Again, the theory of flight is still too much in its infancy to propose anything but a hypothesis in the matter. But I was anxious to show that current scientific data has brought out nothing to discourage inventors. They must keep trying. But even if the experience does not succeed, one thing at least would be gained: that is the recognition that such efforts must decidedly be given up. For one could think of no simpler mechanism, more advantageous in its work yield. If we fail to make such an apparatus work, it will be useless to look for others.

*Art in Animals*

One thing must stand out in the course of this study and that is the amount of skill and ingenuity—the word is not exaggerated—evident in some of the modes of locomotion employed by animals. Some have gone to a great deal of trouble to prove that animals have the seed of the artistic facilities that have been so marvelously developed in man. We have shown that there is in their constructions, in their song, in their preference for certain colors and shapes something which is greatly akin to a sense of beauty. How can one doubt that animals are artistic! Art is everywhere in animal activity, in the flight of the swallow streaking by, in the movement of a beetle crossing a path, in this snake creeping along the hedge, in the tiny fish swimming in the stream. Art started with life itself. Yet we have examined locomotor movements only in their daily practice. What if we really followed the evolutions of an animal and saw it modifying at every moment its specific attitude to contend with un-

expected circumstances and resolving with incredible presence of mind and clarity of conception mechanical problems that would embarrass us!

Children's tales often tell of men changed into beasts. Every child has once asked: "What would I do if I were a cat, a bird, a butterfly?" and thinks it would be wonderful. Yet the child would do nothing more than the animal does, and could do nothing better. I would be tempted to think that practical intelligence is carried to its maximum in each animal. It has been argued, without its sounding unbelievable, that there is infinite wisdom in every instinctive movement.[4] Surely consummate art can be seen there, even something resembling creative genius. The regular undulations of the reptile, the oscillations of the fish's tail, the normal patterns and gaits of the bird and the quadruped may be predetermined, once and for all, by a purely mechanical instinct. But watch a snake climbing a rock, a carp evolving in a pond, crows gliding around a church steeple, a young cat playing! Is that still automatism?

It is possible that the animal is not conscious of being an object of beauty. Of that, later. Let us at least admire it. At any rate, the animal works at combining its movements harmoniously in view of a preconceived end; it arranges them with that instinct for rhythm, with that delicacy of external touch and of muscular tone without which the simplest locomotor movement would not be possible. Thus, without wanting it, it manages to produce real masterpieces; without knowing it, to conform to the laws of the superior logic that is the essence of all

4  Jacques Bossuet, *Oeuvres Complètes*, vol. 1, *Connaissance de Dieu et de soi-même* (Paris: Firmin Didot, 1858); Eduard von Hartmann, *Philosophy of the Unconscious*, trans. William Coupland (New York: Harcourt and Brace, 1931).

beauty. If this is not art, where must we look for it? Is this not how the most genial works of human art have been obtained? We admire a line traced on a piece of paper by the hand of an artist. But there can be not only as much grace, but as much true beauty in the curve described in the sky by the flying bird. Why can't we say that this curve too is a work of art? Is it because it leaves no concrete trace? That may, after all, be the only reason.

# III  The Expression of Movement

*Woman dancing*

When we observe someone's movements, we cannot avoid thinking of the emotions and the various sensations that determine the way that person moves. These emotions, perceived sympathetically, form what is called the expression of movement. It is important not to confuse the *expression* of movement with the *impression* it produces. Impression is made up of the individual emotions of the spectator; expression consists of these emotions objectified, that is, as they pertain to the person who is doing the movement. These emotions form, in themselves, a kind of spectacle, as if they were really perceived.

We will consider successively the expression of ease, the expression of force, and the expression of various emotions, by asking ourselves in what measure they contribute to the aesthetic character of the movement we perceive.

### Grace and Beauty of Movement

The expression of physical and psychological ease of movement is what we call grace. Knowing which movements are the most agreeable to perform and which economize our effort the most, we seem to have in hand all the elements of gracefulness. Not so, for we shall see that grace is reducible neither to a correct use of force, for that is merely mechanical beauty, nor to the least effort in movement.

In his essay on "Gracefulness," Spencer notes that graceful movements are generally those that require the least expenditure of energy:

This connection between gracefulness and economy of force will be most vividly recognized by those who skate. They will remember that all early attempts, and especially the first timid experiments in figure skating, are alike awkward and fatiguing; and that the acquirement of skill is also the acquirement of ease. The requisite confidence, and a due command of the feet having been obtained, these twistings of the trunk and gyrations of the arms, previously used to maintain the balance, are found needless; the body is allowed to follow without control the impulse given it; the arms swing to where they will; and it is clearly felt that the graceful way of performing any evolution is the way that costs the least effort. Spectators can scarcely fail to see the same fact, if they look for it. Perhaps there is no case in which they may so distinctly perceive that the movements called graceful are those which fulfill a given end with the smallest expenditure of force.[1]

Here is another example. Look at a dog thrown in the water for the first time. When the poor animal surfaces, its eyes protruding with fear, it frantically hastens to the shore. Anxious to keep its nose as high above water as possible, it swims upright, beating the water with its paws and making little progress. At last, exhausted and out of breath, it reaches the shore on which it has barely the strength to scramble. See the dog later, after it has taken a liking to the water; it is now horizontal, in the position of least resistance, nostrils barely emerging, and it moves rapidly in a supple, undulating movement which is not fatiguing and gives an impression of ease.

This is a natural procedure. By using my strength judiciously, I spare myself superfluous movements and needless efforts. And this allows me to obtain results more economically. It is no

1   Herbert Spencer, *Essays: Scientific, Political and Speculative*, 3 vols. (London: Williams and Norgate, 1883), 2:315–16.

surprise, then, that by trying to execute an exercise well, I am at the same time executing it more gracefully. Conversely, by trying to do it more gracefully, I will usually achieve an economy of effort. Thus, as we have mentioned before, to play the piano, we will strive for a good posture, eliminate jerky movements, body contortions, and tense attitudes. And we will realize afterward that such control of movement is much less tiring.

Spencer's idea is, after all, correct, if it is taken as a casual remark that applies to many cases. But as a complete theory of grace, as an absolute principle that would measure the pleasure of movements from the economy of force, we cannot accept it. It would bring one of the most complex problems of aesthetics down to a simple question of mechanics. It may be a tempting solution, but a careful perusal uncovers many problems. Gracefulness cannot be reduced just to mechanical beauty. To look graceful, movements must obviously conform with the conditions of beauty, up to a point at least; but something else is needed.

I have seen English schoolboys skating remarkably well. Their goal seemed the same as Spencer's, to obtain the greatest speed with the least effort. However, most of them were not graceful. And that was because, with their precise, energetic shove of the skate, they took no account of the pleasure of the spectators. They were skating for themselves, not for the gallery. Theirs was indeed the most utilitarian, economical method, but it gave no feeling of art. All one saw was great muscular activity, perfectly utilized. It was mechanical beauty, perfect in its way, but purely mechanical. What was needed was a little roundness in the gesture, a little suppleness in the back, a little flourish in the movements, I am not sure what, but something more. It may not be possible to be graceful at such a speed, but then one cannot go so fast if one wishes to appear graceful.

It is evident that economy of forces can only bring to an exercise a gracefulness compatible with that exercise. Try gracefully to hold a fifty pound weight at arm's length. Unless you are remarkably strong, what an unaesthetic impression you will be making on a spectator with the contortions you will have to apply, however well you use your strength! Grace, therefore, cannot be measured by economy alone, that is, by the relationship of the energy expended to the work produced. One must also take in account the actual value of the effort.

## Grace and the Least Effort

It would not even be correct to say that the most graceful movements are those that are the least likely to fatigue. I once watched a well-known runner and was struck by the fact that from the very beginning he was running like a tired man, with a low, slightly dragging carriage and hanging shoulders. This surprised the spectators and they doubted he would succeed. The method was a logical one, however. Effort is costly, so one spares it. The carriage of a tired man is that which fatigues the least and which he can maintain longest. Compare, also, the heavy tread of the mountain guide to the light, elastic step of the tourists he is leading. The guide's gait is infinitely less graceful, but he can maintain it forever; while the novice climber who thinks only of looking agile and vigorous will soon be exhausted.

If you lift a heavy weight, your features tend to contract by muscular sympathy and, when the effort is really intense, the face takes on an expression of pain. But if you want to execute this feat gracefully, the grimace must be suppressed and an effort made to smile, which is no easy task. Gracefulness, therefore, requires extra effort. In the same way, a dancer who must cross the stage will try to do it as lightly as possible, that is, with good elevation and stretched legs. But this will cost her more effort, evidently, than if she were to walk across at a leisurely pace. Again, a gymnast will look more graceful if he uses a rhythmic motion to climb a rope by the strength of his arms, as if this ascension meant nothing to him and each arm contraction were to carry him beyond his goal. Yet it would be more economical for him to climb with a continuous movement.

These examples, which I could multiply, seem to me significant. If the skater saves considerable energy without any appearance of ease, if the runner must display the signs of fatigue in order to prevent it, if the dancer must further tire herself in an effort to look fresh, one must conclude that it is not by the actual economy of effort that gracefulness can be measured.

There is a final, often neglected element in the two theories we have examined. We are talking only of mechanical and muscular economy. One should, however, consider purely psychological ease, which seems to me one of the essential elements of grace.

To avoid such simplification, we must study the conditions of gracefulness in all their complexity. But however hard we try, we cannot prevent their being actually based on outward appearances.

We have a right to hope that it will not always be so. The reasoned study of the mechanical conditions of locomotion exercises an undoubted influence on judgments of taste, by making them more rational. Ideally, aesthetic judgment would be entirely based on reason. It would bring to an end that contradic-

tion we have pointed out beween grace and beauty in movement: that those movements that give us the most pleasure are those that really have the greatest mechanical beauty. Meanwhile, we continue to judge things according to the prejudices of vulgar experience, which reason cannot totally wipe out.

*Physical Ease of Movement*

Several conditions are required for a movement to give us the impression of physical ease. We will examine them in order of their importance.

*1. Conformity with personal habits*   This condition is the most essential one, proving that, though beauty has an intrinsic value, grace is wholly relative. It is possible to perceive the movements of an animal or a man very precisely and to judge if they are adapted to their end; but we can picture other people's feelings only in relation to our own. We imagine ourselves in their place and give them the feelings we would have in similar circumstances. It is evident that such a transfer of personality, which is the essential condition of sympathy, exposes us to many illusions. A very bulky animal will seem to me to have difficulty moving because I, with my available strength, would need considerable effort to displace or support it. But the animal moves with the strength it has. I once watched a country woman sitting on the seat of a wagon, stiff-backed, with her basket on her lap; she stayed in this attitude for the whole trip, which lasted two full hours. It gave me a sensation of cramping, of stiffness, of constraint. I felt uneasy for her but she felt no such discomfort. She had no need to stretch and therefore did not suffer from her stiffness. That is the way she was comfortable. A left-handed person throws a stone with the left arm as easily as a right-handed person with the right. But you, as a right-handed person watching a stone being thrown with the left arm, will find this motion awkward, because you yourself would be uncomfortable doing it. Out of this comes the myth that a lefty is less skillful than a righty. The contrary is true. Good billiard players, magicians, clowns, jugglers, and equilibrists are very often left-handed.

The movements of a snake have everything to make them graceful. Actually, most definitions of gracefulness in attitudes, in movements, in lines would apply to snakes more than to other animals. Yet, due to disgust and fear, one has to pause to take pleasure in a serpent's evolutions. They are incompatible with our own. We understand being a bird. But to be a snake, to have no arms or legs, to advance by wriggling and crawling and curling in and out, this we cannot condone. How awful it is to be a snake!

2. *Absence of visible effort*   When we look at an athlete doing some wonderful feat, what do we watch? His features. Immediately, we want to judge his effort and his vigor. If he performs without frowning, if his veins do not swell or his face get red, we spectators will have a feeling of ease at this display of strength. We have seen how an excess of muscular effort can cause physiological problems and that, in fact, the one causes the other. People in whom these diverse signs are more manifest than in others will seem less graceful in their physical exercises. This is evident among gymnasts and acrobats: those who turn red with their efforts will never give an impression of perfect ease, however agile and vigorous they are. The notable athlete has a neutral coloring. In order to look more comical,

clowns had the idea of making up in an eccentric way. The unexpected result was that they looked infinitely more graceful. For on those whitened faces, with large red and black lines, the signs of effort were no longer visible. During the most incredible feats of nimbleness, their grotesque masks stay impassive, as if unaware of what the rest of their individual does. I remember once attending a dress rehearsal in a circus, in the middle of the day, when the clowns had, naturally, not bothered with make-up. I was completely disillusioned. I no longer had before me those fantastic, rubbery, bouncing creatures who appear in the lights, but common-looking young men, working conscientiously to perfect feats that were evidently very difficult.

3. *Absence of noise*   It is not only with the eyes, but with the ears that we judge the ease with which movements are executed. When we start a machine, we are aware that a great part of our strength is wasted in overcoming interior friction, which makes noise. And in our minds, noise and friction are so associated with one another that the working of a machine which makes noise will seem painful, as if our ear perceives immediately the effort of its motion. Note, for example, the creaking of a knee that does not have enough synovia, or the shriek of an unoiled axle. Under such conditions, it is impossible for the movement to appear graceful.

We are conditioned to judge the violence of an impact by the noise that accompanies it. Any loud noise gives us the impression of a great mass in abruptly arrested motion, of a large animated force suddenly lost. The exterior noises that accompany any movement must be taken into account when evaluating effort. Though they are useful in certain cases to mark a rhythmic beat—the ticking of a clock, walking in time, the tambourine

—or to give the impression of power—the ripple of the waves against a fast sailboat, the rumbling of a thrashing machine, the roaring of a waterfall, a weight lifted and dropped—they are always and directly incompatible with grace. Sometimes they increase the apparent difficulty of a movement—the flapping of a bird's wings in flight, the creaking of boots. Sometimes they give a feeling of heaviness—walking in wooden clogs, jumping on a wooden floor, the rearing of horses on a stage. Conversely, silent movements seem to happen of their own accord—bounces on a thick carpet, running in sneakers, the leaps of a squirrel, the walk of felines, a horse galloping in a meadow, the flight of the owl, the gliding of a hawk, the fluttering of a butterfly. The play of light owes its fantastic apparent lightness to this absence of noise—moonlight on the ocean, the reflection of a vase full of water trembling on the ceiling of a room, the strangely silent fireworks of the aurora borealis.

Conformity with personal habits, absence of visible effort, and absence of noise are the most obvious and immediate signs of ease in movement. Those we will now look at exert less influence on our aesthetic judgments because they imply some thought and because, to interpret them, we must turn to mechanical considerations, elementary as they admittedly are and of the same nature as we encounter daily.

*4. Apparent lightness*    We are quite used to evaluating at one glance the volume and density of bodies. The effort needed to displace or lift an object being evidently in proportion to its weight, the movements of a voluminous and very compact animal will seem more laborious. That is why small animals will usually appear more graceful in their paces than larger ones.

Hard as it is to formulate such general impressions which change so rapidly as soon as attention is paid to them, it seems to me that the prevalent conception of the weight of objects takes into account their density rather than their total mass. A cloud seems light, the rain that it releases, heavy. We ask a child: "What is heavier, a pound of cork or a pound of feathers?" He will ponder over the problem. It proves that for him the weight of things is more a question of density than of mass. These elementary notions are bound to have an influence on our aesthetic judgments.

That is also why animals with a smooth skin, like reptiles and frogs, or with carapaces, like turtles, or with hard wing-covers like beetles all seem at first sight heavier than others, and furry or feathered animals seem lighter. Such coverings do augment the real weight of an animal; but augmenting even more its apparent volume gives it, on the whole, a lighter appearance.

When we look at a bird in flight, we are surprised that it maintains itself so easily in the air: to our eyes, which only judge things superficially, the bird is all feathers and we are tempted to say that it must hardly be any heavier than air. But if we shoot it down with a gun, we will be surprised by the heaviness of its fall and by its actual weight.

The shape of the animal is also a factor in our judgments. The large belly of a cow or a hippopotamus, the donkey's head, the hump of a camel, a bison, or a zebu, the beak of a toucan or a hornbill make them all look considerably heavier. It is because we see there a deadweight which must slow down the animal's movements. On the other hand, the excessive development of parts used for locomotion contributes to an animal's apparent lightness.

*5. Maximum firmness at the point of support*    For a movement to be easy and appear graceful, the point of support of the effort must be firm and look it. Nothing is more ungraceful than walking in mud, in snow, on dry sand, on a spongy terrain. One feels that a part of the expended energy is used to imprint the steps in the surface. The fact alone of leaving visible tracks makes the movement less easy. If the point of support is slippery or moving, it will look even worse, because the wasted effort will be more perceptible. One is uneasy watching a man walking on thin ice or climbing a sand hill, an oarsman rowing against the current, a dog running in the wheel of a turnspit, a squirrel in a cage, a horse walking on a moving plane as in some threshing machines. Here, appearance and reality match, the obviousness of effort corresponds to the waste of strength. On the contrary, and for the same reason, trampoline jumps or an acrobat's springs on the tight rope are very graceful because one feels that the elasticity of the point of support is added to the effort of impulse.

The most elusive point of support is certainly air. The flight of a bird is a continuous fall, compensated by a continuous effort to ascend. It would therefore seem to be the least graceful of all perceptible movements. Because we do not fly ourselves, we do not have a common measure to judge the effort required by flight. As the movement of air driven back by the wing is not visible, our eye cannot perceive the work performed. We simply observe that the air goes fast and we conclude that it moves with ease.

*6. Minimum of apparent resistance*    Finally, the apparent resistance must be reduced to its minimum. A boat ploughing water before it or leaving a heavy wake behind will seem to advance with difficulty. The circus rider's trick of bursting through paper hoops cannot be called graceful. Though there is hardly any real resistance, the apparent obstacle of the paper is enough to make the sight disturbing.

Here a difficulty, specific to swimming and flight, presents itself. An animal moving in a homogeneous medium like water or air finds in it resistance as well as support. The low density or the motility of the element in which it is displacing itself is at once advantageous and disadvantageous. In what way does this kind of mechanical contradiction affect the appearance of the movement?

It seems to me that, according to the circumstance, it is sometimes the appearance of the motility of the support that dominates and sometimes the idea of the anterior resistance. The former occurs to us principally in slow movements, the latter when the movement is fast.

At the instant the bird is taking off, its large wing movements at first produce only a limited displacement and we are aware of the effort wasted. But once it pushes off, as each wing flap carries it farther, the bird will seem to be finding more solid points of support in the air. It is indeed so, for, as a result of this motion, the wing meets at each instant inert layers of air, the very stillness of which produces the resistance the wing needs. But at the same time, the anterior resistance, at first almost nonexistent, has now become an important factor, since it increases approximately with the speed squared. And because we are accustomed to feeling this resistance when we displace ourselves, we pay attention to it. Now it seems to us that the bird requires an effort to go through the air, to fight against the wind.

We see a motor boat leaving a pier. We first observe the

column of water that gushes out at the back, showing the drift of the propeller. When the speed increases, this drift is no longer perceptible, but, seeing the waves beginning to form at the prow of the boat, we now observe the forward resistance of the water. The same thing, depending on the speed, is true of the swimmer.

In fact, the moment when the movement seems easiest is when the speed levels off, because, at that time, the motility of the point of support has become imperceptible and the anterior resistance is not yet accentuated. This observation is in accord with the one we made earlier to the effect that movement has its greatest aesthetic value at moderate speeds. Here as elsewhere, beauty is a question of a happy medium.

In the above analysis, I may be thought to have somewhat exaggerated the effect produced by the sight of these different movements and to have given reasons of no great significance. I freely admit it.

The impressions I describe and imagine having felt in the presence of real objects may not have been so strong. I may, as I speak, be the victim of an illusion. But it cannot be helped. The examples I give are always imagined. One only talks about, and especially writes about, things as one remembers them. This cause for error is constant and must be noted, because it is prevalent in all studies of aesthetics. It is not when one is in the presence of objects that one thinks of analyzing one's impressions; one does it afterward. Literary descriptions are inferior to pictorial ones inasmuch as they are *never* copied from nature.

But imagination always amplifies some aspects while it attenuates the others, effecting a kind of simplification. It is imagination that makes, from a dominant element, a dominating one. It idealizes according to one's bias and suppresses all the accessory sensations that made the object a concrete thing. It is important to state this, particularly when dealing with expression. We must always attempt to distinguish the simplified at the same time as exaggerated expression of imaginary things from the concrete expression of real things. To me, the truth is that the impression produced by a real object is materially much stronger than that produced by a remembered object. But when, after the fact, we think of a thing we have seen, we imagine it moved us more than it actually did, because now the expressive element is re-created, though in a weakened way, while all the intermingled accessory sensations are not re-created in any way. In addition, we hardly think of these things without talking about them, if only to ourselves; it always results in exaggerations.

To take a few examples. Yesterday I saw an animal that repelled me. I want to talk about this repulsion. And, partly to give more interest to my story, partly to express my disgust as strongly as possible, I exaggerate it. It is the same when I describe my pleasure in listening to a piece of music or seeing some extraordinary stunt. The aesthetic feelings described in books and that one attributes to oneself are always, therefore, enlarged and amplified, however sincerely one may wish to report them. We declare that we cannot stand this dissonance or that combination of colors or that kind of movement when, in reality, it is not so very important to us. We think we are describing the emotions released by real objects. But we are actually describing the emotions of an imaginary spectator with a nervous impressionability, a susceptible taste, and a quite exceptional passion for beauty. Nevertheless our exaggerations, when talking about art, are not without benefit to the forming of our taste, just as the scruples we affect when we talk about ethics are not without benefit to the forming of our conscience. They tend to increase the delicacy of our taste.

## Psychological Ease of Movement

The difference between the mechanical and the graceful will be made clearer still when we consider this second category. The more a movement is regular, economical, and rigorously adapted to its intent, the more beautiful it is. But to appear graceful, the rhythm of the movement cannot be monotonous, its intent too apparent, nor its economy too great.

*1. Freedom in the rhythm*   A rhythmic movement that is too regular has the disadvantage of appearing completely mechanical.

To start with the extreme, let us note the effect on a spectator of convulsive movements (fits of hysteria, epileptic seizures, locomotor ataxia, chorea, delirium tremens, and so forth). Such spectacles inspire a feeling of compassion, of fear, of horror. The sight of a poor fellow abandoned to automatic jerks of his muscles, who has become, momentarily, like a machine, shakes one's nerves. It can even, by a kind of contagion, provoke in the viewer similar symptoms. And the instinctive fear of such contagion would make us stay away from the sick person if a feeling of duty did not keep us at his side.

Any repetitive movement will give a similar impression, though to a lesser degree; it will give us the sense of a living, active creature turned into a machine. We suffer sympatheti-

cally at the sight of any tic, speech defect, facial twitch, or gestured habit, such as jiggling one's foot or drumming on a table with one's fingernails. This last kind is the most unbearable, because it is accompanied by an irritating noise. The impression produced is always somewhat the same. Doubtless there is here a certain physical sympathy; we suffer because we feel that these uncontrolled movements are embarrassing for the person who executes them. But putting that aside, even if the person executing regular and repetitive movements seems to be enjoying that activity, the spectacle is not enjoyable, because it does not give us a sense of psychological ease.

The unpleasant effect which is produced only gradually through the successive repetition of the same movements by an individual can be produced immediately and with great strength by their mass repetition. We watch an oarsman rowing in cadence: it may be his fancy to row that way. But if we see a whole crew of oarsmen lifting and dipping their oars in one movement, the mechanical effect of the rhythm will be underlined by this repetition; for evidently this is not a coincidence of whims, but an external law to which all their wills are subjected. The movements of the cavalcade on the Parthenon give an impression of ease, because the horses' attitudes, though somewhat duplicated, are not identical. But certain antique bas-reliefs on which there are four horses harnessed side by side, each lifting a foreleg in the same movement, or a row of men making the same gesture at the same time have a less pleasurable effect. In the Italian ballets that were shown in Paris, those repetitive effects were abused. One hundred dancers all inclining their heads to one side or bending back with their arms above their heads at the same time look more like articulated puppets than dancing women. It creates a beautiful result from the point of view of discipline, but it is an error from an aesthetic point of view.

If social dances, even in gorgeous settings, only offer such an unexciting spectacle, it is because the movements and patterns are set on rhythms that are too simple, too uniform, too mechanical. Knowledgeable judges of choreography think there is more art, individual imagination, and invention in the cancan.

One should note that in most physical exercises and especially in games, there is a tendency to vary the natural rhythm of the movement, just for the sake of varying it. This is not only in compliance with the law of the least effort, but with the law of activity. We want to display our energy, our initiative; we react against the automatism that invades us. Feeling how mechanical movements are that are too regular, we free ourselves from their rhythm, because indeed we do not want to look like machines.

Our movements, then, are graceful only when we feel that their rhythm is not imposed, that we are free, when we wish, to liberate ourselves from their regularity. Room must be left for the play of fantasy. For what is most delightful in observing a rule is the pleasure of breaking it.

Let us take an example from music. It is the measure that marks the rhythm of a melodic movement, and it must be respected. But it cannot be respected in too servile a way. If the conductor beats time with absolute regularity, like a metronome, the music will feel constricted; whereas if he quickens or slows it according to his wish, and even holds it for as long a pause as he likes, one feels he has mastery over it, so that when he does observe it strictly, it is because he wishes to. The music then loses its mechanical character and the movement gains in grace and expression.

One must also take into account the melodic movement that is, to a certain extent, independent of the measure, and that may even be in counterpoint. Finally, even this movement is not determined in an absolute way, since the same motif can reappear with variations and grace notes which give liveliness to the performance and are like its smile. These are the resources that a musician has at his disposal to escape a mechanical performance.

By analogy, the same observations apply to poetry. The rhythm of the verse is to a poet what the measure is to a musician; it must be indicated, but it must not enslave. It is especially important that the thoughts should have their own movement and that the breaks in the sentence do not coincide exactly with the breaks in the verse. One will also understand, without further details, why the most graceful rhythms are also the most varied. Square rhymes are somewhat monotonous. The stanza with crossed rhymes pleases more; and still more graceful is an interlacing with no definite rule. In free verse, one will have the further freedom to lengthen and shorten the lines as suitable, on condition, of course, that they succeed one another according to certain proportions and that they keep a certain cadence within the free variations of rhythm. For the danger is that one can end by losing the sense of the rhythm entirely. Molière's work is a good example of the freedom of rhythm giving the impression of perfect grace.

*2. Freedom in purpose*  The purpose of an activity is as binding as the law of rhythm, for it also constrains our movements into succeeding one another in a determined order. I repeat, therefore, that it is by not conforming too rigorously to this law that we will create the impression of gracefulness.

Play activity will almost always be more graceful than work activity. Random examples from work and play will illustrate this: the roadsman felling stones, the blacksmith hitting an anvil, the rural mailman trudging along a road, a mule pulling a wagon—and, by contrast, a kid gamboling around its mother, a cat playing with a cork, children in a ball game, young people bathing in the ocean. Need one say which are the graceful ones? People who have a task to accomplish, knowing the cost of their strength and time, will spare themselves; and this pre-occupation determines not only the energy they expend in each movement, but also the manner in which they execute it and their appearance. The workman is serious.

> Thoughtful, the mower with his wide blade advances
> Step by step to the last blade of wheat.

When one starts work in good spirits, there may be a burst of gaiety. It does not last. In play, on the contrary, one gives one-self without measure, or one spares oneself without scruple, since there is no other rule but pleasure. The young man in a game has an expression of courageous gaiety, a smile that per-sists even in effort. I readily admit that work activity often has more beauty and always more dignity than play, a thesis that Mr. Guyau defends in his book on contemporary aesthetics.[2] But I cannot concede that it is more graceful. How can move-ments that one executes above all for the pleasure of moving not give an impression of greater ease than those that are bound to a function? If work is graceful, one may say it is acci-dental that it is so. Is not compulsion, which is essentially the only thing that distinguishes work from play, prejudicial from

2   Marie Jean Guyau, *Les problèmes de l'esthétique contemporaine* (Paris: Alcan, 1897), p. 39.

that point of view? The same activity gives us an impression of ease or of effort, depending on whether we perceive it as recre-ation or labor. The expenditure of energy may be the same; the difference of purpose alone suffices to modify the impression produced on the spectator.

This also applies to the movements of animals. I admire a swift flying high in the skies, capriciously meandering in space. Will its flight seem as graceful if I reflect that this is not a display of agility but a chase, and that at the moment the bird is describing one of these lovely curves, it is not doing so for pleasure but to gobble up a fly?

This is partly why rectilinear movements usually lack grace. When I see a bird fly in a straight line, I say to myself that it is going somewhere: if it is flying fast, I will think it is in a great hurry; if slowly, that it seems in no hurry. It will never cross my mind that it is flying for its pleasure. A more varied movement will give me less the idea of a means to an end and therefore will appear freer.

Let us go a step further. One might almost say that this free-dom of movement which pleases sympathetically in animated creatures will please metaphorically in inanimate objects. The oscillations of a branch in the wind, though as limited as those of a clock, seem freer because I cannot predict them as accu-rately; and they will be more graceful. Again, compare the steamer with the sailboat. The steamer navigating in calm water goes straight ahead, ploughing the water effortlessly; a few waves, by varying its motion, will begin to make it look more pleasing; it rises on a crest, makes a lurch and straightens out; it is no longer just a machine. The sailboat will seem even freer because the law of its movements is more complicated. These conflicts of various forces give the appearance of life to an inert body. And is it only an appearance? Is life anything else?

In general, any body moving in a straight line, like a flying arrow or a rolling stone, or like a torrent rushing down the mountain, seems to have a goal we are sure it will reach; but an indirect or sinuous movement—a feather floating on the surface of the water, the fall of a dead leaf, the meandering of a stream through a meadow—gives me a greater impression of fantasy, of capriciousness, of freedom, and, consequently, of grace.

*3. Prodigality in effort*    Not only must economy of movement sometimes be sacrificed to grace, but, from time to time, it is good to sacrifice it in a visible way. Beauty is a kind of luxury. Too much economy of movement is at the antipode of art. In art, one should spare one's strength as much as one can, but it should not be obvious that one is doing so. Certain attitudes, though comfortable, seem ungraceful because they are too comfortable. This fellow reading a large fat book has spread it out on the table and sprawls over it with his chin in his fists. We smile, for he is so obviously afraid of tiring himself. The same goes for movements: too manifest an economy takes away their gracefulness. A certain deliberate prodigality in the spending of energies is sometimes useful to avoid being suspected of parsimony. In all the arts that give, even indirectly, a feeling of gracefulness in movement, we find the gratuitous feats, the challenges to difficulty, the tours de force that, through a substantial increase in effort, actually erase the impression of that effort. A coloratura will end a long phrase with an extra flourish, a sustained note, or a turn of the scale; the more she needs to catch her breath, the more she slows down

her phrase or raises her voice. Why should she breathe? She is above such needs! That is the reason for the vocalizations, trills, and embellishments that are lavished at the end of phrases in popular songs and arias. These explosions of speed are like the leaps and prances of a runner trying to prove that he could go even faster if he wished; when the initial tempo is resumed, the music no longer seems to be racing at full speed, but instead is carried forward or even held back. All impression of effort has disappeared.

Listen to an expert drummer. You will notice that the procedure is the same. First, the regular beat, to establish the pulse; then rolls that, without interrupting it, give it a certain bass; then jumps and syncopations and counternotes and endless variations, in which you can only distinguish the rhythm through a hailstorm of rras and flas; one can hardly follow, the ear loses itself, one asks for mercy. Suddenly the tumult calms down and once more the beat is heard, but this time in a more accentuated rhythm, brisker, as if it were emerging triumphantly from this chase. I remember having seen at a fair a woman playing two drums simultaneously, doing grace notes on the one and playing the beat on the other. Do we not have here a typical example of these gratuitous difficulties that the player imposes on himself to give the impression of perfect ease? The pianist will rain notes in the midst of which the tune comes out. The lecturer will show some coquetry in exchanging glances with a friend, or making a digression over an unexpected incident, or replying gaily to an interruption without losing the thread of his speech. A skillful poet accumulates difficulties as if on a wager, playing with perfect ease with the most laborious-looking meters, juggling with extraordinary rhymes, tripling them for fear of seeming nonplussed by the difficulty. A humorous poet will mingle wit with feeling; in the most lyrical stanzas, he interpolates little ironical thoughts, like Byron or Musset, to show his mastery over his art even when he is most carried away.

## Art and Grace

The above considerations lead us to believe that real grace is not found in nature accidentally, so to speak; it must be sought intentionally. Made of appearances, it implies concern with appearance and with preoccupations that are essentially artistic.

"Grace," said Schiller in his curious study to which we shall have occasion to return, "is a beauty not given by nature, but produced by the subject itself."[3] Nothing is truer. Doubtless, it assumes some natural gifts: an agile, supple, and healthy body; enough plastic beauty not only to prevent the exhibition of one's person from being ridiculous in any way, but to make it look attractive to the spectator; finally, an instinctive sense of rhythm and harmony. With this equipment, it will be easier to be graceful. Without it, however much one tries, one will never succeed. "Whatever he does, a lout will never pass for a gallant."

But all the rest is our doing, the result of our activity; and I may add that it is the conscious, intentional, artistic product of our work, at least in the superior forms of grace. To be graceful, we have to be concerned, if not with elegant movements, at least with avoiding gauche and embarrassed ones. We must exercise a certain surveillance over our attitudes and gestures; we must seek perfection in our movements, partly for the effect we produce on those who watch us, but mostly from self-esteem and, better still, for the love of art.

This may seem in contradiction with a principle commonly admitted: that naturalness is an essential condition of grace. The most elegant gesture will not please me as much if I feel that it is done with a preoccupation with elegance: it is no longer freedom in movement, no longer perfect ease. There is in it, if not physical effort, at least psychological compulsion, which, sympathetically, is bound to produce in the spectator an unpleasant sensation. As a matter of fact, does not experience show us that the more we seek gracefulness, the more it evades us, and that the less we think of our movements, the more true elegance they have?

Watch a shy young man walking along a public promenade: he would like not to appear gauche and he knows well what needs to be done. Yet, as it happens, he is too attentive to what he is doing with his feet, his hands; thence, there exists a constraint unpleasant to observe. Here he is now paying a call. He is already nervous as he enters, his palms are damp, his throat is tight at the idea of appearing before all those ladies who are probably waiting to test him. He sits down. The attention he feels concentrated upon himself stings his face and he reddens. To distract himself from the nervous excitement that torments him, he scratches his ear, swings his leg, chuckles without cause. In all his gestures, in all his answers, he rushes forward feverishly to have done sooner, so that he won't be looked at any more.

Generally speaking, any useless movement done expressly to be graceful destroys grace. You catch sight of a little girl playing with her friends, running, leaping, dancing as gracefully as anything. But she notices she is observed and, immediately, be-

---

3   Friedrich von Schiller, *Complete Works*, vol. 5, *Aesthetical Letters and Essays* (Boston: Aldine, 1910), "On Grace and Dignity," p. 173.

comes mannered. The charm is broken. A woman who wishes to look distinguished will lift her little finger in an affected manner; the village coxcomb coming to town in his best clothes will inevitably swagger as he walks to give himself a carefree look. It is all the same lack of taste. You admire a circus acrobat doing trapeze tricks: she springs, grabs the trapeze in motion, swings; and while she thinks only of showing her skill, she gives a feeling of perfect ease in her movement. But once she ends the display and is about to take leave, she skips a few times in the ring, takes a bow with her hand on her heart: now, she is trying to be graceful and so no longer is.

It is very true that to acquire grace, one must not seem to be too preoccupied with it. But I feel that, by taking early the habit of watching one's movements, one can become free from that preoccupation. The faults mentioned above are beginners' faults. They are not due to making one's movements too artistic, but rather by not making them artistic enough.

The affectation noticeable in people who wish to appear graceful is due to the fact that this preoccupation is something new or unusual to them. They suddenly take it into their heads to give us a spectacle of supreme elegance, of perfect distinction. That is doing things too fast: they are not equal to it. A hostess who is not used to entertaining feels she must use formal expressions with pretentious turns of speech. A practiced hostess displays polished manners effortlessly, because she has learned early to express herself well. It is the same for elegance of attitudes and gestures. In addition, one should not forget that there is a kind of acquired gracefulness, which tends to make affectation disappear. A mother gives her daughter good advice. Friends undertake to correct errors of taste with a smile. Stiffness is much harder to cure when it is caused by in-

nate shyness. However, timidity is often due to the consciousness of one's inexperience and will disappear as one is aware of improvement. Nothing gives more security than getting used to being in society. Once the apprenticeship, both mental and physical, is over, the bad moments are behind.

In acquiring gracefulness, whether simply concerned with body exercises or with that much more complex grace of bearing, there is a time of transition, an ingrate's age, when natural grace is lost and acquired grace not yet found. When one starts to do things deliberately and on principle, one does them badly at first. The elegance to which one aspires may negate the little one has. Spontaneous movements become constrained as soon as one thinks about them; the attention that is turned on them paralyzes or exaggerates them. They only take on their new grace when they become habitual enough to happen by pure reflex. Then one no longer has to worry about the placement of a foot or the position of the little finger; and the result is a sensation of ease in the whole body.

Spontaneity is indispensable. Indeed, perfect harmony of movement requires the coordination of a great number of partial movements. But our attention, being narrow by nature, can only be directed to a few of them at a time, leaving the others free to follow their natural flow. We must, therefore, train successively the different muscles to function in the desired manner. When each has caught the routine and can execute it instinctively, we only need to tell our body to do the movement for it to obey instantly.

When one studies a movement methodically (dance, gymnastics, fencing), it is best to break it down according to each measure. Then each motion can be perfected. When, later, it comes to executing the movement, it can be done as fast as one wishes without risk of getting mixed up. The beginner taking his first fencing lesson is anxious to get to the moment of attack. The methodical exercises to which the fencing master subjects him try his patience. But it is only when he learns to lunge slowly and correctly that he can do it fast during an attack. The impetus of his legs will follow his arm in an almost instantaneous impulse.

These examples show the relationship of reflex actions to the manifestations of grace. But it is important not to forget that even in these movements that have become natural by habit, something is left to the will. When talking of spontaneous, unconscious gestures, one must not take these expressions too literally. If, in order to acquire ease, one should no longer have to pay express attention to the movements in detail, it does not follow that one can let them happen purely automatically. Acquired grace is not mechanical grace. The will must always participate to keep the body alive, attentive, ready to obey any command. The will must maintain harmony between all these different forces which would become discordant if left to themselves. It must hasten or moderate their play, according to circumstances. In an orchestra, when each musician knows his score, the leader has less to do, and that enables him to do more: he regulates the timing, sees to entrances, indicates nuances, centralizes all the partial movements to make them contribute to the ensemble. Superior grace always has something intentional. From beginning to end, it remains a product of art.

But, one might say, at least this art must give the illusion of nature, by concealing itself as much as possible! I am not at all of that opinion.

One should note that a gymnast has a tendency to mark the timing of the movements he executes. He does not do this because he needs to, but for your enjoyment as a spectator. Movements thus executed cost more physical effort but give a greater impression of psychological ease; by holding back the movement, by making pauses, he shows that, when he proceeds, it is not because he is propelled by impulse, but because he wills it and is in control of what he does as well as of the speed at which he does it. His movement is more graceful because beauty can be better appreciated. You must have enough time to perceive the gymnast's successive attitudes and the play of his muscles. If he goes too fast, with no pauses, you will be aware that the movement has been done, without knowing quite how; by delineating its various stages, he makes you understand. In this way, you will have an artistic enjoyment of this skillful decomposition of efforts. You will realize the justification of each gesture, designed with an eye to the end result. Methodical movement is to natural movement what logically ordered and analyzed ideas are to a confused phrase where thoughts are presented in a jumble. To make a musical comparison, natural movement is like a plain chord of which one feels the resultant harmony without knowing the elements that compose it; and methodical movement is like an arpeggio in which the notes file by the ear rapidly, before melting into a harmonious whole. Grace, then, is obtained not by giving the perfect illusion of nature, but, on the contrary, by underlining the methodical elements of the movement.

The more I reflect on the theory by which art, in its various manifestations, has to be concealed and appear absent, the less it seems to me in accord with the real requirements of taste. How can the idea that the real beauty of a work is due to the formal intent of its author depreciate it in our eyes? It should, on the contrary, increase its value. When I hear a nightingale singing in the calm of the night, should I, in order not to spoil my pleasure, think that there is nothing intentional either in the hour or in the song? That the bird sings simply because the moonlight keeps it awake and that the nature of its song is only determined by the law of the least effort, or some other mechanism—instinct, chance, whatever—as long as it is not taste? Surely not. First, it would be unjust. I consider myself poetical because I deign to listen to the nightingale and notice the harmony of its song. But the true poet is the bird who, not needing to exalt its imagination with poetical phrases, felt, before I did, the charm of this beautiful night and was inspired to compose its song. And does not this way of looking at things augment my pleasure? The idea that grace in movement is absolutely natural, that it is fortuitous and automatic, and that taste has nothing to do with it would prevent me from admiring it. I do not wish grace to appear too designed, too prepared; but we still must be made aware that it is intended.

Let me go further. In my opinion, a little coquetry is not unbecoming to grace. I cannot see why any form of art should affect disinterest and seek to please without appearing to care for our opinion.

In effect, complete disinterest is impossible. How can beauty not be aware of the admiration it inspires, and, when observing it and enjoying it, why should it not seek it? The primitive man dancing a war dance knows he is beautiful, and does not forget that many eyes are fastened on him. The most modest young lady who is startled by the least glance always feels observed. If she were indifferent to the effect she produces, she would not suffer as much from her awkwardness. Even in animals, at least in the higher species, it is unquestionable that the instinct of coquetry exists. A kitten that fails in a trick perceives that she is being laughed at and retires, vexed; a greyhound has movements that are deliberately graceful, sometimes even mannered. A horse whose pace is being slowed paws the ground, straightens up, and prances as if dancing in place.

One remembers what advantage Darwin took of this instinct of coquetry in his studies on sexual selection. It is through this instinct that he partly explains the beauty of the shapes and adornments that we admire in animals. We might also turn to this instinct to explain the grace they have in their movements. In a great number of animals, the male parades before the female to seduce her by movements that may make us smile but that are evidently aimed at attracting her attention by enhancing himself; the peacock spreads his tail feathers and makes them quiver and glitter; the pheasant struts back and forth in front of his hen, always lowering his superb necklace toward her; the pigeon inflates his gullet and turns around himself; the grouse in the wood clearing does a real dance in honor of his female.

At least in the human species, it is incontestable that grace of movement is one of the most powerful elements of seduction; that it is deliberately sought to this end; that it appears especially among young girls as they become young women; and finally that there is always in the feeling of grace a portion to be given to sexual attraction.

For all these reasons, it is very difficult to believe in the artless, spontaneous, unconscious development of grace. What is the harm, after all? One would have to be pretty badly disposed to reproach beauty for making efforts to please and to resent its being concerned with our good opinion. Is not the desire to please an added charm? Why should it be absent from grace? Everything concurs in a conclusion that grace is artful.

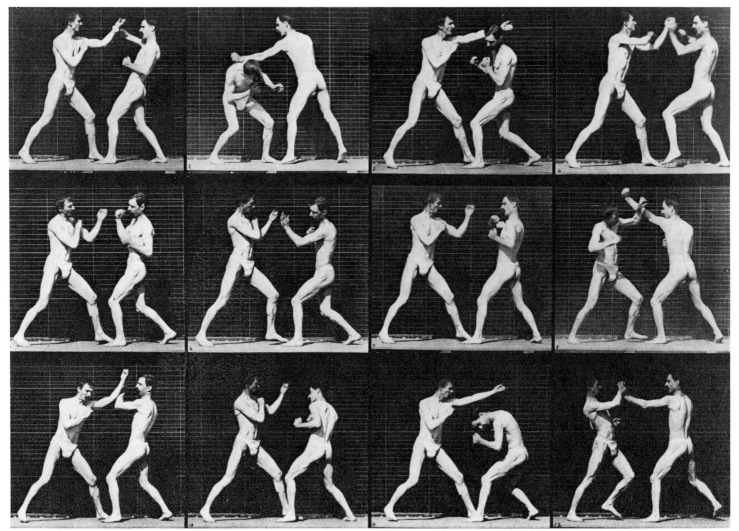

*Men boxing*

The idea of force evidently comes to us as a result of muscular effort. If, metaphysically, force is only the unknown cause of movement; and if, geometrically, it is measured only by the acceleration that is communicated to a given mass, in practice it is impossible for us not to picture it as effort. I am holding another person by the hand and make an effort to draw that person to me; he resists and I can only picture his resistance as an effort of withdrawal, opposed and equal to my effort of traction.

The impression will be the same with an inanimate object. If I push it, I imagine it opposes me with a force of inertia, that is, an effort to cling to the ground. If I raise the object, it seems to me to be making an effort to fall. One of the most curious impressions we can experience in this respect is that given by remote attraction. If I bring a piece of iron to an electromagnet, the moment the electrical current passes through the coil, I feel my hand abruptly drawn by a mysterious, almost immaterial force against which I must struggle. We get the same impression in regard to gravity, by picturing it as a power of attraction, though we are so accustomed to seeing bodies fall that it prevents us from realizing how strange the phenomenon is.

We shall now see how this idea of exterior effort or force which occurs at the moment we make a muscular effort tends toward complete objectification. When I stretch a bow, I feel the effort I make to bend it and I imagine it is making a similar effort to spring back. Now the string is in place and I relax, but, in my mind, the bow continues its effort. Thus the idea of force,

which was first conceived only as a function between the object and me, has become completely objective, surviving the opposition that caused it. It is of course an illusion, for the piece of wood has no need to spring back; it only has a tendency to do so. Or, to be more precise, I can assert only that if the string breaks, the bow will spring back. Nothing tells me that this virtual release corresponds to anything else but a certain arrangement of its molecules. And yet, I cannot help picturing in these molecules a force of tension, an activity, an effort of a permanent nature.

If, finally, I witness a collision of heavy masses, if I see a body push or crush another, it will give me the idea of a conflict of forces which I will picture to myself as antagonistic efforts.

Is there not already in this notion of force, however primitive, a kind of poetry? Is it not a result of our tendency to lend our feelings and sensations to objects and to personify them? In any case, we shall see that it plays a great role in the images we have of the material world and that it can provide us with the highest aesthetic emotions.

We have a kind of sympathy for every force in action, which makes us interested in its conservation. When I make a movement, the law of inertia should extend it indefinitely. But though physics teaches us that force is conserved integrally, that in nature the quantity of movement neither increases nor decreases, common experience, on which our aesthetic judgments are actually founded, contradicts this. If there is a fact fully demonstrated by our senses, it is that any force wears itself out and disappears sooner or later; that any mass in motion comes back to rest if it does not receive a new stimulation from the outside. The stone you throw hits the ground and suddenly all its movement is lost. If you roll it on the ground, the distance it goes depends upon the smoothness of the terrain, but it will always stop. It is the same for the ripples of water when it is disturbed, for the vibrations of a bell when tolled, for the impetus you take to jump. It is possible that this energy, which appears lost, can be found in totality in the vibrations of the ground and the air or in released heat; but it is no longer manifest in any visible motion; in my eyes, it no longer exists.

This being the case, it is understandable that we take a particular interest in extending the movements we have produced: this force that we see acting outside us is a part of ourselves. But, even when the movement is not made by us or by others whose feelings we can share in our imagination, it still awakens our sympathy, because of our tendency to personify the objects when they move. One might say that force is the spirit of matter in motion. When our eye follows a revolving top, a projectile flying through the air, a ripple crossing a sheet of water, a whirlpool of dust rising along the road, does it not seem that matter becomes alive before us? And when those forces that animated the object for an instant withdraw, do we not, when the object returns to inertia, get the impression of something dying?

This same sympathy explains the particular pleasure that the movement of elastic bodies gives us. Look at a marble falling on a tile. Nothing is more graceful than this movement, not only because of its alternation and rhythm, but especially because of its dynamic vitality. Nearly all the force expended in the fall is once more available for an equivalent ascent. A lead pellet falling on the stone flattens itself heavily; a stone thrown in the sand plunges in and becomes still: this is a force abruptly destroyed. But the rubber ball gives us the spectacle of a force always reborn: the instant this material mass, which was

immobilized for a moment, rebounds, we cannot avoid the impression that it does so automatically.

We always take sides in the conflict of physical forces which is like the drama of inanimate nature. When a flooding river beats on the facing of a wall, when waves assail a cliff, when a tree struggles against the gusting wind, we side with the wall or the river, the cliff or the waves, the tree or the wind, according to our disposition at the time; and we await the result anxiously; we follow with passionate, almost wild interest the vicissitudes of the battle.

Of all the forces of nature, the most challenging to us, as we have said before, is the force of gravitation. So we will nearly always take sides against it, reserving all our sympathy for the forces that resist gravity, that seem to be fighting against the fate of falling.

A building I am observing is not to me just a visual image, a combination of lines, surfaces, and colors. If it were so, I could, without any disadvantage, substitute a canvas reproducing its likeness superficially; the impression would have to be the same. But when I find myself before the building itself, other notions, namely dynamic ideas, enter into the image I have. I do not picture these stones as geometrical solids, but as hard, weighty masses, piled one on top of the other; the entablature weighs down on the column which makes an effort to support it; the vault weighs down on the facings which in turn lean against flying buttresses, to resist this pressure. The architect must have calculated all these pressures and counterpressures; the spectator just estimates them, and his impression is one of security or disquiet, according to how stable or unstable the combination appears to him. What do we admire in a Gothic church? Is it only the purity of its lines, the grace of its curves?

No, it is also its victory over gravity; it is the understanding between these forces which are solidary and unite to fight against a common enemy. It seems to us that if a single stone were to be withdrawn from the edifice, the whole thing would immediately collapse. But all the stones support one another, returning the pressure they receive by an equivalent counterpressure, obtaining their cohesive strength from these very pressures and standing in suspension through a miracle of balance.

Any fall or collapse gives us the sensation of a force irretrievably lost, of a waste of energy, so that descending movements will, by their very nature, be less aesthetic than ascending ones. Compare for instance the high jump to the long-distance jump, or the ascension of a balloon to its descent! Even putting aside all extrinsic reasons that may exercise some influence on our judgments, you will find a particular attraction to the ascending movement; whereas, if descending movements have any allure, they owe it to the same reasons. If, for example, we take pleasure in the steady fall of a cascade, it is because of the freshness it brings us, the milky whiteness of its foaming water, its ceaseless movement which captivates the eyes, and the gentle, almost lethargic sounds of water falling into water. But this fall is in no way agreeable in itself; and the proof is that it will please us only if it is light, and delayed or attenuated, as it were. What is taken for the pleasure of the fall is only the pleasure of a lesser fall (e.g., a dandelion seed, a dead leaf, a snowflake falling gently to the ground, a bird gliding down to a stop, an acrobat spiraling down a rope). But if the mass of plunging water is great enough to fall in one block, the impression will be totally different: then it is just a heavy, ceaseless fall; it is the obstinate action of gravity. We imagine ourselves crushed on those rocks, engulfed in those whirlpools; and the total impression is one of horror.[1] If, nevertheless, we seek such emotions, it is out of curiosity, out of a kind of mental intoxication which attracts us to tragic spectacles.

The Epicureans thought that all atoms have a tendency to move downward, colliding only because of imperceptible deviations in their fall. They do not seem to have realized that if that were the case, the whole world, which is made up of these atoms, would be falling in space, as in a bottomless abyss. If they had thought of it, they might have been less complacent about their hypothesis. Let us just imagine a rock perpetually falling in space: it is an untenable thought, a nightmarish idea.

Independent of any mechanical beauty, of any gracefulness, force in itself, by the very fact that it takes energy to evolve, evokes in us a feeling of admiration. In the somewhat brutal world we inhabit, where rights may have the last word, but where, certainly, the reason of the strongest always prevails at first, one understands without difficulty that the object of our ambition and envy is above all physical power. Every child dreams of being strong. We all admire an exceptionally vigorous man and certainly the expression of force is among the attributes of virile beauty.[2] Some animals, such as the bull, the bison, the rhinoceros, or the elephant, are admired in spite of their lack of grace; in the absence of structural beauty, there is a dynamic beauty.

---

1   See Charles Bigot, "De Paris au Niagara—Journal de voyage d'une délégation," *Revue politique et littéraire*, Jan. 15, 1887.

2   Sculptors of antiquity have usually erred in giving Hercules too heavy a shape. That is not the way to personify virile strength, which should rather consist in muscular energy. The Hercules of poets was as agile as he was vigorous. That of sculptors might have been capable of striking a blow with an enormous club, but he would never have caught up with the bronze-footed doe.

We extend this admiration to the brutal forces of inanimate nature: a steam engine,[3] a hydraulic wheel, huge waves beating against a cliff, the wind blowing in a storm, the flash of lightning. All undoubtedly give us an aesthetic emotion.

We also extend it to forces that are not active, but are potentially so. For example, when we see a heavy mass of rocks protruding above our heads, we have the sensation of an immense energy ready to develop into a formidable crash.

We extend our admiration to the results of effort, which are like the permanent witness of its power: a tree broken and twisted by a hurricane, an enormous rock jutting in the middle of a plain like the hand of a giant, a monumental construction, a cathedral spire reaching upward into space. The great iron constructions which are the glory of modern architecture should produce the same impression. In fact, they do compel our admiration, in spite of the scorn heaped upon them by conventional aestheticians who never fail to condemn the present in the name of the past and refuse to see art where there is industry. One knows of the strange request presented by a number of artists to the engineer Jean Alphand, protesting in the name of good taste the erection of the Eiffel Tower. "Will the City of Paris associate itself much longer with these baroque, mercantile fancies of a builder of machines and dishonor itself by becoming irreparably ugly? For the Eiffel Tower, which even commercial America would not accept, is, without doubt, the dishonor of Paris." Mr. Eiffel replied:

I will tell you my whole thought and hopes. I believe my tower will be beautiful. Because we are engineers, do you think we are not concerned with beauty in our constructions and that when we strive for solidity and durability, we do not also strive for elegance? Do not actual conditions of strength always conform to the secret conditions of harmony? The first principle of architectural aesthetics is that the essential lines of a monument be determined by their perfect appropriateness to their intent. What conditions have I had, above all, to take into account for my tower? Wind resistance. Well, I claim that the curves of the four ridges in my building, as supplied by my calculations, will give an impression of beauty, for they will translate to the eyes the boldness of my conception.... There is furthermore an attraction in the colossal, an intrinsic charm to which the ordinary theories of art hardly apply. Will one argue that it is by their artistic value that the pyramids have struck the imagination of men so strongly? What are they, after all, but artificial mounds? And yet, what visitor stays cold in their presence? Who has not returned from a visit to Egypt filled with irresistible admiration? And where is the source of this imagination if not in the immensity of the effort and the greatness of the result? My tower will be the tallest edifice ever erected by man. Will it not also be grandiose in its way? And why would something admirable in Egypt become hideous and ridiculous in Paris? I try to understand but confess I cannot.[4]

Yes, any colossal force, by the side of which ours has little meaning, awakens in us this complex feeling—made of imagination and dizziness—that one calls the feeling of the sublime. And one could even argue that in everything that appears sublime, whether in moral or in material greatness, whether in a heroic action, a work of genius, or a gigantic building, it is the mightiness of the effort that awakes our admiration; in other words, the truly sublime is the dynamically sublime.

3   In his book on *L'expression dans les Beaux-Arts* (Paris: Alphonse Lemerre, 1898), René Sully-Prudhomme also seems to confuse force with mass when he says that modern machines are less expressive of force than the old machines, because they are less voluminous. It is a somewhat outdated idea.

4   *Le Temps,* Feb. 14, 1887.

My will never totally determines my gestures or attitudes. If I wish to turn my head around, I have no thought for the angle or the speed of the rotation. If I do think of it, it will be in an imprecise way. The most precise volitional act is always somewhat undefined; it only regulates the bulk of the movement and always neglects some detail of execution. One can say that it only determines in what general category the premeditated movement belongs. But if our ideas are always general and sometimes very vague, nothing is general or vague in nature. Each actual movement is absolutely determined, down to its smallest detail. Whence comes the additional determination required to make the movement finally occur? From causes outside our volition, from the spontaneous release of our muscles, from simple reflex actions. That is how feelings determine our movements and attitudes. Painters of the French School have been justly reproached for giving their characters attitudes that are overly emphatic, exaggerated, and artificial. It is principally because they have sought expression in volitional attitudes, that is to say, in those attitudes we take to show our feelings on the outside. There was a confusion between mimicry and expression. Really expressive attitudes are those that do not intend to express anything, but are unconsciously determined by a deeply felt emotion.

Let us take some examples. Consider the simplest gesture in the world, that of seizing a goblet. Imagine this gesture being made by the ailing Alexander the Great, tossing down the beverage offered by his doctor, Philip, which he had been warned might be poisoned; by Socrates about to drink the hemlock; by Faustus in his despair at the nothingness of things; or by a child resigned to drinking a glass of medicine. In every case, the intention is the same, the hand always moves toward the cup. But how varied are the nuances in the gesture, according to the feelings that inspire it! What great differences in its expression! In one case, it will show firmness, loyalty, with a touch of defiance and bravado; in another, contemptuousness, indifference, not without irony; in yet another, desperation, and the sudden frenzy of destruction; and in the last, resignation and distrust. Replace the gesture with a sentence, such as: "Well, let us die if we must!" and think of how it will be pronounced in each case. The words will always be the same; but the tone will vary. These specific nuances in gesture and attitude, which complete the determination of a volitional movement, form what Schiller aptly calls the *tone* of a movement.[1]

It is not my intention to embark on the broad topic of expression. Not that it is totally foreign to our subject, but it is so complex that we must set ourselves limits. Furthermore, the problem of expression has been the subject of studies so detailed that they now form a distinct branch of aesthetics. I will not, then, inquire into the gestures and facial expressions that correspond to each feeling, nor into why these gestures take their particular shapes, nor into how we come to interpret them. I only wish to say a few words on the influence they have on the beauty and grace of movement.

When we see someone being affected by an emotion, our attention may be drawn particularly to three things: (1) the

---

1   Friedrich von Schiller, *Complete Works*, vol. 5, *Aesthetical Letters and Essays* (Boston: Aldine, 1910), "On Grace and Dignity," p. 186.

movements of that person; (2) the emotion the person feels; (3) the relationship of those movements to that emotion. To judge how the expression of feelings influences our judgments of taste, we will take each point of view in succession.

Let us first consider the expressive movements in themselves, that is, by trying to eliminate whatever attraction the feelings they express may have for us: for the time being, we are only concerned with the way these feelings modify the execution of a movement.

Certain feelings have the effect of exciting nervous and muscular activity, others of depressing it. The first are more often expressed in gestures, the second in attitudes. Compare, for example, the expression of gaiety, which is an exciting feeling, to that of sadness, which is a depressive one. The merry person cannot hold still, stirs about, and speaks with vivacity. The sad person remains preferably sitting and silent.

The best way to see how a given feeling influences our activity is by observing the different effects it has on some recurrent movement which is by nature quite regular. While observing this, we will note that rhythmic movements are only expressive when their rhythm varies; for it is these variations alone that reveal the influence of feeling. Let us choose, for instance, the rhythm of the walk. As long as it is normal and regular, it expresses nothing. A stroller is walking straight ahead, neither fast nor slowly, neither dragging her feet nor stepping high. What on earth can her walk tell us? This mechanical movement of the legs is no more expressive than the turning of carriage wheels. But if her step accelerates or slows down, it will immediately take on some expression; for it is evidently some feeling or sensation or an intention of some kind that is interfering with the composition of the movements and disturbing their

mechanical rhythm. Acceleration will mark impatience to get to one's goal; deceleration is a sign of fatigue or discouragement. The finest nuances of feeling can be expressed by an alteration in the rhythm. Merriment manifests itself by a certain exuberance; self-satisfaction, by a characteristic way of throwing the legs to the side; aggression, by the resonance of the step. Sadness walks downcast, fear is hesitant and advances as if retreating; desire has sharp impulses which carry it forward; guilt has sudden stops; reverie wanders, and so on. Whatever the mechanical task, such as turning a wheel, carving a piece of wood, cutting up a beam, or copying out a page, there will be the same differences, corresponding to the same sentiments.

It would be quite difficult to say why a given feeling acts on our actions in one way or another, especially since the same feeling can take an active or a passive form, according to its intensity or to the amount of energy in the person who feels it. But generally speaking, it seems to me that feelings are more active as they pertain more directly to the present. Thus anger and terror are active feelings, because the thought that produces them always relates to a recent or imminent event. On the contrary, feelings whose object is distant, such as regret which turns toward the past, hope which turns to the future, or happiness which places itself outside time, can be categorized as passive or turned inward. They imply an interior meditation; we have to withdraw into ourselves to savor their sweetness or bitterness. How could they excite us, when they do not present us with an immediate goal or an effort to be accomplished on the spot?

Active or passive, all these feelings are compatible with gracefulness, but only if they are moderate enough not to rob us of our self-control. As soon as they take a certain intensity, they prevent our mind from exercising its usual control on our movements and from adapting them to their intent in the best way possible. Our gestures become more nervous, more automatic, less thoughtful: the involuntary element which we have noted in volitional movements becomes preponderant.

When our feelings become excessively intense, all grace is destroyed: such is the case for hysterical laughter, despair, rage, terror, intense suffering. Large movements which are the expression of these emotions are like an effort we make to shield ourselves from their effect. We relieve ourselves with cries and convulsions. Under such conditions, reflexes are extremely violent, nervous discharges brutal, and the natural rhythm of the movements is completely broken. Or else there is complete exhaustion, a prostration that is painful to watch.

Sometimes, in states of mind that are more complex, excited feelings conflict with depressive ones. For example, consider the coward who gets insulted and trembles with powerless rage: anger pushes him forward, fear, backward; and this psychological conflict is expressed by vibratory gestures of an unpleasant effect.

Active feelings may, however, acquire a certain beauty by their exaggeration, the beauty of strength. While complete despair offers a lamentable spectacle from all points of view, there is something powerful about heavy gaiety, a vital exuberance which can still be admired. Fear is only tolerable on a very attenuated scale, like that of a timid child; in its extreme manifestations it takes on an abject character. Anger, on the contrary, when it is taken to its paroxysm, has superb attitudes; it looks you straight in the face and, gathering all its forces, gets ready to pounce: see the threatened bulldog, the infuriated bull, the lion stalking, the cobra when it is being teased. Paul de

Chaillu, in his travel narratives, vividly describes the attitude of a gorilla facing the hunter:

Suddenly, as we were yet creeping along in a silence which made a heavy breath seem loud and distinct, the woods were at once filled with the tremendous barking roar of the gorilla. Then the underbrush swayed rapidly just ahead, and presently before us stood an immense male gorilla. He had gone through the jungle on his all-fours; but when he saw our party, he erected himself and looked us boldly in the face. . . . He was not afraid of us. He stood there and beat his breast with his huge fists, till it resounded like an immense bass-drum, which is their mode of offering defiance; meantime giving vent to roar after roar. . . . The roar of the gorilla is the most singular and awful noise heard in these African woods. It begins with a sharp bark, like an angry dog, then glides into a deep bass roll which literally and closely resembles the roll of the distant thunder along the sky. . . . His eyes began to flash fiercer fire as we stood motionless on the defensive. The short hairs on the top of his head stood up and began to move rapidly while his powerful fangs were shown as he again sent forth a thundering roar. . . . He advanced a few steps—then stopped to utter that hideous roar again—advanced again, and finally stopped at a distance of about 6 yards from us. And here, as he began another of his roars, and beating his breast in rage, we fired and killed him.[2]

Does not this description awaken in the reader's imagination a certain aesthetic emotion? Setting aside the emotion that his courage produces, do we not admire the hideous animal for his strength and his powerful anger? And is there not here something very much akin to what Kant called the dynamic sublime?

Now let us consider the emotions that people feel. When we

2   Paul Belloni du Chaillu, *Explorations and Adventures in Equatorial Africa* (London: John Murray, 1861), p. 70.

observe a person who is moved, our imagination always pictures that person's emotions; we will take more or less pleasure depending upon whether we are disposed to share them or not, whether we are sympathetic or antipathetic. This emotional impression will contribute to our finding it more aesthetic or less so. In some cases, the effect produced by the feeling being expressed only adds to that produced by the movements themselves: if, for example, a smile is graceful, it is not only because it animates the countenance, but also because it awakens in the viewer feelings of gaiety and good will similar to those it expresses. In other cases there will be a conflict. The expression of physical pain is never graceful, however plastic the attitudes may be by which it is manifested; for the symmpathy we feel for that suffering inevitably overshadows and, by contrast, obliterates the kind of physical sympathy which induces pleasure in the rhythmic play of the muscles and in the freedom of their contraction. Emotional suffering can leave an impression of grace, if the conflict is not too immediate and if the distress is of a light nature only. One would have to be steeped in aesthetics and greatly in love with appearances as well as indifferent to reality to look at pain as an artist in order to admire its expression. One knows where this kind of dilettantism carried Nero. There is already a certain depravity in a refinement of taste that permits people to maintain their sense of beauty at the sight of even the slightest pain. Nero admired Junia, "sad, lifting to heaven her eyes brimming with tears/shining among the torches and the swords."

As soon as feelings become intense enough and acquire a real emotional value, they become our only concern and determine our judgments of taste. If their intent is only to stir our pity or indignation, we cannot possibly admire the movements they express. If they are beautiful, generous, or heroic, they must arouse our admiration, whatever their physical expression.

When we see a movement being executed, remarks Guyau, we empathize with the body and limbs executing it,

but we empathize still more with the will which moves the body and limbs; the energy of this will may seduce us more than the easy play of the members; and the ends it seeks be more attractive than a movement without a goal; finally, there comes a moment when one almost totally discounts the limbs which are reduced to the role of instruments, tense and bent like a bow ready to release an arrow, sometimes even spent by their effort. The messenger of Marathon, represented by Greek sculptors, may have been covered with sweat and his features may have expressed exhaustion from his effort and the beginning of agony, but he was nevertheless transfigured by the branch of olive he was waving in his hand and he became sublime; that man, spent but triumphant, is like a symbol of human labor, of that supreme beauty which comes not from parsimony but from munificence, not from ease but from effort, when movement no longer appears to be the evidence and measure of the force expended, but the expression of the will and the means of appreciating one's inner energy.[3]

This truism could not be expressed with more eloquence.

Finally, we will examine the relationship between movements and emotion. In expressive movements, we may admire the quality of the expression itself, that is, the way the body adapts to the emotion being felt. There are some rather coarse temperaments that are never moved by moderate feelings but must be shaken by violent passions in order to become expressive. And there are more delicate temperaments that vibrate at the least emotion and are affected from head to toe. It is then

3   Marie Jean Guyau, *Les problèmes de l'esthétique contemporaine* (Paris: Alcan, 1902), p. 42.

a real aesthetic pleasure to see how the most fleeting nuances are reflected in their mobile, transparent faces. Any particular expressive gesture, for the very reason that it is expressive and whatever the importance of the feeling expressed, has a specific, superior beauty, for what it interprets for us is no longer just material life, but the life of the soul.

It is true that in real life, we hardly think of comparing movements to the feelings they express, especially when the feeling has an interest in itself. But what we do not have a right to do in the face of nature, we do without scruple in the face of its artistic expression.

When it is only a question of paintings and statues, we take pleasure in looking at an abandoned Ariadne, a dying soldier, a mother holding the corpse of a dead child, an athlete devoured by a wild beast, whose entire body is shriveled with pain. At the theater, we see an actress sobbing and twisting her arms; but unless we are deep in the grip of the drama, we do not take her suffering seriously. We have for the sentiments she expresses only an attenuated sympathy which leaves our mind free. And we admire, in the impersonation before our eyes, the elegance of the actress's lines, the grace of her shape, the plastic beauty of her attitudes, and the trueness of her expressions.

Acting is certainly a very difficult art; nothing is less easy than grasping the proper expression of feelings that are unusual or transitory and, when the right nuance is found, making it look natural. Seeing how difficult it is for an actor just to walk back and forth across the stage like everyone else, it becomes clear how much art and study the portrayal of passions requires.

This brings me to say a few words about a little comedy we play, sometimes without being aware of it, every time we speak of something that means a great deal to us. I am speaking of the comedy of gestures. There are two kinds of gestures: expressive gestures and descriptive gestures. Expressive gestures correspond to our own feelings, past or present. Take, for instance, this sentence: "The robber aimed at me, I was terrified." The narrator can mimic the fear that he felt at the time, or even the feelings that his past fear inspire in him now. These gestures are the essence of oratory. We know the importance that was given to them in ancient rhetorics. Lawyers still practice this art with its real power as well as with exaggerations which sometimes make us smile.

Descriptive gestures are not intended to underline the tone of the sentence, but to complete its meaning, by actually showing, in a more or less picturesque way, the object or the scene being described. We can, for instance, imagine the gesture the narrator would make to represent the robber who is aiming at him. We also know how an obese person would be described or a woman of opulent beauty. Generally speaking, these gestures have little nobility and it might be best to eliminate them entirely. Numerous sculptures have familiarized us with Mirabeau's great gesture as he pronounced the famous phrase: "Go and tell those who sent you that we are here by the will of the people and that we will leave only by the force of the bayonets." His arm advances in a threatening gesture, imperious, and of the greatest effect. Imagine him in the same situation, miming that phrase with descriptive gestures!

# IV   The Perception of Movement

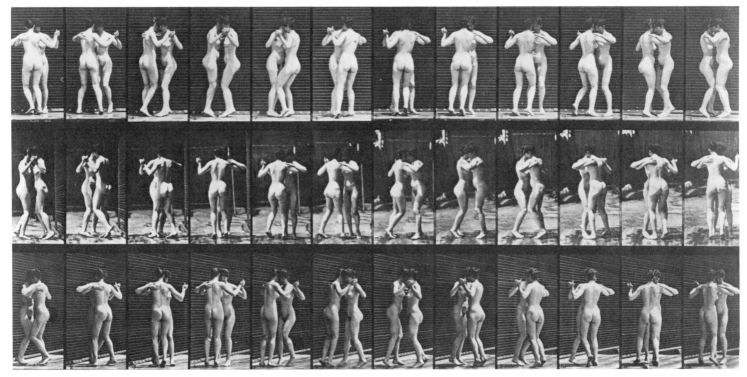

*Two women waltzing*

To perceive the movement of objects, one must be aware of their placement at each moment during their transit through space. Any objective localized sensation will therefore help us perceive the movement. The more precisely it is localized, the more accurate the perception is.

We shall disregard taste, for its sensations totally lack the characteristic of externality. Nor will we examine smell, because although its perceptions are objective enough, they are too poorly localized. What are odors in themselves? A kind of vapor that detaches itself from objects in long trails and capricious eddies. With each breath, we inhale a large whiff of an odor without in the least knowing where it comes from, unless the object from which it emanates is under our eyes. It might be different were our sense of smell more developed. Many animals are evidently aware of the direction and distance of odorous bodies and can, by smell alone, perceive their movement to a degree. A dog following a trail soon recognizes on which side the traces are freshest and never fails to follow its direction, which it can therefore evaluate. But in humans this faculty is so little developed that we can hardly conceive it.

We come to tactile sensations, those we feel from the contact of an object on our epidermis.

When a hard object hits me abruptly, I get the notion of movement in a very energetic, even rough way. A gentle contact, such as that of a blunt point tickling my skin lightly, will be even more informative: it will give me a series of quite distinct sensations, well enough localized to allow me to perceive its exact path and the approximate speed of its course. From this point of view, there is between tactile and visual perceptions an analogy that will be interesting to examine further. When my fingers skim the surface of an object, the impression is the same as if the object were moving at the contact of my fingers. I could therefore interpret this impression either way. If I am well aware of my own movements, the object seems motionless; if I execute them without being conscious of doing so, the object seems to be in transit.

I am walking along a wall, brushing it with my hand. Though I know the wall is actually stationary, it seems to be running away under my fingers in the opposite direction of my walk. But if, without stopping, I press my hand against the wall for a moment, the illusion disappears. We will see that visual perceptions give us similar illusions.

Another analogy worth noting has to do with the duration of sensations. If I touch the back of my hand with a blunt point, does the sensation cease the moment the point is withdrawn? No, the impression is sustained. And even when all local trace of the impression has disappeared, the nerve centers continue to be affected. (In the course of experimenting with this, I have had the impression, without being able to guarantee it, that this aftersensation is not continuous, but rather made up of recurrent twinges that grow weaker and weaker. The instant the point leaves my skin, I feel a circular wave of sensation which returns several times.) Let the point now be placed again against the back of my hand and made to glide softly over it. These circles of diffuse sensation of which I spoke and which occur around the point of contact will overlap one another and give me a continuous linear sensation. If a circle, a triangle, or a letter of the alphabet is traced on my hand with my eyes closed,

I will be able to indicate the shape of the figure, especially if the tracing is fast enough and long enough for the tactile sensations to be continuous.

The sense of touch can therefore serve, in a certain degree, to perceive a movement. But it has the disadvantage of almost always modifying the perception by virtue of the contact itself. Furthermore, its range is somewhat limited. That is why we usually use it only to perfect and control our visual sensations.

Muscular sensations, which are sometimes quite wrongly attributed to the sense of touch, serve mainly to regulate and direct our own movements. Though we have given them a great deal of importance earlier in this work, we must now assign them to a secondary role. They are just about useless in perceiving external movement. They do, however, mingle with visual perceptions and contribute in determining their aesthetic character. We will speak of this later, when we discuss optics and motion.

## 14 Visual Perception: The Movement of Objects in Our Visual Field

Of all the organs of perception, the eye is unquestionably the one that is most suitable for discerning objects in motion. It can perceive them at any distance, recording all their movements without any modification. Finally, and this is the main reason that must determine us to study it in greater detail, visual perception has, from our point of view, a far greater value than any other means of perception. There is not a single one of its features that does not contribute in some measure to determining the aesthetic character of movement.

Visual perception of movement is very complex. We will therefore break up the subject by examining first the perception of the eye when it is still; then we will consider the eye's movements and the illusions that take place when we ourselves move. This is not the order in which we have gradually acquired our pieces of knowledge, for our senses do not develop methodically. In practice, our early visual perceptions are accompanied by eye movements and body displacements. From the start, we are thrown into the heart of the problems and it is up to us to find our way out. But if in practice we always go from the complex to the simple, in theory it is better to go from the simple to the complex.

Suppose, then, that the eye is quite motionless and let us see what the perception of movement becomes under such conditions.

Sight can give us a prodigious number of perfectly distinct

and localized sensations at the same time. Cast your eye on a printed page. You distinguish with absolute clarity all the characters that are close to the point of fixation. Beyond this zone of direct vision, the position and range of which correspond to the position and range of the yellow spot in the retinal field, stretches the region of so-called indirect vision, in which the objects appear less sharply. We have difficulty reading the characters situated on the edge of this region and we could not possibly distinguish those at its extreme outskirts. But if these images are unclear, they are nevertheless localized. And they still appear separate from one another. In the final analysis, the number of perceptions that our eye provides us at one time is so great that we could spend the day describing everything we see in our visual field in one look.

This localization of visual perceptions and acuity of vision have their limits, however, and it is important to define them in order to determine in what measure and under what conditions we can perceive movement.

*Localization of Visual Sensations*

Up to what point do we realize the location of the retinal elements receiving luminous impressions, or rather, since visual sensations are always immediately objectified, the location of luminous objects in our visual field?

Because the impression that luminous objects make on me varies according to their position at the center or on the periphery of my visual field, I can tell fairly well their distance from that center. I will also know whether they are on the left or the right, the top or the bottom of my visual field. For this field is not only quite well centered, it is also well oriented, as the direction of gravity serves as a compass to fix its cardinal points. With these indications alone, I can already determine to a certain extent the position of objects and, therefore, their movements.

This kind of localization is still too vague, but I could not localize better without having more data. We will see, anyway, that in using my perception, I tend to ignore it somewhat, rather than make it sharper. As I have to move my eyes constantly and therefore at every instant, to make objects pass from the right to the left and from the bottom to the top of my visual field, I try not to notice this change of appearances. My attention detaches itself from it, as from all that is purely subjective in perception, so that, in our present state, we have only a very weak sense of the true localization of images in the visual field. And if it is theoretically true that we possess this sense, in practice, we act as if we did not.

It has been surmised at times that we are conscious of the direct source of luminous rays. Because the viewing line that joins a luminous point to the element of the retina that is impinged upon is more or less perpendicular to the concave surface of the retina, the law of localization of visual sensations has been thought to be as follows: each sensation is, so to speak, projected outward, perpendicularly to the surface of the retina. However, visual localizations do not have this geometrical precision. Given the image of a luminous point, we see it clearly outside us, in a certain direction, that is to say, somewhere in the visual field. If, then, another point becomes visible, we will see it somewhere else, in another direction. But the angle of both directions or the distance of the objects in the visual field will not be determined at all. Finally, suppose the visual field is filled with luminous points. The only thing our vision tells us is that they are all placed outside one another. The number of visible points that compose an image is the only measure of its size. The proof of it is that an expanse that is clearly divided always seems larger than a uniform surface.

The only serious objection to this hypothesis is that if the visible expanse is evaluated not by the size of the visual angle formed by the viewing lines, but by the multiplicity of perceptible points, two objects of equal size would appear unequal when one is perceived directly and the other by indirect vision, which is much less well differentiated.[1] To that I answer that because we are in the habit of seeing the same object move from the zone of direct vision to that of indirect vision, experience has taught us to take this change into account; it is precisely because the object perceived indirectly is *seen* to be smaller that it is *judged* to be as big. Wundt's reasoning could prove just as easily that it is not by their visual angles that we perceive sizes, since, if it were so, two objects of equal size would have to appear unequal when they are not at the same distance, for their angles would be different.

In return for perceiving only poorly the absolute position of objects, we appreciate their respective positions very well, that is, the order in which they are distributed in the visual field. Is this localization innate or is it acquired as a result of the movement of the eyes? The second hypothesis is much more likely. The fact remains that we have this faculty. Even when our eye is motionless, we are conscious of the respective positions of all the objects making an impression on our eye at the same time. In that, but in that alone, the localization of our visual sensations is perfect.

1   Wilhelm Max Wundt, *Éléments de psychologie-physiologique*, French ed., 2:77.

This has an unexpected consequence: to perceive the movement of an object, we need two points of reference.

Say we have a luminous point A, which makes an impression on a specific retinal element, producing a sensation a. I postulate that the rest of the visual field is absolutely empty, or dark, which comes to the same thing. Where do we see this luminous point? Since there is no other sensation to which we can attribute the sensation a, it is quite impossible for us to localize it and the position of A is undetermined, not only its distance, but its direction. It is like an isolated star floating in the immensity of space. The only thing we can say is that it is outside us; even then this notion of exteriority, which is still imposing itself on me by force of habit, will end by disappearing too when I fully imagine the conditions of the hypothesis.

Now, suppose A displaces itself. Its image will slide on my retina and will give me, as it passes over a new retinal element, a new sensation a'. But this sensation, not being distinguishable from the previous one in any way and following upon it immediately, will seem to be only its extension: my consciousness will not be changed and the sliding of the image will not be perceived.

In fact, this experiment is almost impossible to realize because, in practice, the background on which the objects move is never quite dark. Even in the most opaque night, the phosphenes that my retina produces spontaneously will make it conscious of itself: the luminous object will always appear on a motley, quivering background and will never be completely isolated. But in the measure that the experiment can be realized, we see the loss of the sense of localization. When we see a light in the dark, our appreciation of its movement is very imprecise, as long as it moves slowly. We will see why later. We even have great trouble judging whether it is moving or not.

Let us take our hypothesis one step further. Suppose that instead of one luminous point, we are dealing with a real object that gives us a group of very differentiated sensations, as, for example, the image of the moon. This image might glide all of a piece in the visual field, even turn around, but, without a point of reference, its movement will not be perceived.

Suppose that instead of one luminous point, we see two. There is now in the visual field another point B, which either stays motionless while A is moving or else moves independently of A. This will still not suffice. We will not be able to note if the two points are getting closer to or farther from each other. How indeed do we estimate the distance between two objects? By the number of objects in between. But it is impossible for us to evaluate a distance in emptiness: two luminous points striking elements of my retina, however far from each other, would only appear distinct from each other, but would not give me the notion of the interval between them unless the intermediary elements are stimulated (for example, the points situated to the right and to the left of the blind spot). Furthermore, it is easy to verify that this notion is still quite imprecise, when the background against which the spots stand out is a solid color, that is to say, when the intermediary elements give me only homogeneous sensations: the objects indeed appear to be far from each other, but we cannot say how far. Consequently, it would be quite difficult for us to evaluate their relative movements.

But if a third object C appears in the visual field, then and only then there will be some order in my sensations and they can be localized in relation to one another. Suppose the three spots ABC are distributed in that order on the surface of the visual field and that they then present themselves to me in the order of ACB, then CAB. Even if the exact position of each of these points is indeterminate, I am nevertheless certain that their positions have been inverted and that a movement has occurred. It is therefore a first consequence of the principle of visual localization that, to perceive a movement, there must be in our visual field at least three luminous points, distinct from one another, in the order of which we are able to note an inversion. In other words, to establish that a mobile object is displacing itself, we need not one but at least two points of reference. If one is inclined not to recognize this condition in the perception of movement, it is because, in fact, it is almost always realized. In practice, we see objects move on a background that, though it does not itself attract our attention, is perceived indirectly and furnishes a largely sufficient number of references. If we relate their movement to another body that serves as a point of reference, this body is almost never, truly speaking, a point but a surface on which we can take the needed coordinates.

A second consequence of this principle is that our eye, being immobile, can only gauge well angular or perspective movements of objects. Say O is the optical center of the eye and A a luminous point shining in space (fig. 17). The line AO, extended to the retina, determines a spot a, which is the image of the object or its perspective projection on the retinal surface. Suppose the object moves along the line AO, approaching or retreating from the eye. The image a will not move, the order of my sensations will not change in any way, no movement will be perceived. Now if A changes to A', the image a, sliding transversely on the retina, will take the position a' and I will perceive a movement. But, as we can see, this transverse movement of the retinal image which makes me believe in an equivalent movement of the object does not correspond to the actual

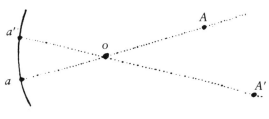

*Figure 17*

movement of the object, but only to its angular movement. They would correspond only in the exceptional case of the object moving without changing its distance to the eye, that is, on the surface of a sphere with the eye as its center.

From these principles result a great number of illusions to which we are exposed at every instant. I shall content myself with citing only a few. At equal speed, the farther objects are, the slower they appear. When we look at a line of luminous points passing before us at a uniform speed, such as a train going by, each point seems to get faster and faster as it nears us, reaching its maximum speed when it passes right in front of us, then gradually slowing down again. An object coming toward us on a flat terrain at a constant speed seems to descend in our visual field at a uniformly accelerated speed, and so on.

We can, it is true, modify these judgments by learning to interpret the illusions of perspective. But this makes the error, not the illusion, disappear. For our senses continue to err even as our intelligence interprets their manifestation correctly. Only where very close objects are concerned do we perceive their true distance by the adjustment or the convergence of our eyes.

As a result, the movements that cost us the least effort of perception have to be those that are projected in silhouette in our visual field. As it is from this projection that we immediately judge their speed and direction, it is also on this projection that our first aesthetic impression must depend.

### Acuity of Visual Perceptions

If our retinal elements were of an infinitesimal size, the smallest displacement of an image in our visual field could be perceived. But this is not the case. Even in the yellow spot, where they are closest together, they are still of an appreciable size, so that there is inevitably a limitation to our perception of movement. A luminous point moving uniformly would appear to be moving only intermittently, its movement becoming perceptible only at the instant the image, after having traveled over the expanse of one retinal element, passes on to the next.

Most of the time, we cannot even be conscious of this passage, because it does not happen fast enough to be noticed. Our eye is not built perfectly enough to gather all the beams emanating from a luminous point onto a single point of the retina. Were it able to do so, it could not adjust to all the points of an object at the same time, but only to those that are at the same distance or of the same color. Hence, in practice, the retinal images are never perfectly sharp: a diffused circle that spreads over several retinal elements at the same time, not a geometrical point, corresponds to each point of the object on the retina. To illustrate the result, compare the visual field to a pointillist watercolor painted on wet paper rather than to a mosaic formed of small hexagonal tiles. Consequently, even considerable displacements of the object may produce no notable change in the visual field, especially when the object moves on a solid background which gives us sensations that are very little differentiated.

When the movement of an object is slow and continuous, it can only be registered after a series of observations that show me its different positions in space in relation to nearby objects. Thus I see the globe of the sun appearing above the horizon. A few moments later, I note that half of it has emerged. Then it rises completely above the horizon. I will notice even slower movements by a similar procedure, such as the progression of a glacier or the growth of a tree.

Can we call this perception of movement? No, it is induction based on memory. From time to time, I compare the present position of the object to its anterior position, as I remember it. But the changes occurring in a few seconds of observation are too small to be perceived. Though I know the object is in motion, it is impossible for me to catch it in the act. Only after I have lost sight of it for a few moments will the differences accumulate enough to become perceptible and allow me to conclude that a displacement has truly taken place.

But it is different when the movement, without becoming faster, is jerky. Then, indeed, the differences of placement will all accumulate in a single instant and will be perceived, instead of spreading in infinitesimal quantities over the whole duration of the movement. Watch closely the second hand of a watch, which breaks up the second into a number of fractions. It seems to be rushing along very fast, especially if, at the same time, you hear the "tick, tick" marking its path. Remove it far enough so that you can no longer discern the divisions of the dial. At this point, your perception becomes quite indefinite and there are moments when you wonder if the hand is moving at all.

Someone in front of you is waving an arm slowly. Blink your eyes rapidly, or better still look at the motion through the chinks of a revolving disk (Stampford's stroboscope, Plateau's phenakistoscope, or a zoetrope). Because the movement has become intermittent and therefore more easily perceptible, it seems considerably accelerated. The figures seen in a zoetrope which represent an object in the various phases of a movement give us a strange impression of mobility: with their febrile, jerky movements they seem to have a supernatural activity. This last experiment will help us to understand how a series of still images can give us the illusion of movement. If the retinal images were perceived for themselves, we would only register the appearance, in our visual field, of a series of objects placed in various positions. But they are only the reflections of an anterior reality. We therefore interpret this appearance by saying that it is the same object which appears to us successively in different places.

Finally, the movement of the object will appear continuous if the images follow one another so fast that we cannot perceive any pauses between consecutive ones. At each instant, an instant being our briefest possible sensation, the object shows itself to us in a new position, and that is exactly what we call a continuous movement.

### Persistence of Retinal Images

So far we have assumed that the retinal images last just as long as the luminous impression that produced them. This is not quite true. Though the retina is constantly working to repair and reconstitute itself after a light has impinged on it, it does not achieve this immediately. An instantaneous impression will leave on our eye an image that will persist for an appreciable time.

This fact is well enough known, so we shall recall it only

briefly. Suppose we have a luminous impression brief enough to be considered instantaneous. It will give us a sensation of a certain duration which will decrease continuously without our being able to determine exactly the moment it ceases. For about a thirtieth of a second, the decrease will not be perceptible, so that luminous impressions that are repeated thirty times a second give us a certain sensation. But it would take much longer to erase the last traces of the impression. According to the sharpness of the impression, the image can stay visible for a second or more.

This fact is of major importance in the perception of movement. Everyone has experimented with moving a light in the dark. If the movement is quite rapid, you will see not the displacement of a luminous spot but a kind of comet. Its head is the actual impression you have at this moment and its tail is the extension of the luminous sensation. I can, in this way, trace in space whole circles, loops, numbers, or letters in lines of fire.

What happens in the dark for a quick movement will also occur, to a certain extent, in full daylight, even with a very slow movement. Any luminous point displacing itself in the visual field leaves behind it a visible wake, the existence of which we can easily ascertain if we make sure to keep our eye really motionless.

The result is that an animated object moving rapidly will become completely invisible. For, when the object displaces itself, each of its points leaves behind it a wake into which enters the next point, so that all of them tend to melt into a continuous line; for this to happen, the speed need not even be very great. When you are in a train, look through the window at very distant objects, taking care to fix your eyes on a spot of the window in order to ensure its immobility. You will see these ob-

jects getting almost as muddled as if you were looking at the hedge lining the railroad track. Imagine we have a wheel turning faster and faster. Its spokes seem to widen and melt into one another as their speed increases, until they melt into one continuous, transparent sheet. Or make a stick or your arm swing rapidly: I will only be able to discern it at the two extremities of its path.

It is on this principle that is based the electric measure beater constructed by Carpentier for the Paris Opera. In a blackened panel there are two ridges in the shape of a V. In each ridge is placed a square ruler, the faces of which are painted alternately black and white. A simple mechanism turns at will each ruler a quarter turn, so that the first shows its white face and the other its black face which becomes invisible. You think you are seeing a wand oscillating like the baton of an orchestra leader. The illusion is striking.

This leads me to believe that in the zoetrope, one could give, with much less trouble and more clearly, the illusion of an alternative movement by representing the movement only at its extreme phases and replacing all the intermediary positions by a single diffused image.

Without multiplying the examples, we can see that, as a general rule, a body cannot be perceived distinctly as long as it is moving in the visual field.

But if the duration of luminous sensations makes it very difficult for us to perceive clearly a body in motion, on the other hand it is an advantage when we wish only to ascertain its mobility. It enables us to catch several of its phases at the same time. Phenomena, which in reality occur successively, are presented all at once, like a synoptic tableau. Incredible as it would seem, we are able to have an immediate, instantaneous perception of the movement, for the image of a moving object differs at every instant from that of a still one.

Suppose there is a dark object moving, even very slowly, on a light background (fig. 18). Its contours will be more sharply defined in its posterior section than in its anterior one. For in its anterior portion, the background against which the object advances is not eclipsed at once, but continues to be discerned for some time, as if seen in transparency through the object. Behind the object, on the contrary, the background reappears instantly, the luminous impression requiring almost no time to produce its effect; it even reappears with greater luminosity, as the retinal elements on which it impinges have had a rest during this short eclipse.

If, on the contrary, the object is more luminous than the background, it will evidently look like figure 19.

Here, now, are three soap bubbles, one being blown up, the other losing air, and the third remaining the same (fig. 20). One can see that the very aspect of the object at a given moment can show whether it is moving or not and can even indicate the anterior phases of its movement. I will be aware of the speed of

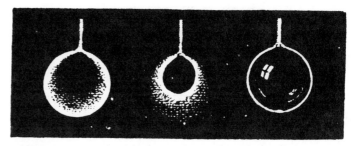

*Figure 20*

an object passing before my eyes from the length of the colored wake it leaves behind. Usually this wake is not noticeable, because it is pale and our attention is directed to the object itself. But it is nonetheless perceived indirectly and suggests a more or less rapid motion. One can, as a matter of fact, bring this wake out by making the image intermittent, for example, by lighting the mobile object with a series of electric sparks or by looking at it through the slots of a turning disk: there then appears in the visual field a whole series of images of uneven sharpness, the palest corresponding to the more distant phases. From the number of simultaneous images given to me by an object moving intermittently, I am able to judge the rapidity of its movements. Thus, when I watch a bird in flight, my eye perceives simultaneously a certain number of its wing beats; the faster its beats, the more numerous these retrospective images will be. One must state, however, that this is not seen so clearly when the bird is outlined in black against a very light sky, since total black leaves no trails on the retina; it will therefore be clearer when the bird is gray, like the swift, and clearest with brightly colored ones such as the kingfisher[2] or the oriole, or white ones, like the pigeon.

*Figure 18*　　　　*Figure 19*

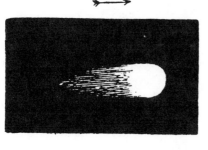

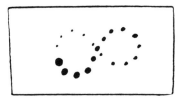

*Figure 21*

Finally, this duration of the retinal image allows us to recognize easily the actual trajectory of bodies in motion. If, to discern it, I had to make a series of observations and compare them, this method would be both tedious, as it requires an effort of memory and attention, and insecure, because the points of reference would often be lacking. Suppose you have a point describing a figure 8 as it moves (fig. 21). This diagram shows immediately the direction and nature of the movement, whereas if the point were to be drawn at a different phase of its movement on each of twenty sheets flipping before your eyes, you would most likely not understand its manner of displacement. It is the same for all perceptible movements. Owing to the duration of the luminous perceptions, the object literally describes its trajectory and permits us to appreciate its nature extremely well by leaving with us not just a memory but an actual image, a persistent tracing of its successive positions. Were it isolated in space, in order to localize each of the sensations it gives us, we would only have to bring them back together; the object would act as its own point of reference.

This method is used a great deal in physics experiments to show up movements that by their rapidity and complexity would escape the eye. A pearl attached to the tip of a vibrating rod describes symmetrical figures of great elegance (experiment of Wheatstone); a luminous ray sent out on a tuning fork carrying a little mirror will trace its vibrations on a screen (method of Lissajous); by gilding the tip of a bee's wing, one can ascertain by its vibrations that it describes a double loop (experiment of Marey).[3]

### Applications to Fine Arts

The persistence of the retinal images that prevents the sharp perception of moving objects has important consequences from the aesthetic point of view.

It explains the false attitudes that we note so often in paintings or sculpture that have the pretension of representing animals or people in motion. It might be horses galloping as horses never gallop, with their leg joints bent at right angles; or it might be men running with their torsos leaning forward, an attitude that occurs only at the initial departure, but which must inevitably straighten up as soon as the body reaches its full speed; or again, it might be birds all flying with their wings turned upward, as if they never lowered them and always flew in synchronization.

These errors should no longer be tolerated, now that we have at our disposal the technology of photography. The camera, pointed at objects in motion, is like an ideal eye that sees everything at one glance and permanently retains what it has seen.

2   The European kingfisher has brilliant blue-green upperparts and chestnut cheek and underparts, unlike the American one, which is gray with white cheeks—Ed.

3   Jules Marey, *Animal Mechanism: A Treatise on Terrestrial and Aerial Locomotion* (New York: Appleton, 1874), p. 186, where he also cites Sir Charles Wheatstone's experiment.

Ingres demanded that a painter be capable of sketching a roofer as he was falling from the fourth floor. His astonishing drawing virtuosity permitted him to do feats of this kind when he had to make a rapid drawing of a model in a pose impossible to hold for any length of time.[4] But such a result would be attained much more easily with an intelligent use of photography, which should now be used by all painters as an instrument of work. It would not prevent them from observing nature directly, far from it, but it would permit them to observe it fruitfully. Having in the eye, so to speak, the series of attitudes that an animal or a man takes when in motion, they would recognize them as they go by and seize their rhythm and sequence better. As the philosopher Tyndall remarks somewhere, you can only see a thing well when you know in advance what is going to happen. And that is even truer about movement perception than about any other kind of observation.

The only danger that the use of photography may present for the fine arts is to tempt artists to reproduce literally. That would be a grave error. We see examples of this from time to time in our exhibitions. Some artists, with a kind of bravura, take pleasure in representing animals, preferably horses, in absolutely implausible, sometimes grotesque poses. If one protests, they are ready to prove, photos in hand, that these attitudes are true. It is possible the attitudes exist in nature, but the artist should not have caught them. If a galloping horse stays a moment with a leg forward and its crump in the air, that is no reason to represent it thus. There are, in the gallop, positions that are better balanced and, above all, more plausible. The first duty of a painter is to make a choice among truths.

Not only are these representations ungraceful, one might also say they are false, as they make us see things differently from the way we see them in nature. What is lacking notably in giving the impression of movement is what we have indicated is its real token, that is, the luminous tracing that moving objects leave behind them.

Is that to say that we should represent objects exactly as we see them? Not at all. The literal representation of appearances would be no less implausible than that of the truth. For the watching eye, the flying bird does not have two wings, it has at least four; the trotting horse does not have four legs, it has at least eight, since, in any rapid alternating movement, the eyes conserves at the same time the image of both extreme phases of the oscillation. Add that in a painting thus conceived, there would inevitably be holes. How effective would be these blurs, these diaphanous images of objects in motion among the sharper images by which motionless objects in the composition must be represented? We are now in a quandary.

One radical solution would be to give up the fight! What is the point of representing movement if we can obtain only approximations? Léon Dumont declares on the subject: "This whole class of representations should be banished from the plastic arts; they should limit themselves to suggesting indirectly the idea of movement and grace by enduring signs and never try to represent a suddenly interrupted movement, unless the artist has as his goal to paint the act of interruption itself."[5]

But this is not the way to solve questions of aesthetics. Good taste is made up of good measure, nuances, and even compromise. What of *The Marseillaise* of Rude? And *The Victory of*

4   Amaury Duval, *L'atelier d'Ingres: Souvenirs* (Paris: Charpentier, 1878).

5   Léon Dumont, *Le sentiment du gracieux* (Paris: A. Durand, 1863), p. 208.

*Samothrace?* In these works, the movement is not just indicated, it is rendered directly. And surely, they are great works of art.

I would therefore refrain from imposing any kind of restriction on artists. I would only say "Take care." To represent a movement, you will inevitably have to cheat to some extent. You have the right to do so, for art lives on expedients or rather, to avoid any offense, on conventions. But at least these conventions should be acceptable. You cannot paint things exactly as they are, nor as they seem, but we shouldn't be too aware of it! You want to paint the ocean crashing on the beach? Spread your colors widely, push them with a large brush, let the movement of your hand follow and indicate the undulations of the waves; do not apply the foam heavily, but toss it on their crest! Otherwise you will paint a sea of zinc or, like Courbet's famous *Wave*, it will be a sea of plaster.

Do you want to paint a tree shaken by the wind? How do we see it in nature? The trunk is perceived in all its details: the waving branches are less sharp, tracing multiple images; the leaves, lashed by the squall, make thousands of incoherent movements that the eye cannot follow, and they are scrambled in a quivering confusion. If you want to paint this tree, since you cannot paint the movement itself, you will have to give it its optical equivalent. It may not be easy. But who obliges you to paint the blast of the wind?

The problem will be even greater when painting people or animals in motion, because their shape must be recognizable. Without being defined by too sharp a contour, which makes a painting look like stained glass or cloisonné, the subject must however be sensed by a correct outline. How, then, can our figures seem to be moving?

The simplest expedient, to give movement to a painting, is not to push its execution in too great detail. "Sketches," remarks Eugène Véron,

are generally more alive than finished drawings. We saw a striking example of this a few years ago. *La Gazette des Beaux-Arts* had published the facsimile of a number of sketches by Paul Baudry for the great foyer of the Opera. They were full of animation and life that have largely disappeared in the finished painting. Gestures are not lacking, however, in Baudry's work; one might even say they are lavished, yet it does not move. All these characters, in spite of their big arms and spread out legs, are fixed in a stillness all the more unpleasing because it is in contradiction with the movements. To what is this disastrous transformation due? To the fact that in the sketches, the gestures are indicated vaguely by a multitude of little lines which, by their closeness, animate the figure by indicating several successive moments or attitudes perceived simultaneously in each movement, whereas this mixture of succession and simultaneousness has completely disappeared in the unique and precise line of the final attitude.[6]

The remark is very true. I will add a psychological explanation to Véron's reasons. In a rough sketch, the figure that we have before our eyes is only a token intended to suggest the idea of the subject. We look at these lines and then imagine the subject. Where do we see it? Inside, or in that vague region where we localize imaginary objects. The more the execution comes close to nature, the more we will be tempted to look upon what we have before us as the actual object of our contemplation; so we become demanding and complain of the immobility of the figure. Suppose an artist is sketching a dancing woman. As his hand moves across the paper, in his mind he imagines this femi-

6   Eugène Véron, *L'esthétique* (Paris: Bibliothèque des Sciences Contemporaines, 1883), p. 296.

nine body coming and going, an unseizable ghost, and he moves to the rhythm of a mysterious orchestra with the lightness of a dream. But as the features become more precise, the image attaches itself gradually to the paper; when the drawing is finished, it is completely stiffened into it.

The difficulty is not, therefore, to impart movement to a sketch, but to a painting. The rule to follow, it seems to me, is to give the parts that must appear mobile a more sketchy execution; and in order that these blurred parts should not make a hole in the painting, give them a secondary place. In this way, we will not be tempted to look too hard at something we are supposed not to see well. That is what Morot did very successfully in his *Charge des Cuirassiers* in the Luxembourg. In this turmoil of rumpled men and horses, jostling one another, what do we look at? The horses' legs? No, they are lost in a cloud of dust, where we distinguish, however, the actual attitudes of the gallop. Our eye goes straight to the heads of the men, to their eyes shining with the flash of hate, to their mouths twisted in a grimace of effort. We have the right to see that in the painting, for we would also see it in reality. Our eye, attached to these horsemen rushing by, would immobilize on our retina the image of the points to which it would be drawn; and it is those very points that have been clearly delineated.

Though sculpture does not have at its disposal as many artifices as painting, it can also have recourse to a more summary rendering to give the impression of movement. You will suggest the idea of motion better if your execution is the more boldly figurative: indentations of the thumb, fragments of pellets crushed into the mass of clay clearly show that we have before us a fictional representation. In etchings, it is recommended that one "allow the paper to do the work." In a statue being modeled, one must also allow the clay to do the work, which means, in both cases, that the imagination of the viewer must be allowed to work.

But, in general, we are better off avoiding movements so rapid that they are not perceived in reality. Being alternative and therefore intermittent, our most rapid movements must go through a dead point on which they stop for a moment, and that constitutes an attitude. That is the moment at which they should be caught. This advice seems to me even more necessary when the work is larger and arrests the eye longer. The more animated works please best at first, but tire faster; they do not stand up under too long a contemplation, because after a while the contrast between their actual stillness and the movement they picture bothers the eye and disconcerts the mind. A small statuette can laugh: it is made only to be looked at briefly; a larger statue will please more by its expression of quiet happiness; a gigantic statue should be peaceful. Even in landscapes, it is good to follow this rule. It is wiser to reserve large canvases for serious subjects that show us nature in its austere and solemn aspects. Besides, artists, without realizing it, nearly always follow this rule. It is due to a quite technical reason. When one makes a simple sketch, one can catch the passing effect or scatter the figures according to one's whim. But for a work of some importance, which must be executed more slowly and requires longer preliminary studies, one will be naturally inclined to choose more lasting effects, attitudes that in nature can be found more enduring.

## 15 Optics and Motion: The Movement of the Eyes

We will now examine perception as it relates to the movement of the eyes. This theory is quite complex, but fortunately we will not have to do any personal research because it has already been studied in depth by physiologists. We only need to choose from the accumulated observations on the subject those that concern us particularly and interpret them.

The eyes have a double movement: one of adjustment, in which they adapt themselves to perceive objects distinctly; the other of rotation, in which they turn in their orbit.

We will not say much about eye adjustments, not because the subject is unimportant, but because it offers few problems from the point of view of aesthetics.

Left to themselves, our eyes adjust for vision to infinity, that is to say, the crystalline lens stretches to the maximum and the viewing lines of both eyes become parallel. If the object we are looking at comes nearer, we have to make a rather strenuous adjustment, as can be ascertained by looking first at an object very far away, then immediately at a close one. Consequently, the movement of an object will be much more perceptible when it is approaching than when it is going away. And the most painful movements to perceive will be those that oblige us to readjust repeatedly. That is why it is unpleasant to watch merry-go-round types of movements in which the object, turning on a vertical axis, moves alternately nearer and farther away from us.

It is the rotation of the eyes that interests us more particularly. Our eyes move incessantly. They move to recognize the source of luminous impressions, to scan objects in detail, to follow them in their displacements. They move in order to rest, one after the other, the different parts of the retina that get quickly exhausted from fixing on an object. Add to that the almost continuous motions to which we subject them when we turn our head, modify our position, approach or leave objects.

Up to what point are we aware of these movements? When I roll my eyes in their orbit, I am conscious of a certain effort. What does it consist of? The tactile sensations that usually accompany muscular efforts are almost totally lacking here, so smooth is the gliding of the eye in its orbit. For the same reason, the muscular sensations must also be very small, as there is almost no resistance to overcome and the mass of the eye is insignificant. That is what enables us to read for hours at a time, letting our eyes travel from word to word with no fatigue. At the most, we will notice a feeling of tension in the muscle of our eye when it strays a great deal from its primary position or when we contract antagonistic muscles simultaneously, as when we try to look at something fixedly with one eye or converge both eyes. The element that dominates by far is the volition of the movement. It is at the instant that I decide to move my eye, to modify its direction, or to check it that the effort becomes perceptible. We can therefore establish as a rule that the movements of the eyes are conscious only as they are volitional.

This sensation of effort has great practical utility, as it enables us to control our looking and direct the movement of our eyes. But can it inform us with precision on the nature of the movement of bodies?

## Visual Attraction

The movement of the eyes is frequently, perhaps even most of the time, produced by a simple reflex action, our eyes going to the brightest points of the visual field and following their movements automatically. This is a curious fact which has a bearing on aesthetics and requires an explanation.

The interest we have in the movement of objects is first of all practical. Animals who live in a perpetual state of war must be immediately aware of everything happening around them. Any unusual movement—a leaf that stirs, a shadow that passes—attracts their attention at once. It might be an enemy approaching or a possible prey. It is the same thing with man in an underdeveloped state. Through heredity, this necessary curiosity must have become instinctual in modern man. Children who live in the perfect safety and peace of their families jump at a sudden movement. The sudden sight of unexpected objects will make them cry out in fright. They are afraid before they even know that some things can harm them. They feel danger before they have acquired that notion through experience.

Later, this interest becomes more theoretical, and, one might say, contemplative. Any perceived movement stimulates in us a feeling of pure curiosity, immediately, without thought. We see a workman at work: we want to know what he is doing and how. Here is an ant running in the grass: where is it going? what is it looking for? A few people are running down the street: what is there to see? This interest in resolution may also be applied to the movement of inanimate objects. Here, naturally, we no longer speak of intentional resolution. But we are interested in the result of movement, in its direction, which is still its resolution, however unconscious. Our intelligence is always at work, asking questions. The boy Gribouille in *Les Misérables* looked at the water running under a bridge, waiting for it to stop running. We all have such naïvetés. Used as we are to seeing all mobile objects stop, we cannot see a movement without awaiting its end. And as waiting, which supposes an effort of mind and a beginning of anxiety, is in itself painful, we feel a sort of relief when it ceases. We even make a kind of game of this wait. A stone is falling down a slope before us. Immediately, we make a bet: it will reach here or there, and we keep our eyes on it, to see if we have guessed right. If it stops too near or too far, we feel a little vexed.

The mobility of objects also sustains the interest by entertaining the eyes constantly. The most beautiful object tires us quite rapidly, because it is always the same and because we are passive when we contemplate it. Give a child a magnificent toy: he will admire it an instant, then will leave it where it is; whereas a puppet moving its arms and legs or a top spinning around will have inexhaustible appeal. We are all children in that. We take pleasure seeing a banner undulating at the extremity of a mast, or the smoke of a factory chimney rolling and unrolling endlessly in the wind, or the snow falling from the sky. This occupation, at first intentional, soon becomes automatic; and we understand therefore the real fascination that moving objects exercise on our eyes. If a light suddenly shines in our eyes, we cannot help looking at it. If it moves, our eyes follow it spontaneously, by a movement of pure reflex: the longer they fix it, the less they can detach themselves. Which of us has not lingered, in mindless rapture, to watch the sails of a windmill, the eddies in a river, the quivering of a fire? We could stay for hours gazing at a steam engine, the stretching and shrinking of its connecting rod, the turning of its flywheel, the constant coming and going of the leather strap. It seems as if our eyes are caught by the gear in motion and are drawn forcibly into it.

Let us now choose a few examples in nature that have an aesthetic value: a stream running over gravel, the moon gliding among the clouds, the light ripples wrinkling the surface of a pond, the deceptive moire of a field of green wheat undulating in the wind. Do we admire them only for their beauty? I am inclined to think that if they hold our eyes that way, it is because they cause a kind of visual dizziness which has a hypnotic effect on our mind.

This contemplation is so mechanical that it often lasts longer than we intended and long after its interest is exhausted. In the end, this mobility of objects and the ceaseless movement of our eyes can give us a feeling of nausea and vertigo; yet, in spite of ourselves, carried away by habit, we go on looking. A small effort is all we need to turn our eyes away, but we are powerless. Worse still, giving in to a kind of mental vertigo, to what Edgar Allan Poe terms the spirit of perversion, we prolong wantonly this painful sensation, feeling the approach of hypnosis, to see what will happen.

Our eyes have taken therefore the habit of following moving objects spontaneously. Accordingly, we can only become aware of their movements through passive muscular sensations; but we have seen that eye rotations give us virtually none.

*Visual Illusions*

Even volitional movements, though conscious, give us muscular sensations that are not strong enough to make it possible to distinguish between them, and, therefore, to be used in determining the path of our eyes with precision. When we move our eyes volitionally, it is always with sudden jerks and at maximum speed. (One can only make the eye move slowly and continuously by attaching it to a moving object that it follows automatically.) The reason is that, because the time during which our eye moves is completely lost to perception, we have taken the habit of making it as short as possible. If we are conscious of the angular movement accomplished, it is either from the number of perceptible points that our eye has caught or, supposing that the speed of rotation is constant, from the time elapsed between two consecutive appearances of distinct images, that is to say, from visual sensations, not muscular ones.

In the final analysis, one can assert that it is not our awareness of the movement of our eyes that helps us take cognizance of the movement of objects, but, on the contrary, it is almost always the changes that have occurred in the visual field that tell us what movements our eyes have actually made.

Glance, for instance, at a line on this page. You are quite conscious of the movement you have made from left to right. But what sensations have told you this? Are they muscular ones? No, they are visual sensations. While your eye was turning in its orbit, you saw new images appearing in your visual field, which, little by little, by jolts, passed from the right to the left of the zone of clear perception. Without this parade of images, you might also have been conscious that your eye was moving from the effort you needed to keep on casting it to the right, but you would certainly not have perceived the direction and speed of this movement distinctly.

When my eyes are open in the dark, I completely lose consciousness of my eye movements, since I have no objects on which to fix them. You may even mark a fixed point on your retina by developing on it a positive image, then looking into the night. Where do you see this point? In such an undetermined direction that you could not possibly put your finger on or even near it. Now, roll your eyes in their orbits; the image will indeed seem to move, but only a little with large eye motions.

One can even say that if our muscular sensations make us conscious to any degree of the position of our eyes, it is by their association with visual sensations which alone are capable of localization. If I had never had any visual sensations, how could I tell what movements I have made or if I have even made one? If I have a sensation corresponding to the contraction of the eye muscles, am I aware of the structure of this delicate instrument, with its ingenious mechanical devices? Do I even know that I have eye muscles?

In short, we have a certain awareness of the movement of our eyes when it is volitional, but it is a general awareness which does not serve to determine, even approximately, the movement of the objects we follow with our glance. And I will show that in most cases this awareness is quite useless. In normal perception, a correct interpretation of visual sensations is enough. In abnormal cases, when the consciousness of ocular movements would be useful in preventing errors, it is lacking and the illusion occurs irresistibly.

Let us first examine the way motionless objects appear as the eye travels over them. I am looking straight ahead, then I suddenly shift my glance to the right. All the images glide in my visual field in an angular movement at the same speed and in the opposite direction to that of my eye, and are fixed on the left. It appears exactly the same as if the objects had moved instead.

But am I taken in? Independent of my awareness of having made the movement, my interpretation of appearances suffices to tell me that I have moved and that the objects did actually remain in place. First of all, I did not see any object move, since I could not discern anything when I made my rapid eye movement: my vision was eclipsed only for an instant. Then the image that now strikes my eye in its new position shows no change in the relationship of the objects. If they had really moved I would have seen a marked change in their outline, size, and position. But when the motion of images is due to the rotation of the eye, the perspective of objects remains the same, whatever the direction of the eyes, at least within the limits of normal oscillations. At most I might think there has been a movement of a quarter of a turn around me of all the objects in one block. But that is too incredible to be accepted for even an instant. Generally speaking, changes produced in the visual field by the jerky movements of the eye are always interpreted as eye movements, *never* as the movement of objects.

But it is quite different for continuous eye movements. They *always* give objects whose images shift in the visual field the appearance of movement. Suppose there is a fixed object from which my eye is departing with a continuous motion, slow or fast, no matter how. Its image will not only take different positions in the visual field but will get blurred and leave behind it the luminous wake which is the characteristic of movement. Inevitably the object will take a virtual movement of translation. Even though I know it is motionless, I will see it move. The awareness I may have of my own movement will not destroy this illusion. At best, it might lessen slightly the virtual movement of the object. That is how a great number of well-known illusions are explained; for instance, the ground seems to run away under our eyes when we have fixed them too long on moving objects: in this case, the movement of the eye, which is at first volitional, is followed by an involuntary one that produces the illusion, not because it is instinctive, but because it is continuous. A decisive proof that this hypothesis is correct is the illusion that takes place when I press my finger into my eyeballs: this is one time when I am conscious of my eye movements and yet, even in this case, there is no way to correct it.

Can I not, however, let my eyes wander over an object without attributing a virtual movement to it? For example, let my eyes travel over a flowery carpet with a continuous movement. The images do not appear blurred and no illusion occurs. Nevertheless, there has been a most significant illusion, which shows us how little we are aware of the actual movements of the eyes. In this experiment, we think we are moving our eyes in a continuous motion, but in reality we are jerking them. First we fix our eyes on a flower on the carpet, then we jump to another. And we think this displacement of our eyes is continuous because our attention goes successively to the different points of the subject; we may simply be thinking we are shifting our eyes when we are just shifting our head. But ensure the continuity of your eye movement by making it follow the tip of your finger traveling slowly above the carpet; immediately, the images get blurred and will take a virtual movement. We will recall this remark when we deal with the grace of lines, which are often explained by alleged eye movements that are incompatible with the most elementary conditions of vision.

Let us now consider what happens when we attach our eyes to a moving object. When an object passes in front of me, if I want to perceive it clearly, I must follow it with my eyes. The point at which I am staring no longer moves in my visual field;

it is seen with perfect sharpness and the characteristic signs of movement are completely lacking. Let us just cite as example the classic illusion of a moon that seems to be running through the clouds. Let us note that the illusion does not occur when I make sure to look at the moon itself. But when I look at the clouds, they appear motionless, while the moon seems to be running in the opposite direction, not only by contrast, but because its image is really moving on my retina.

Should I therefore establish as a rule that any object we follow with our eyes has no apparent movement? Probably not. For the objects we look at are never just points. We note that when they move, there is a change in their apparent size, which tells us they are going away from us. If, from the window of a train, I look at a house going rapidly by, since I am following it with my eyes, I am not aware of its translatory movement; but the fixity of my gaze, which removes the illusion of its angular movement, maintains that of its movement in depth. I may even note that as it recedes the house seems to revolve by a number of degrees exactly equal to the angular movement of my eyes. The real movement of the point I am fixing can also be revealed to me by extrinsic signs. Whether it is a man walking, or a dog running, or a carriage going by on the road, the object has such complicated movements that I cannot follow them all at once. Certain parts will therefore displace themselves on my retina and their motility will permit me to appreciate the movement of the others. Furthermore, an object never moves in a void, but against a background to which I attribute a virtual movement, since my eyes move in a continuous manner in relation to it. Knowing that this background, by its very nature, must be motionless, I will conclude that it is the object that is moving.

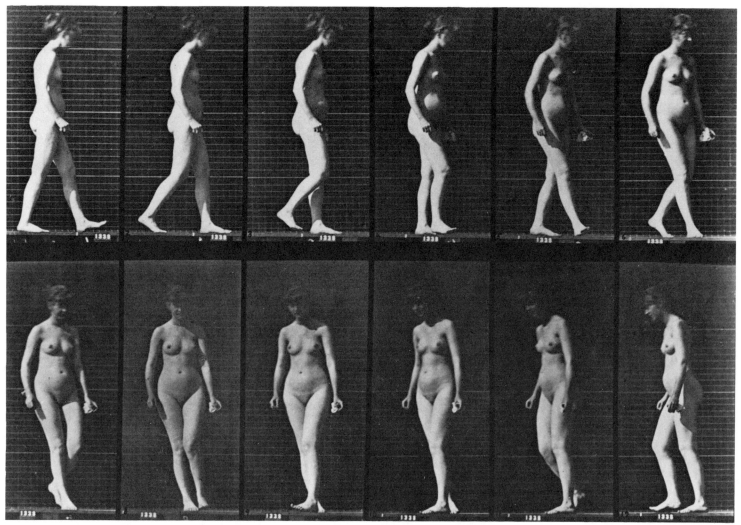

*Woman walking*

Finally, however indistinct my awareness of my eye movements may be, it does tell me at least that the objects that my glance follows have some kind of movement. In the illusion mentioned earlier, even if I attribute to the moon a great apparent speed, the clouds do not really seem completely motionless. When my gaze follows a bird flying in the sky, I am, to a certain extent, conscious that it is traveling.

The illusion therefore rarely occurs in an absolute way, because it is difficult for the necessary conditions to be fully realized. But they are usually realized closely enough for us to underestimate the movement of objects our eyes follow. When you look at a woman walking, you are well enough aware of the actual movement of her head. But are you aware of the actual movement of her arms? They do seem to be swinging back alternately, stopping for an instant at the extreme point of their path. However, if you think it over, you will acknowledge that it is only an illusion and that this apparent movement is only a relative one, in which you happen to take no account of the translatory speed of the walker. At the instant the hand reaches the extremity of its swing, it is indeed motionless in relation to the body, but since the body is in motion, the hand's actual speed is the same as that of the woman's displacement. If there is any time when it could be motionless, it, in any case, would only be at that point on the return when it reaches its maximum relative speed, that is, at the moment it crosses the line of the leg.

Here is another simple experiment that shows to what extent the movement of the eyes diminishes the apparent movement of objects. Say we have a disk rolling on the ground. As it revolves around itself, it advances by a distance equal to its circumference. The movement of each point on the circumference can therefore be broken up into two relative movements of equal speed, one circular, the other rectilinear. Let us now compare what appears to take place in the perception of this movement with the actual movement which can be determined geometrically. As the disk is rolling, we concentrate on the movement of a point marked on its circumference. Our first impression is that it turns regularly in a circle. On second thought, we realize that when it reaches the highest point of its path, it will have twice the speed of the disk's translation, for at that point the two relative movements are added together; by the same token, when it touches the ground, its speed will be zero, because the two relative movements are then neutralized. Yet, even forewarned, all our eye can tell is that the point is moving slower in the latter case than in the first.

The illusion is identical for the trajectory of the movement. In fact, it works according to the cycloid in figure 22. Reason will prove it to me. But however much I know it, I cannot perceive that movement. At the instant the point, after touching the ground, continues its motion, I cannot escape the notion that it is first thrown backward, describing in space a series of closed loops and its apparent trajectory looks something like figure 23.

It would be, in fact, the trajectory of the point if the disk were skidding on the ground, that is, if the speed of translation were inferior to that of rotation. The very shape of this illusory trajectory enables us to determine how much we underestimate the movement of translation.

Again, look at a cart moving rapidly on a muddy road. You will inevitably see the mud being hurled back, though the above analysis proves that such a projection is materially impossible.

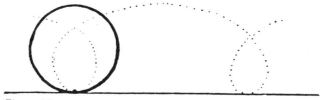

*Figure 22*

*Figure 23*

This tendency of ours to underestimate the movement of a luminous point that we are following with our eyes is the key to most of the optical illusions concerning movement. It explains particularly why certain illusions happen somewhat capriciously, holding off for a while and then bearing down on us irresistibly or modifying themselves in the course of the experience without our knowing why. The cause of both capriciousness and reversals lies in a movement of our eyes to which we were not paying attention. For instance, when we step along a plank over a torrent, we only feel dizzy as long as we look at the water. To the vision, our body, just like any object, appears motionless if we look at it, mobile if we fix our eyes on a surface that moves in relation to it.

If two objects slide against each other, first one, then the other will take an apparent movement; that is because, without realizing it, we are looking at them in turn. Once forewarned, we can, by volitional eye movements, achieve this reversal at will. When you are at the edge of a quay and a boat passes alongside, you can, at will, become aware of the boat's motion or see it in place and attribute a virtual movement to the quay itself. Or, when we are in a train stopped at a station and another train beside us starts moving, we think it is our train which is in motion. We should err only part of the time. Yet we

make the error every time. It is because, when the other train gets going, its movement attracts our attention and we fix our eyes on it, which makes it appear motionless, and we attribute the relative motion to our train.

Finally, we come to the illusions caused by the movement of the viewers themselves, that is, those that occur when we turn our head or when our whole body is in motion. The above detailed explanations allow us to be brief.

It is evident that if we are not warned that we are making a movement or being carried into space, we will be exposed to absolutely every illusion caused by the virtual movement of objects. Therefore, on a ship in mid-ocean, all our movement perceptions are falsified.

If our movement is volitional, we will be brought back to the conditions of normal perception. The only difference is that here the muscular awareness is much greater and must play a more important role. It will be taken into account not only in interpreting appearances but in shaping them. It will explain to us, for instance, why a very distant object that we are following with our eyes while we are walking seems to go along with us; or why a close object toward which we turn our head as we pass by seems actually motionless. These appearances can be conveniently reproduced and interpreted by the following experiment. Look at a white wall through a tube. You have the impression of a kind of motionless moon at some distance away. It will move to the right if you move the tube in that direction. It will move to the left if you walk to the left, making sure to keep the tube on a parallel line: in other words, from the very fact that you are aware of your own movement and that the moon is not moving in relation to you, it must seem to be following you. Now do both movements at the same time: the two illusions will neutralize each other and the moon will again seem motionless.

But there is a visual illusion against which our consciousness of our own movements cannot prevail. It is that which makes us see objects moving when their image shifts in our visual field. Muscular awareness may help us reason with this illusion, but it cannot modify it. Thus, when I walk, however much I feel I am walking and know that the objects in relation to which I am moving are actually still, let their image move ever so little on my retina and I will have to attribute a virtual movement to them. For, by getting blurred, they give me the essential sign which characterizes movement. The only way to see them motionless is to fix my eyes on them as I go by, that is, to really immobilize their image. I do this instinctively to ascertain the immobility of the ground over which my carriage is rolling, or to correct the illusions produced by a merry-go-round, or to avoid the dizziness caused by waltzing. But if I am carried by too rapid a movement, the dizziness is bound to appear sooner or later. Not, as is sometimes asserted, because I lose consciousness of my motion (when else would I be more aware of it?), but because my eyes get tired of the constant escaping of objects on which I seek, in vain, a point of support; they end by staring straight ahead. Then, inevitably, it is the objects whose

images are streaking by in my retinal field which will seem to be moving.

We have seen with what ease these illusions of movement perception are produced. It can provide some amusement for a while. But it is a rather dangerous game to play, which should not be abused. Besides giving rapidly a sense of dizziness, there remains a tendency to give in to illusions more easily a second time; it weakens our feeling of reality. It would be wiser, when we get these feelings of vertigo, to attempt to stop them immediately.

When illusions occur in spite of ourselves, they nearly always have a painful character. Throughout our life, we use our eyes to give us a precise awareness of things. We work at it. As soon, therefore, as we have to do with a phenomenon of an equivocal character, we make an effort to try to interpret our sensations sanely, to fight the illusion that tends to occur. And this effort makes the perception of the object unpleasant. When I watch the moon running through the clouds, or a half-submerged rock that seems to rise and sink with the waves, I resist the illusion, then I give in to it, then I get undeceived and this uncertainty and the perpetual deceptions are fatiguing.

Some will say that if I am not conscious of the illusion, I cannot suffer from it and that if I become aware of it, it will disappear. But between absolute consciousness and absolute unconsciousness, there is a peculiar state: it is when a person is deceived, knowing full well he is being deceived. Let us go into this further.[1]

We are used to interpreting sensations a certain way; these judgments, at first deliberate and volitional, eventually become

1   For more details, see Herman Helmholtz, *Optique physiologique*, French ed., p. 564.

a habit. The association becomes irresistible. We then have what is called acquired perceptions. These judgments have the spontaneity and unawareness of reflex actions to which they are totally comparable. Like them, they give us no feeling of effort or fatigue; like them, they happen unavoidably, even as our will might resist them. For instance, I have taken the habit of closing my eyes when a threatening body approaches. If someone threatens my eye with his finger for fun, I know my eye is not in danger, but the eye itself judges it is and closes. Likewise, an object seen through the fog which consequently appears farther away is deemed larger than it is: I realize this is an illusion, but still the illusion persists: I make the error with the full knowledge I am doing so. Thus the mind, like the body, has reflex actions that are independent from its volitional acts and may find themselves in conflict with them.

But when there is such a conflict between volitional and reflex judgments, the discordance is painful; the harmony that we have been attempting to establish between them is upset; we feel there is some warped machinery in our brain. Any conscious hallucination worries us more as it is more conscious; we feel an anxiety close to madness. An object that I know is motionless seems to be moving: for a moment, I feel I am losing my reason. Humboldt explains that the particular anxiety that earthquakes produce on all animated beings is occasioned by the sudden loss of our hereditary belief in the stability of the ground. Is it not even worse to lose faith in the testimony of one's own senses, in the solidity of reason?

But the illusion becomes especially painful when it deceives us about our own movements because it causes a feeling of nausea and dizziness. For example, if we are in a canoe and anchored in the middle of the river and we fix our eyes on the ripples that wrinkle the surface, we seem to be going in the opposite direction; we make an effort to catch our equilibrium and that effort makes us lose it. Or, tired after a long trip and already sickened by the smell of the train, we feel nausea whenever the train slows down or starts off again. This feeling is very strong when we do not look outside, because then the movement occurs without warning and without our being able to understand our loss of stability. In the cabin of a ship, we are much more seasick when we feel ourselves moving without anticipating or understanding the oscillation. The downward movement of pitching is more nauseating than the upward one, because we lose our own point of support. All these sensations are explained in the same way: it is only because of our visual perceptions that we maintain our sense of balance, so that when these perceptions are absent or falsified, the sensations relating to the position of the body become abnormal and inexplicable and, therefore, unpleasant, at the same time as our equilibrium is compromised.

These remarks show that in order for the movement of objects to be pleasant to look at, it must be clearly perceptible; that is, it cannot expose us to any error of interpretation and especially not to dizziness. Knowing how the illusion occurs, we can easily see under what conditions we can avoid it.

Suppose there are only mobile objects in my visual field. I fix my eyes on any one of them. How will I perceive its actual movement? By comparing it to nearby objects? But since the premise is that they are all moving, I will seek in vain a landmark among them. By the shifting of the object's retinal image? But, in order to do that, I would have to be certain my eye is staying motionless, which is very difficult, not to say impossible, under such conditions. Then by the movement of my eyes?

But we have seen that we only have a very indistinct awareness of that.

There therefore have to be in the visual field a few motionless objects, not only in fact but in appearance, on which the eye can be anchored in order to judge the movement of the others. To the extent that this condition is realized, the movement will take on an aesthetic character. In a first trip to sea, when you reach the open water, you experience a very painful impression as soon as you are surrounded only by those green waves rising and falling, tiring your eyes with their perpetual motion, although these same waves charm when seen crashing against a cliff. From my window, I watch a parade, a cavalcade, a passing regiment: the effect will be much more pleasant if the parade advances between two rows of motionless spectators than if the whole crowd turns around to follow them or forms a crosscurrent. In both cases, I lose the notion of the actual movement of the cortege and, at the same time, the effect of the contrast which increases its visual interest.

Furthermore, the motionless objects that serve as landmarks must occupy the major part of the visual field or they will, by contrast, take a virtual motion, because of our natural tendency to attribute to objects of a lesser surface the totality of the relative movement. In a few cases, we ourselves can determine the appropriate proportions by choosing our point of view carefully. For example, if we wish to contemplate a cascade from its most advantageous viewpoint, we will step closer or farther, giving it more or less background. And, instinctively, we will stop at the distance where the moving surfaces are the most aesthetic in proportion to the fixed surfaces.

By experimenting, I might establish some figures, a kind of magic formula that would determine this proportion. But the subject is not so precise. In matters of aesthetics, overly strict formulas are often but dust in the eye.

All we can say is that mobile surfaces must occupy a small portion of the visual field in relation to fixed ones; the more so as the opposite relationship would be fatiguing for the retina, since the movement of objects gives us a vibrating, twinkling sensation when perceived indirectly.

For objects to make the most favorable impression on my eye, it is also best that their movements be symmetrical. When an object crosses the visual field, it tends to attract our eye and, therefore, to produce the illusions inherent in dizziness. But if, at the same moment, another object describes a movement that is exactly the reverse, the two actions nullify one another and our eye keeps its equilibrium. Say we have two objects, A and B, which we establish are of the same size and are placed at a short distance, *ab,* from one another: the center of gravity of the two objects is placed at point C, center of *ab.* It is on this point C that we have a tendency to fix our eye in order to see both objects together. Suppose, now, that B starts moving to the right; the distance *ab* increases in proportion to the speed of B and point C will be displaced in the same direction at half the speed, carrying our gaze with it. But if object A starts moving at the same time and at the same speed as B, but in the opposite direction, the distance *ab* may increase but, as it is lengthening equally in both directions, point C remains the same: the optical equilibrium of the system will not be broken.

Let us now take a few examples from nature and from art: one will recognize that the sight of movement always has the more charm as this condition of symmetry and equilibrium is best observed. Nothing is more graceful than a fountain whose jets rise, spread out, and fall symmetrically. A single column of water, especially when the wind inclines it, will not have such a good effect. Throw a stone in a pond: you will produce a system of gradually widening ripples, but they will not attract the eye, since their center remains in place; this is a pleasant movement to look at. It will not be so satisfying if the same experience is made in a river, where the system of ripples undergoes a general movement of translation. The effect will be more unfortunate still if you look at the parallel ripples made by the wind on a lake: they advance in a continuous movement, attracting your eye, which persists in following them, then returns to its starting point to seek new ones, and so on. In these conditions, sooner or later, dizziness will inevitably appear.

An artificial sun turning slowly draws the eye to its gyration and the effect is unpleasant; it is much better when it turns faster so that only an emission of sparkling rays is seen. This is why builders of machines make, for aesthetic reasons, the spokes of flywheels curved rather than straight: when the wheel turns very rapidly, the curved spokes give an impression of irradiance, their apparent movement going from the center to the periphery; but with straight spokes, the vertiginous impression of gyration remains. At the theater, a cortege coming toward the spectator will be much more effective than a transversal one across the front of the stage. The symmetrical movement of the two arms is more graceful than the pendular movement of one arm. In general, pendular movements, such as that of the pendulum of a clock, have very little aesthetic value, unless they are fast enough for the eye to stop following them, as in the vibrations of a tuning fork. But of all movements, the most dizzying and therefore the most unpleasant is indisputably the merry-go-round kind of movement (circus horse, wooden horses, dancers' pirouettes). However agreeable the

waltz is to the dancer, it is very tiring for the spectator: the sight of couples turning around and around in a drawing room is not particularly aesthetic. It is the same for circling movements. The above principles might be of value to choreographers. By analyzing the aesthetic effect of a very few simple movements, and, if necessary, by making a few experiments—in other words, by establishing the theory of what we have just outlined —one could perfect this art to a great extent and obtain much more effective results.

Finally, for a movement to be pleasing to the eye, it can be neither too slow nor too fast. But how can this maximum or minimum be measured? The movement is too slow when it obliges us to make an effort of attention to follow it. Suppose there is a wheel, at first motionless, which starts to turn at a gradually accelerating speed. First its rotation will not be perceived. Then a moment will come when you ask yourself if it is moving or not; at one moment, the movement will be perceived, then it will seem to stop, probably because the eye, having followed it, has unconsciously immobilized its image. Then we reach what we might call the aesthetic speed. Having gone beyond it, we enter a period still more unpleasant than the first, because to the effort of attention is added a physical effort of the eye, in which it must make very rapid movements to still discern the spokes. The image will seem to be quivering, sometimes clear, sometimes confused. Finally, we give up following it. We keep our eyes on one point and the image of the spokes will melt in a continuous sheet which can be pleasing to view.

Difficult as it may seem to extract a formula from this succession of pleasant and unpleasant periods, it operates, however, according to a quite simple law. There are two limits, one of slowness, one of speed, beyond which movement is not perceptible. The most agreeable movements are those with an average speed, those that are at about equal distance from the two extremes. When the movements near these limits, they will become more and more displeasing until they cross the limit: then, all effort of perception ceasing, the unpleasantness will disappear. All this can be condensed into a simple formula: a movement of variable speed becomes especially unpleasant as it nears the limits of perceptivity.

This law would apply just as well to the effect produced by a pendular movement. If it is too slow, it will not be perceived. When it is a little faster, the eye will follow it without being conscious of doing so and the surrounding objects will take on a relative movement which may produce a visual vertigo. Then the movement accelerates further until it reaches the aesthetic speed, then exceeds it by crossing a second limit as unpleasant as the first, until finally the oscillations are too fast to be perceived or even to give the impression of any movement at all. That is what happens when they succeed one another at the rate of more than thirty per second. Past that limit, the oscillations can increase indefinitely, a hundred, a thousand times per second; not only will it not change the aesthetical effect but the appearance of the oscillating object will remain exactly the same. We will see only two motionless images, at the two extreme points of the oscillation.

One should also note that the most aesthetic speeds must be the most constant ones or those that vary at a uniform progression. Jerky movements disconcert the eye by escaping it suddenly, and the effect is especially troublesome when these jerks are irregular, because, since the mind is unable to anticipate them, the eye does not always have the time to be prepared.

But we are beginning to stray from the subject of perceptions caused by the movement of the eyes to considerations of the appreciable pleasure we find in such movement. That is what we shall examine more thoroughly in the next chapter.

We have concluded from the preceding study on visual perceptions that the most pleasing movements to view are those that are in no way equivocal, that do not require that we make a great effort of correction, that are grasped at once, in one word —that can be perceived with the least intellectual effort. But we have in no way taken into account the affective quality of these perceptions, that is to say, the varying pleasure of the diverse sensations on which they are founded. We shall now examine this new element. We can assume in advance that it must play a definite role in the aesthetics of movement. The luminous objects that cross our visual field give us specific colored sensations. When our eye follows a moving object, its movements correspond to those of the object, giving us specific muscular sensations. Let us find out what influence these totally subjective sensations have on those judgments of taste that relate to movement.

## Attraction of Color and Movement

Everyone knows that when we keep our eyes attached to a brilliant object for a long time, the retina gets tired and reacts less and less to the impression it is perceiving.

Fix your attention closely on a star shining in the night sky. After a few seconds, your vision seems to blur and little by little to dim. The stars whose scintillating glitter you perceived indirectly will seem to go out one by one. Now they have all disappeared and you only discern the central star, shining with a hard glow in the dark sky and giving you the impression that a metallic point is being pressed harder and harder onto your retina. Then it too disappears in the dark; you no longer see anything. Your eye makes an imperceptible movement to find it again: immediately, all the stars reappear together.

This experiment proves that an overprolonged impression on a retinal element can end by blinding it, especially in the area of indirect vision. As the same effect is produced on all the points hit by the rays emanating from the luminous object, the total image must diminish gradually if we stare at the object too fixedly.

The result is that, given equal luminosity, an object moving in our visual field will seem brighter and more vividly colored than a motionless one. That fact alone, independent of any feeling of curiosity, explains our fascination with objects in motion.

In the aesthetics of painting, one talks mostly of the charm of color, considered, so to speak, at rest; but the most beautiful thing is the movement of colored objects, or color in motion. Is this special charm due to the movement or to the color? To both at the same time. It is then that the eyes experience the most vivid and durable satisfaction. They are diverted by the motion just as much as by the diversity of colors that pass before them.

Nature is prodigal with such spectacles. It may be rainbows rising and falling in a waterfall with the clouds of pulverized water; the throat of pigeons and hummingbirds; the scintillating of dew drops; the ocean sparkling in the sun; the sun setting behind clouds. A sunset lavishes all the harmonies of color, but what creates its magical charm is that these harmonies change. You never tire of them because they are never the same; the sun, gliding through strata of clouds of varying depth, modifies all the nuances; long rays of light hit distant clouds and scattered billows floating, almost invisible, high in the sky, and inflame them all at once. The spectacle is constantly renewed.

A mere soap bubble will give us a small replica of these impressions. Let us follow it in its growth. At first, it is only a diaphanous sphere, shining like glass; little by little, limpid light pink and green hues appear and condense in colored clouds; then come images with clearer contours, marvelous ocelli, tears, palmettos, streaks of paisley. The colors deepen; whirls of deep blue in copper yellow appear, wild spots of stormy, somber aspect; by now, black spots are scattered here and there, precursors of the end to come, and, suddenly, nothing. The bubble has burst, leaving the eye still enchanted by the phantasmagoria.

I must also mention a spectacle often spurned as idle entertainment but of first-rate value aesthetically: I speak of fireworks. Recall those rockets describing graceful parabolas; the bombs bursting in a rain of tricolored stars; the zigzag of serpents; the whirling of catherine wheels; and the final bouquet that rises in an immense puff, spreading above all its sonorous, crackling, blinding canopy. We might as well admit it is an exceptional sight, perhaps even too beautiful, as the eye tires quickly before such splendor and prefers quieter beauty. Lean over the railing of a bridge on a moonlit night and watch the luminescence playing on the water; it is a sight you never tire of. The eye, fascinated by the constant movement of the reflections, is also charmed by their gentleness. Another spectacle, among the most beautiful, is that of the waves, reflecting various images in pleasing chromatic combinations. I once admired this effect on the edges of the lake of Le Bourget: the

sheet of water reflected a wall of reddish, salmon-colored rocks; and over this background, tiny waves passed by in iridescent moires and gentle wrinkles, reflecting the pure blue of the sky: the movement of those two colors was quite ravishing as they intermingled without blending and seemed to frolic together.

This is a charm that a painting cannot render, since it presents the harmonies of color at a standstill. Instead of giving a symphony of colors, a painter can only thump out a chromatic chord; however beautiful it may be, it will tire us in the end. Whereas in nature's mobile scenes, the chords succeed one another, impressing the eye with a rhythm and harmony analogous to that produced on the ear by a musical movement.

I also tend to believe that a certain mobility is an essential condition for the charm of color, even in painting; and that the aesthetic effect of any chromatic combination would be nonexistent if, by an unconscious movement of the eyes, we did not make the various colors, presented in simple juxtaposition, pass sequentially on the same point of our retina. Let us, for instance, take the chromatic combination whose value is best known, the juxtaposition of two complementary colors, like red and green, or blue and yellow. As long as my retina has not been impressed by any color, I have no desire or need to look at one rather than the other. But if I have been looking at green, I must transfer my eye to red in order to recover the freshness of my sensation and at the same time relax the retinal elements strained by too long an impression; and it is because I have created this need for myself that I will feel pleasure when I finally encounter the desired color. If I am shown red and green, or blue and yellow, in juxtaposition, my eye will move from one to the other with an ever-renewed pleasure. But one cannot conceive what pleasure a retinal element would get from perceiving a nuance while the element next to it perceives its opposite. My perception therefore owes its pleasure to the rhythmic succession of these contrary impressions on the same point of my retina.

It is now clear that, by modifying the brightness and expanse of colored surfaces, one can vary the strength and duration of impressions; that by spreading a single color over a large surface, a painter gives the sensation of a stagnant light; that by hammering tone upon tone on a canvas, he gives the eye glancing over it rapidly the equivalent of sudden variations of luminosity; and that it is good to make the light glisten and scintillate that way. When you look at a canvas by a colorist such as Rubens or Delacroix, you realize that the colors you have before you are not simply juxtaposed, but in motion, waving, vibrating, fading into one another or brightening by contrast, thus producing, within the light, new heightenings of brilliance. And it is our eye, moving successively from one point of the canvas to the other, in an order predetermined by the artist, that gives the colors spread out on a motionless surface their own motility. Maintain your eye in one position for an instant and all the nuances will fade and get tarnished with surprising rapidity. As soon as they move freely, the colors light up again and their magic play recommences.

## The Direction of Movements

The anatomical construction of our eye enables it to turn in any direction. But all the movements it can make are not equally easy.

Left to themselves, the eyes tend to place themselves in the primary position, straight ahead and a little below the horizon. The farther they stray from this position, the greater the effort they must make. For extreme deviations, the effort becomes almost painful, whereas to return in place, the eyes only need to suspend all effort of innervation. From this peculiarity must result a preference for external movements that bring the eyes back to this center of fixation, and, by the same token, an antipathy, probably unconscious and as feeble as you like, but not completely negligible, for the movements that turn the eyes away. In other words, convergent movements are preferred to divergent ones.

If after having strayed from this primary position the eyes come back to it with some speed, the elasticity of the muscles tends to make them overrun the position before getting back to it. Thence, there is a tendency for the eyes to make a movement of simple oscillation. "It seems to me," says Helmholtz, "that among the preferred eye movements are those that travel in the visual field along meridians passing through the primary position. These are also the movements where there is no apparent rotation of the objects and that is probably the reason for their preponderance."[1] Objects should therefore be followed more easily by the eyes when they move in a straight rather than a curved line. For when their movement is rectilinear, one can always make it go through the primary position, by orienting correctly the direction of one's head, and therefore perceive it by a simple oscillation of the eyes; whereas that is impossible for a curved movement. This is a further reason for the unpleasant character of merry-go-round movements.

Among rectilinear oscillations, the horizontal ones are cer-

1   Hermann Helmholtz, *Optique physiologique*, French ed., p. 653.

tainly favored. This may be due to the structure of the muscular apparatus, perhaps, even, to the arrangement of the eyelids which forms a horizontal slit in which the salient ball of the cornea slides; or perhaps, simply to the habit of reading. This habit would explain also our tendency to look from left to right rather than from right to left when we examine a series of objects. (According to Delaunay, this tendency is more developed among superior races.)

Next come vertical oscillations, which cost a greater effort of innervation and the resistance of which we are still inclined to overestimate, out of habit. Last, we have diagonal oscillations, which are especially difficult because of our tendency to return to the nearest vertical or horizontal: our eye, tempted by those forces that tend to make it stray from its primary direction, can only maintain itself there with a special effort and with muscular vibrations which will be evidenced by the sinuous trajectory of the eyes.

## The Aesthetics of Lines

From this preference of the eye for certain movement directions, some have attempted to draw a whole aesthetics of shapes and lines.

Charles Henry, in the *Revue contemporaine,* has said: "The problem of the aesthetics of shapes comes down evidently to this: which are the most pleasant lines? But a little reflection proves immediately that a line is an abstraction; it is the synthesis of the two parallel and opposite directions in which the line can be traced; the reality is the direction. I do not see a circle, I see only circles going in one direction or another, what we call *cycles.* The problem comes down to this new statement: what are the pleasant directions?"[2]

I have cited this entire preamble because it is the clearest explanation I have found of a doctrine I believe is quite false. Without doubt, figures that we can perceive with the least effort must, all things being otherwise equal, have our preference. Knowing in which directions our eyes go with the greatest of ease, one quite naturally deduces that the most aesthetic lines are those that take our eyes in those directions.

But there is a preliminary question that does not seem to have been considered: it is whether, when we perceive a line, we really follow it with our eyes. There seems to be no proof that we do. I would say, on the contrary, that we follow it only in very exceptional cases, and that, to judge the shape of a line, we seek on the contrary to embrace it as a whole, at one glance.

First of all, the movement of the eyes would be a very poor way to appreciate the direction and therefore the shape of a line, because its own direction is poorly judged.

Suppose my eyes are directed to some point of my visual field and I want to move them to a given direction. Will this movement, started in the desired direction, continue in the same way? In order to do that, my eyes would have to tend to move in a straight line; that is to say, the rotating movement of my eyes would have to tend to occur along fixed axes. But that is approximately true, as we have seen, only for vertical and horizontal movements that occur from the primary position of the eye. Oblique movements are made preferably along sinuous lines, which, however, would be of no use to express the gracefulness of these lines because it is evident that there is no likeli-

2  Charles Henry, *Revue contemporaine* (1885), p. 445.

hood that a line we are perceiving coincides exactly with this trajectory of our eye. As to the eye movements that tend to make it describe curved lines on the surface of the visual field, they maintain the original impulse very poorly. Hence there are almost always, in the volitional movement of the eyes, deviations in direction, of which we are not conscious.

As we have a tendency to assume that points that our eyes scan without being conscious of a change in direction really form a straight line, one can see to what errors one is exposed by this procedure of surveying the visual field.

Second, it is evident, from all we have said of the effect of continuous eye movements on the clarity of visual images, that we cannot take absolute cognizance of the shape of an object if we follow its outline this way: the image would get completely blurred under our gaze and would take on a virtual movement, which would be reverse to that of the eye and would have a most unfortunate effect. If, as you are reading this line, you can discern every one of its characters, it means your eye is not scanning it in a continuous motion, but is moving in little jerks followed by a pause, which is the only thing that counts for perception. But if you pass the point of a pen over this line and follow it with your eyes, you will see what happens.

Finally, direct observation shows that, in fact, this is not the way we look at objects. Ask someone to look at some object and watch the movement of his eyes while he is studying it: you will discover that his eyes do not *draw* the object, but stop here and there, seeking points from which he will get the best total view; and they never settle on a contour, but always on a central spot. The same observation holds true for a simple line. A visible line is an object like another, that we look at in our usual way, by seeking a spot from which our vision can embrace it most easily, and then fixing our eyes on it. It is not even at all necessary for this spot to be on the line itself. This happens for straight lines only. To look at a curved line, we will preferably choose our principle spot in the center of the surface it circumscribes. Generally speaking, the first glance we cast on a figure goes to its center of gravity: that is where we are best placed to embrace the whole figure at one glance.

This fact seems to me to have important aesthetic consequences. It informs us first that, in a painting as in nature, what determines our aesthetic impression is not the outlines, it is what is inside these lines, what, in terms of painting, is called the masses. Even in a line drawing, the lines are only made to lay down the masses, to indicate them summarily.[3] Yet it is not on them, but between them that our gaze falls. The true lines of the human body are the medial lines. The human figures that young children trace in their exercise books with a dot for the head, a stroke for the body, and a single line for each arm and leg have more life and movement and give a better impression of nature than those they trace with double lines.

We can also understand now from where our preference for centered, rayed, symmetrical figures comes. Half a regular hexagon is not pleasing to look at. Re-establish the other half: our eyes will go to the center of the figure and will embrace it wholly at one glance. Symmetrical figures will have an even better effect when their axis or center of symmetry is actually indicated, so the eye will not even need to look for its point of fixation.

3   This explains why we recognize immediately a figure cut out of paper, but have trouble telling the shape of the void left by this cutout. The contours are exactly the same but our eye is not accustomed to looking at a void; it sees shapes only where they are filled. One could make, on the subject, a psychological study on the kind of picture puzzles in which objects and people are hidden.

Thus a straight, continuous line allows the gaze to drift away without knowing where to settle. Put a simple transversal dash in the middle: the effect improves from the mere fact that you have given the eye a point of fixation.

The favorable impression produced, under certain circumstances, by parallel lines comes less from their actual parallelism than from their optical convergence: they lead the gaze toward their common point of escape which provides the eye with its center of fixation. This effect is especially perceptible for horizontal lines whose point of escape coincides approximately with the primary position of the eyes. Suppose, for example, that I am in a room at a distance OA from one of the walls and that my eye is settled on point A: I will pay no attention to the convergence of vertical lines which have their point of escape at the zenith; but all the lines of the floor and ceiling which, being parallel to OA, escape at point A into the point of fixation of my eye will be shaped like a kind of double fan whose symmetry will please me before I have even realized the reasons for my pleasure.

Finally, can we not explain identically the special charm of paintings in which the eyes are irresistibly attracted, either by lines of recall or by a particularly bright spot, toward the center of the painting from which they cannot detach themselves, almost to the point of hypnosis? It has been said that a good painting should be painted with one stroke of the brush. I would add that a good painting has to be seen at one glance.

In all of this, evidently, the influence of the movement of the eyes contributes in determining our aesthetic judgments only in a sort of negative way, since all we require of a figure is that it spare us any movement.

But then, how can we explain the special aesthetic value that we attribute to certain lines? For we cannot deny that curves are more graceful than straight lines; and among curves, some seem particularly elegant. Consider a starred polygon, a circle, an oval, a cross, a square, a triangle. Each of these figures answers to the conditions mentioned above of being well centered and visible at one glance. But how different their effect! Let us examine this difference.

The difference lies in the expression and sympathy which are the muscular sensations that the sight of a line evokes indirectly for us. For we are disposed to look at it, not as a geometrical boundary, but as a solid, material object, like a thread more or less stretched, whose shape indicates its tension. Thus a straight line will give us something of an impression of rigidity, of effort; a sinuous line will appear somewhat relaxed; the curve described by the garlands of a chandelier is very graceful, because it corresponds to their natural fall.

Sometimes the aesthetic character of a line is determined simply by the attraction that the objects recalled by its shape have for us. Because angular shapes are found mainly in minerals and rounded forms, in living creatures, we find in curves a *je ne sais quoi* that is more animated than in straight lines. You watch a draftsman tracing a line on paper: it is a rather complex curve of which you cannot find the clue; as long as this state of affairs lasts, the aesthetic effect is zero; a simple square traced with a rule would be just as acceptable. But little by little, you see: the line represents the silhouette of a woman's body. Now you look at it with different eyes; and the images it brings to your mind give it all at once a grace it did not have of its own.[4]

4   About the expression of shapes and lines due to the association of ideas, see Gustav Fechner, "Introduction à l'esthétique," *Revue philosophique de la*

More immediately, the grace of lines has its reason in the idea of movement which is inseparable from the notion of line. A line, by definition, is a trajectory, a passage from one point to another. By considering it from that point of view, we find ourselves again on familiar ground. All we have said about the aesthetics of movement in general can be said about the aesthetics of lines. The graceful lines will be those that have been traced with an easy, free, supple hand; although they have a goal, they must not seem too hurried to get there; their direction cannot exclude a certain variety. Léon Dumont remarks in *Le sentiment du gracieux:* "This condition excludes from gracefulness all straight-lined directions, at least when they last too long; or, to speak more precisely, it excludes all the prolongations of the same lines, even of curved lines. For the regularity of the latter is no more pleasing than that of straight ones. But it often happens that one considers as a single curved line a series of different curves and it is this confusion that has made one say that curved lines are more prone to be graceful than straight ones."[5] Thence, the charm of fantasy lines, such as accolades, foliage, interlacings, and of those arabesques in which, as Lammenais has said so well, "the eye gets lost pursuing a symmetry it keeps thinking it is seizing, but which escapes it in a perpetual graceful movement."

But what is most important in lines as in movement in general is not grace, but beauty. A line will be beautiful when its trajectory is justified, when this passage from one point to another occurs along a curve of least effort. Given two vertical lines that must be connected, the most aesthetic curve is that which passes from one to the other without jerks, without sudden changes of speed or direction, and without needless deviations. But to carry this to its logical conclusion, it would seem that because the most economical line is the straight line, it also should be the most beautiful. In general, I would agree. If the serpentine line is the line of grace, the straight line is the line of beauty. It is the straight line that, by its predominance, can give style to a simple piece of furniture and to the most majestic edifice. The marvelous curves of the Parthenon which have been so written about were designed only to forestall the optical illusions that would have inflected the principle lines of the monument, and to give them a perfect apparent straightness. The straight line is the rule. Curves are the exception. They are used only as connections or to break up from time to time the barrenness of straight lines. Such is their role in Gothic architecture of the great epoch. As soon as they are multiplied profusely and become dominant, as in flamboyant Gothic, they mark a decadence in art.

But I do not like to indulge in reasons of pure sentiment which make us arbitrarily attribute beauty to this line or that. One cannot decide on the aesthetic value of a line as long as it is considered by itself: it must be seen in the whole of which it is a part, in the object of which it determines the shape. A line is not beautiful in itself. It is beautiful—or not—according to whether it is well adapted—or not—to its specific end.[6] We have to admire it only according to whether it is justified for

*France et de l'étranger* (Paris: Germer Baillière et cie., 1878), 6:181, and James Sully, "Les formes visuelles et le plaisir esthétique," ibid. (1880), 9:498.
5   Léon Dumont, *Le sentiment du gracieux* (Paris: A. Durand, 1863), p. 82.

6   Excellent articles can be found on this aesthetics of lines in Eugène Viollet-le-Duc's *Dictionnaire raisonné d'architecture française du XI^e au XVI^e siècle* (Paris: A. Morel, 1861–75). Read also *A Manual of Decorative Composition,* trans. J. Gorino (London: Virtue & Co., 1898). It is, regarding method, one of the best books of aesthetics in recent years.

reasons of local suitability. If, in general, hand-traced curves or "curves of sentiment," as they are called, are of better effect than those traced with a compass, it is because they are better adapted to their specific goal; I would even say they are more "intelligent." A building has beautiful lines if every one of its lines indicates good construction.

One sees, therefore, that it is not difficult to explain the aesthetics of lines while ignoring the movement of the eyes. I would be tempted to say: explain as you wish, as long as it is *not* through the movement of the eyes! It would be a mistake to believe that, in a matter as fundamental as that of the beauty of lines, we let ourselves be guided by reasons of this nature. If our aesthetic judgments rest on such a fragile base as the tendency of our gaze to turn one way or another, such triviality is really not worth our while.

That this subjective pleasure should have a certain influence on us, fine! We have to acknowledge it. But I deny completely that this influence should be predominant and primary. What is passed off as the basis for judgments of taste are rather the subtleties of an over-refined taste. When we must judge the shapes of an object, is it of any use to know which are the most pleasant directions for our eyes? The important thing is to ask what is the use of these lines, why they have been so traced, what is their raison d'être, their justification. And it is our reason alone that must decide. As to our eyes, which are mere instruments of perception and the humble servants of our mind, we can only require one thing of them: that they give us precise data.

So the conclusion of this examination brings us back to the essential principle we posed in the first place and which we would like to see included in all discussions of art and taste:

true beauty is in the intelligent adaptation of things to their end. And so, with some relief, we have completed the full cycle and, after traveling through the dimmer areas of aesthetics, once again we see the light for an instant.

Without question, auditory sensations contribute in a large part to determining the aesthetic value of the movement of objects. We have seen that they are not indifferent to the expression of grace; that more than any other sensation, they are expressive of force through the dynamic ideas they awaken in our mind; and that they have a certain influence on the expression of feelings. We must recognize that by the pleasure they give, they may, through the addition of a musical element, considerably increase the attraction of visible movement. They mark their rhythm; they give them their harmony. When we contemplate a waterfall, waves in motion, trees whose foliage is undulating and shaking in the wind, we cannot say if it is our eyes that feel their charm rather than our ears. Finally, thanks to the sense of hearing, all the movements that the eye perceives have, so to speak, their specific tone which characterizes them and adds to their pictorial value. To imagine what the spectacle of nature would be without auditory perceptions, we need only picture a ballet without music.

But if auditory sensations serve to qualify movement, can they serve to perceive them? To answer that, we must find out if they are sufficiently localized and if they even have any relation to space.

## The Auditory Perception of Movement

Let us suppose that we have no other sense than hearing. What would become of our auditory sensations in such an eventuality? Our ear would undoubtedly perceive noises as sonorous objects, each having its individual character which would permit us to distinguish between them and, if need be, to recognize them. But setting aside the visual images that they suggest, would we have any reason to picture them as something external, situated a certain distance from us and in a determined direction? Reduced to purely auditory perceptions, would we be living in a world of sounds with no notion of space? For my part, I am inclined to believe that, even under such conditions, we would have a perception of movement. When we see with what ease the different senses can, when needed, supplement one another, we arrive at the conclusion that, whatever range of sensations we have as instruments, the mind would manage to reconstruct every essential thing in the edifice of human knowledge.

Let us even admit that, by themselves, auditory perceptions are completely devoid of the character of externality. One cannot deny that, at this point, they have acquired it from their association with visual perceptions. As soon as children begin to pay attention to noises, that is, to perceive them, they get used to localizing them in the tangible, visible objects from which they notice they emanate. Sonority appears to them to be a quality of an object on the same level as its hardness or its color. This association is the more understandable as their attention goes only to objects that are very close, so that, at the moment they hit them or see them in motion, they simultaneously perceive their noise.

But a sonorous object does not affect our ears identically, according to whether it is placed to the right or left, in front of or behind us, close to our head or at a great distance. To each movement of a visible object, there corresponds a change in its sonorousness. We have also gotten the habit of this correspondence from the beginning; we have used it to judge, by our hearing alone, the position of sonorous objects, so that, actually, the localization of our auditory perceptions is precise enough to permit us to complement or in some cases supplant our visual perceptions. A horse canters by in the street, under my windows: I listen to it as I watch it. And once I have lost sight of it, the rhythmic sound of its hoofs, getting softer as it recedes, will continue to make me perceive its movement. The sonorous rhythm which is an inseparable part of recurring movement serves to scan them and preserves my notion of their speed even as their too great rapidity takes them beyond my gaze. Who can measure with the eyes the speed of a trill executed by a professional pianist? But our auditory sensations remain distinct enough for us to evaluate it. A spinning top or a turbine turning at full speed appears motionless: we would not even suspect they are gyrating if it were not for the rumbling or clinking that accompanies their movement.

Finally, and this is the greatest service it can give us in practical terms, the sense of hearing is a kind of warning system. Its perceptions, less precise than visual sensations but of a more extensive field since it is really spherical, signal the approach of objects and indicate the direction in which we should turn our eyes. They play, in relation to vision, the role of the finder of a telescope.

### Acoustical Illusions

Like all acquired perceptions, the localization of sensations has, out of habit, taken the character of an immediate perception. We cannot hear a noise without localizing it: it has hardly hit our eardrum when immediately, by a reflex association, we assign it some position in space. This tendency is especially evident when there are continuous changes of sonority that correspond to an actual movement of the objects: a weak sound will not always seem to me far away, but if the sound gets weaker, I will inevitably picture it receding.

This being granted, we see how acoustical illusions will occur. If these characteristic changes happen under abnormal conditions, we will, out of habit, continue to attribute them to their usual causes. The telephone furnishes us a good example of these errors of interpretation. When, to take part in a telephone conversation, you put a receiver to your left ear, for example, the voice of the speaker will seem to come from far away to the left. If you then put a second phone to your right ear, the voice will seem to be getting nearer and moving from left to right; then it seems to settle at a short distance in front of you. In fact, that is the spot from where the voice would be coming under ordinary circumstances, for us to receive the same auditory sensation. Our ear attributes the sound vibrations to their apparent source in the same way as it usually attributes them, under normal perception, to their actual source. It is an illusion more or less similar to that produced by the eyes, when, in a convex mirror, we think we are seeing, close to the surface, the images of the most distant luminous objects.[1]

The theater uses these illusions constantly. We imagine we hear a triumphant cortege advancing, a barge departing with a

---

1    The effect of the echo, usually cited as the typical acoustical illusion, is, properly speaking, an error rather than an illusion. It does fool us as to the actual situation of the sonorous object, but we do really hear the sounds in the direction from which they seem to be coming.

chorus of voices and instruments, a distant echo moving from one hill to the other; but these effects are produced by a few chorists or musicians hidden behind the backdrop. It goes without saying that the illusion will be all the more perfect if pains are taken to reproduce the changes of tone that go with moving away so that they form what you might call the aerial perspective of those sounds. Since the luminous objects become paler as they get farther away and eventually get lost in the fog, so the sonorous objects, heard at a distance, lose the characteristics of their timbre. Listen to the music of a military band going by on the boulevard: the sound of the diverse instruments which all hit your ear at the same time are first united in a single sonority, powerful, vibrant, richly toned, which is the characteristic voice of the fanfare. Then the music recedes; the weaker sounds get lost; the blare of the cornet, the loud tones of the trumpet, and the rattle of the drums reach you still with a degree of clarity; then they all get blurred and the wind brings you puffs of indistinct vague sounds which end up disappearing in the distance. What is true of the whole band is true of each of its instruments: their tone alters in the same way, by the gradual disappearance of the harmonies of the sound; it becomes more uniform and therefore more impersonal.

Another kind of change is produced by the interposition of reflecting surfaces which break up the sound, or of inert bodies which absorb its vibrant force. For instance, there is a man talking behind a wall: all the secondary vibrations which gave a bite to his voice will be powerless to move this enormous mass of stone and the voice will reach us muffled and sepulchral. These modifications of timbre are perhaps still more characteristic than the changes of intensity in the sound. When they are reproduced exactly, even reason cannot destroy the illusion. Though we know how this sound is produced, habit is stronger and our ear continues to deceives us, however much our judgment warns us of our error.

But what will happen if we have before our eyes the object itself from which the sounds are coming? In that case, it is clear that our visual perceptions, by expressly correcting our auditory sensations, counteract the illusion. We do, however, resist the evidence of our eyes, persist in our error, and prolong it at will to give ourselves the spectacle of it. Without really being taken in, we endeavor to act as if we were and to play at the illusion, so to speak.

As a matter of fact, certain natural and familiar illusions have prepared us for this artistic illusion, by loosening the ties which originally united our auditory perceptions to our visual ones. For example, we see far away, in the country, a hunter shooting: if the noise were simultaneous with the visible explosion, we would not think of separating one from the other. But because it reaches us only after a few seconds, we therefore picture it as something immaterial which detaches itself from the object and goes out into the air. Or, on a very windy day, you enter a forest: at every gust of wind, you hear a loud voice rising, which passes above your head, then sinks into the woods with a prolonged resonance. What is that noise? Is it the wind blowing? Is it the leaves shaking? No, it is something intangible, invisible, very real, however: it is a voice passing by.

The phenomenon of the echo contributes a great deal in producing this illusion. A person near us cries out; a distant hill sends the sound back to us: the sound that came to us on one side now comes from the other. In these conditions, how could we avoid picturing it as a sonorous object, distinct from the visible one, lighter and capable of moving rapidly with its own movement, whereas the material body from which it has detached itself stays in place?

One can now understand how much easier it is for us, when we want to be taken in by a musical illusion, to ignore the visual perceptions that would correct it. We are at a concert. The instruments are still tuning up. Finally, the orchestra leader taps his stand with his baton, the hall becomes silent, and the symphony starts. From that moment, the orchestra does not exist for us; if we continue to look at it, we do it mechanically and to do something with our eyes; but we totally exclude the orchestra's presence. What we hear is not the sounds coming from the strings of a violin, the tube of a clarinet, or the stomach of a double bass: it is a storm approaching with its muffled growls that suddenly bursts over our heads; it is a hunt going by in the distant forest; whatever. It might be a good idea to hide the orchestra in order to augment the illusion. Wagner did just that at Bayreuth. Grétry says in his *Mémoires:* "I would like the orchestra to be veiled and that neither the musicians, nor the light of the stands be seen from the spectators' side. The effect would be magical. And we know that in any case the orchestra is never supposed to be there."[2] But even with the orchestra there, the illusion remains. The resonances in the hall remove the idea of the origin of the sounds, and more surprising, even of their reality.

In fact, contrary to the ordinary hallucination that makes us attribute reality to images, it is sometimes the real sounds that give the effect of imaginary ones. Suppose, for instance, a soloist is playing the horn. By gradually softening the sound of his horn and muffling it, he gives so well the impression of distance

2   André Grétry, *Pages choisies des mémoires* (Liège: Wallonia, 1915), p. 317.

that if I heard him without seeing him, I would think he were actually going away; this would really be a hallucination. But I can still evoke the image that would then come to my mind and delude me, with the full knowledge that it is an image. I imagine a horn receding from me; and it is to this imaginary horn that I attribute the sounds that are hitting my eardrum. From this moment, the sounds lose for me their characteristic of being local and appear only as simple representations; and the less their actual source is indicated to me, the easier it will be for me to idealize them in this way. A few violin chords harmonizing in calm, pure, ecstatic notes can give the effect of a celestial vision, of unreal and purely imaginary sounds.

It should not be thought, on the other hand, that this illusion is something of an artistic convention. Here also, its origin can be found in natural illusions. Any sound soft enough to make us wonder if we are really hearing it or if our ears are ringing, or undetermined enough to prevent us from finding its source, will seem almost imaginary. I remember having felt this very clearly while listening to the echo in a valley: when I called out, I heard a plaintive voice rising, a voice with a timbre so strange, so mysterious, such an aerial voice that it seemed from another world; even my dog (we know that these animals have a sense of the supernatural) looked at me with an anxious air and started to howl.

### Diagramming a Melodic Movement

This brings us to an illusion of a less precise, less characterized nature, whose nuances would have been difficult to grasp if we had looked at it first. I am speaking of the proclivity to represent a melodic phrase in terms of space.

This tendency has been explained in many ways. The simplest seeming explanation is drawn from our system of musical notation. As we hear sounds of increasing or decreasing acuteness, our mind pictures its visual diagram or graphics and we see notes climbing or descending the degrees of the musical staff. It is indeed quite plausible that the habit of reading music must increase this tendency. But the question is to find out why this system of notation was adopted and seems immediately so natural.

It may be because deep sounds have the tonality and timbre of a voice coming out of the depths, whereas high ones have the timbre of open air noises. One could also say that we emit high tones more easily if we lift our head and deep sounds when we lower it. Again, one could say that to make the voice rise, we have to stretch the vocal chords more, whereas to lower it, we need only relax them, which corresponds approximately to muscular sensations that we feel when we lift a weight or let it drop down. All these reasons, as well as others that have been advanced, seem to have merit. The truth must be that they all contribute, to a certain extent, to giving this impression.

The illusion, moreover, may, according to circumstances and individual temperaments, occur in a more or less characteristic way. We know that for some people, auditory sensations are accompanied by visual sensations, to the extent that to each level of sound corresponds a special nuance and that even vowels seem to have a specific color. Without going so far, one can have a special disposition to associate visual images with sonorous ones. Here, for instance, is a quite remarkable example of this intuitive perception of sounds. The entire passage must be quoted for its literary and psychological interest:

If you wish to get an impression of the ancient city that the modern can no longer produce, climb, just before sunrise of an Easter or Whitsun morning, to a high point where you overlook the whole capital and attend the awakening of the chimes. At a signal from the skies, for it is the sun that gives it, you will see these thousands of churches all coming alive at once. First, scattered bells pass from church to church, as when musicians indicate they are about to start. Then see, for the ear, at times, seems to have its own sight, see of a sudden like a column of sound, a cloud of harmony rising at the same moment from each belfry. At first the vibration of each bell rises straight, pure, as if isolated from the others in the splendid morning sky; then, swelling by degrees, they melt and mingle, they enshroud one another, they unite in a magnificent concert. Now, it is but one mass of sonorous vibrations released unceasingly from the countless steeples, floating, undulating, leaping, swirling over the city and extending far beyond the horizon the deafening circle of its oscillations. But this sea of harmony is no chaos. With all its vastness and depth, it has not lost its transparency: in its midst, you see each group of notes coiling away alone as it escapes from the belfries. You may follow the dialogue, alternately hollow and shrill, of the bourdon and the high bell; you see the octaves leaping from spire to spire; you watch them spring, winged, light, and sibilant, from the silver bell, or drop, broken and limp, from the wooden bell; you admire among them the rich gamut that the seven bells of St. Eustache are incessantly ascending and descending; and you see clear, rapid notes dart across them, make three or four luminous zigzags, then vanish like lightning. Yonder, there is the shrill, frail voice of the Abbey of St. Martin; here, the sinister, crusty voice of the Bastille; on the other side, the great tower of the Louvre with its bass voice. The royal chime of the Palais throws out resplendent trills incessantly to all the winds, on which fall at regular intervals the heavy staccato notes of the Notre-Dame belfry which make them sparkle like the anvil under the hammer. At intervals, you see sounds of every shape floating by, coming from the triple peal of St. Germain-des-Prés, and again, from time to time, this mass of sublime sounds opens up and gives passage to the *stretto* of the Ave Maria, glistening and crackling like an aigrette of stars. Underneath, in the deepest tones of the concert, you dimly discern the singing inside the churches seeping through the vibrating pores of their arches.[3]

Admitting that there is some partiality and stylistic effect in this description, it is nonetheless true that it is possible to represent things thus, if you put into it some imagination and good will. Is there not a *soupçon* of complacency in all these illusions?

In other circumstances, and this happens most often, I think, the sounds that vary in tonality will not necessarily take an apparent movement in space, but will only make us think of such a movement. Thus in descriptive music, the listener will have an impression of rocking, of falling, of rising, of enchantment. Language, with its overprecise terms, renders the vagueness of these sensations with difficulty. To describe the impression that a descriptive symphony makes on us, we always exaggerate a little. We say we hear the sounds climbing, descending, spreading, coming together, interlacing, disuniting; sometimes they crash all together in a vertiginous abyss, then rise again and spiral up to infinite heights where the ear loses them. That is approximately correct; but such expressions should be taken metaphorically rather than literally. The illusion almost happens, but it does not really, and these visual images remain too imprecise to intermingle with our auditory perceptions and modify their appearance. When we listen, with our eyes closed, to an arpeggio played on the piano in order to isolate ourselves better with our auditory perceptions, we have the clear impression of an ascending sonorous movement. But we do not, for all that, picture the various notes of the arpeggio piled up one upon the other or actually placed at different heights. All we can say is that that series of notes evokes in us the same dynamic ideas as the sight of an ascending movement would produce. A cord being stretched and released as it vibrates will produce on my ear the same effect as the dips of a flame fluttering as it goes out; but it is nothing more than an analogy.

Finally, this last illusion, slight as it is, will definitely disappear as soon as the sound takes on an expressive value, for there is then an incompatibility, a contradiction between the two kinds of effects. For the illusion of the apparent movement to happen, the variations in tonality and sound have to be interpreted as a simple effect of perspective and the sound itself be conceived as objectively invariable. Conversely, for these variations to be expressive, they have to maintain their specific value, be perceived in their own terms, and the sound must no longer seem to rise or go away, but to vary in place.

3   Victor Hugo, *Notre-Dame de Paris* (Paris: J. Hetzel, 1832), pp. 155–57.

In fact, the illusions we have mentioned are only of limited aesthetic importance. The veritable movement of sounds is not their apparent movement in space, but the sound of their movement, their sonorous rhythm and melody.

The study of this other kind of movement and of the perceptions related to it departs too much from the subject at hand to be treated in detail. It is, however, as qualified to be part of a general aesthetics of movement as that of visible movement. We must therefore say a few words about it. Besides, our detailed analysis of visual perceptions will allow us to be brief in this case, for there are remarkable analogies between both kinds of perception.

### The Perception of Sonorous Rhythm

The persistence of auditory sensations plays at least as great a role in the perception of sonorous movement as that we have attributed to the persistence of the retinal images in the perception of visible movement.

Auditory sensations have an appreciable duration, independent from the duration of the physical impression. When I hear a sudden impact, it continues to tingle in my ear long after the vibrations in the air have finally died out; and when the sensation itself has disappeared, we can still discern in our consciousness something like an image resonance which is the consequence of the sound and which lasts longer still.

These few examples will show to what extent this persistence

can go. When we are preoccupied and someone speaks to us without warning, we hear unconsciously the sentence that was addressed to us; we ask that it be repeated, but even before it is said again, we recall it within ourselves. When a clock strikes the hour, we often notice the chimes only after the series has begun; we take care not to start counting at that point; we wait until the end, then, returning in our mind to the beginning of the series, we recall and count these sonorous images one by one. They were therefore all still present in our consciousness. This can be reproduced experimentally: without warning the people around, strike a glass a few times and ask how many times you have hit it. You will observe that when the series does not go over seven or eight strikes, it is very easy for them to tell by retrospective hearing. Yet the test is made under unfavorable circumstances, as the successive sensations are homogeneous and therefore tend to overlap.

We shall now see how this persistence of auditory images explains the sonorous rhythm and permits us to determine approximately the limit of speed, slowness, and complexity beyond which it ceases to be perceptible.

*1. Limits of swiftness*   At what point do we cease to perceive the rhythm of a sound being reproduced at shorter and shorter intervals? Evidently, it will cease to appear repetitive the moment the sonorous sensations begin to melt into one another, giving us the impression of a continuous sound. For instance, a gong is being struck faster and faster. At first, the rhythm is perceived clearly, the impression produced by each stroke is very energetic and, as the sound is allowed to expand, a maximum of sonority is obtained with a minimum of effort. But now the sounds follow one another more and more rapidly; they then overlap partly, forming a continuous drone in which thinnish sounds detach themselves, corresponding to the feeble reinforcement of sound produced by each stroke. Finally they fuse completely and we hear only a kind of prolonged howling: all rhythm has disappeared.

It is acknowledged that the fusion of auditory sensations starts to occur at the speed of about thirty times a second and that the extreme limit of perceptible rhythms is reached at the speed of 1/100th of a second.[1]

However, that speed is far from being reached in practice. An interval of 1/30th of a second is even much too little. From personal experience, I postulate that a series of sounds repeated more than seven or eight times a second no longer gives us the feeling of the rhythm, although our ear may observe that they are objectively rhythmic.

This can be proved by scraping the bars of a fence with a stick or by scraping a card across the teeth of a comb. When you go beyond the speed I have just indicated, you can observe that the auditory sensations following one another in the consciousness no longer appear intermittent, though they are perfectly distinct. Since our attention is not brought to the current sound more than to those preceding it, we can, at no moment, tell what point of the series we have reached. In fact, we do not hear a series of noises, but a continuous crackling one; and, strangely, this continuity even makes us lose the sensation of the present, of the moment. The succession of sounds will only become perceptible again when the rhythm slows down sufficiently for us to pause an instant at each new sound and ob-

1  Hermann Helmholtz, *On the Sensations of Tone as a Physiological Basis for the Theory of Music*, trans. Alexander Ellis (New York: Dover, 1954), pp. 174–79.

serve its actuality. Then the notion of interval, of intermittence, will reappear and the sounds will again form a rhythm.

*2. Limits of slowness*    Now, given a sound that is reproduced at slower and slower intervals, at what moment do we cease to perceive its rhythm?

The extreme limit is evidently found in the maximum duration of the consecutive image of sounds. If a periodical sound is repeated at intervals so slow that at the instant it is heard again, the impression left by the preceding sound has completely disappeared, it will no more give us the feeling of a rhythm than did the old cannon of the Palais Royal which went off every day at noon. To appear rhythmic, a sound must be repeated at short enough intervals for the tones, prolonged by their resonance, to be connected; and there should be no hiatus in the series of our states of consciousness.

But that is not enough, for, in addition, we must first be able to compare the intervals, and second, find in the sounds themselves the measuring of the time elapsed between two successive impressions.

To realize the first condition, there must be at least three units of rhythm present in the consciousness at one time. At least two are needed to give the notion of an interval, but to ascertain whether the intervals are regular, we have to compare their duration and, therefore, when we reach the next one, we must have kept a more or less precise notion of the first. This makes three units of rhythm for two successive intervals.

To fulfill the second condition, since we cannot measure time in a void, the intervals that separate two rhythmic units must be filled by some sonorous sensation; on the other hand, since a continuous, homogeneous sensation would give us practically no consciousness of duration, this sensation will have to be varied. It is the sum of these variations, immediately recalled at the instant we move to a new rhythmic unit, which forms the duration or size of the interval.

Suppose there is a series of instantaneous sounds following one another intermittently. Objectively the time interval between them is empty; but subjectively it is filled by the sonorous image of the sound, which decreases while it lasts until it becomes imperceptible. This decreasing image is what divides the actual sensations in our consciousness and makes them appear separate from one another. But this decrease is rather sudden, so that under such conditions we will only be able to perceive a very rapid rhythm. As usual, this rapidity will be proportionate to the energy of the sounds. It goes without saying that any attempt to determine the precise rate of this speed is futile. However, one can determine by trial and error the length of time a sound of a given intensity remains in our hearing. There is no need for complicated apparatus to do this.

For instance, I place my watch in front of me, and as soon as the second hand reaches sixty, I close my eyes in order to isolate my auditory sensations completely and begin a series of short taps on the edge of the table, endeavoring to space the sounds far enough apart to almost lose consciousness of their periodicity. After perhaps forty taps, I open my eyes: seventy seconds have gone by, which makes it just under two seconds per sensation. If I begin the experiment again, I can reach this figure or even surpass it, but not by much; the limits in variation are very narrow.

More intense sounds, such as loud hammering on a board, will give me more durable consecutive images and therefore can be spaced further apart by four or five seconds perhaps; but

this time I think we have reached the extreme limits, not because the consecutive images of the sounds cannot last longer, but because, beyond that, the size of the intervals would be very poorly evaluated.

Now, let us have a rhythm formed by a sound whose intensity increases and decreases regularly, like the voice of the wind screeching under a door. Here the intervals can be much longer than when we dealt with discontinuous sounds, since they happen to be divided into two symmetrical phases, one of crescendo, the other of decrescendo; moreover, these variations of intensity give us a stronger feeling of rhythm, because of the dynamic ideas they suggest. But it would be preferable if crescendo and decrescendo were not absolutely continuous; the variations in intensity, like those of tonality, are more easily perceived when they are produced by fits and starts. It therefore seems to me that it is a sound like that of a bell, in which vibrations and throbbings are discerned as the sound fades, that should provide the slowest among perceptible rhythms.

3. *Limits of complexity*   When we hear a series of somewhat rapid sounds, we very rarely listen to them one by one. Our tendency is to group them, to scan them, to shape them into rhythmic phrases. This tendency can be explained by our lifelong habit of counting things; by forming groups of sounds, we are better aware of the number of auditory sensations that are passing through our consciousness, because we no longer need to count units, but their multiples. One must also make use of the instinct of imitation, which tends to make us automatically follow with our voice a sound that we hear. When for instance we listen to the noise made by a steamboat engine, we join it in unison and try to follow its rhythms in our heads. But the natu-

ral rhythm of the voice being much slower, we cannot match its speed. We will therefore divide the series of sonorous pulsations into rhythmic phrases and mark the end of each period with some break in our throat. Because it attracts our attention, the sound on which this extra effort falls takes on an increased value, and the rhythm, chosen arbitrarily and quite subjectively, will seem to have an objective reality. In the same way, we hear rhythmic periods in the vibrations of a train, which might be determined only by the refrain of a song going through our mind. The train itself seems to catch this refrain, marking it with its jolts, accompanying it with its clatter, repeating it endlessly until it becomes obsessive.

When we thus aggregate into a phrase sounds that already have a rhythm, we form a rhythm within a rhythm or what might be called a rhythm to the second power.

To be easily perceived, these rhythmic periods cannot, in my mind, exceed more than eight or nine units. As a matter of fact, that is the longest period used in our verse. Already the inexperienced listener has enough trouble detecting a verse of seven feet from one of eight, when listening without counting the syllables. The nine-foot verse, attempted by a few contemporary poets, is almost impossible to grasp, unless, of course, it is divided into shorter segments.

Finally, taking the shorter segments themselves as units, we can aggregate them also into rhythmic groups, which will give us a rhythm to the third power. But I think that we cannot go any further than that. For, in order to perceive these various rhythms included within one another, we have to detect a difference in the intensity of the accents. And it would be difficult to distinguish more than three degrees of intensity. In a rhythm to the third power, the units consist of the weaker sounds; the phrases are marked by somewhat louder accents, and the groups of phrases by accents of maximum intensity. If one tried to reach a degree of greater complexity, the result would spell confusion.

There will also be a limitation in the number of units that the longest rhythmic groups can include. If the loud accents that mark these groups were separated by too long an interval, the feeling of the rhythm would be lost. The total length of each group is therefore limited. And since, on the other hand, it is impossible to produce, in a given time, an indefinite number of units, because all sonorous rhythm is limited in speed, one sees that the most complex groups can only be composed of a restricted number of rhythmic units.

Some experiments have been attempted to determine this number accurately. Here is one devised by Wundt on the subject.[2] You start a metronome and after a determined number of beats, you ring a bell to indicate the measure. The point is to know how many units can enter into these groups without losing the sense of their equality. You find that you cannot group more than twelve beats into a series, at a speed of three or four per second. The experiment is interesting, but one should not exaggerate its precision. If the concern is to find out the number of beats that can be evaluated without being counted, the figure is too high. If the listener in the experiment is allowed to count this series, with a little practice he could certainly go much farther. This figure of twelve rhythmic units in each series is therefore only an approximation.

2   Wilhelm Max Wundt, *Éléments de psychologie-physiologique*, French ed., 2:240.

## The Perception of Melodic Movement

Just as visible movement consists not in a succession of different images but in a succession of images that presents one object in different positions, melodic movement does not consist in a simple series of different sounds but in the variations of one same sound. It therefore assumes, at the same time as a difference in our sensations, a certain identity, at least in appearance, in the object we are perceiving. The notion of this identity is suggested to us either by the fact that the various sounds come from the same sounding agent, or by the similarity of their tone, as when we listen to a musical instrument, or to the voice of a singer, or to a tune on a chime. But in this last case, in order to maintain the impression of a melodic movement, one must disregard the fact that the notes are jumping from bell to bell. Finally, it would be almost impossible to recognize a tune in a series of sounds emitted by instruments of very different timbre, which would each give one note in turn.

Melodic movement also has this resemblance to visible movement: it is very poorly perceived when it is continuous. Suppose we have an acoustic siren whose disk gets into motion at a uniformly accelerated speed. We first hear a very deep tone that rises little by little in a continuous way. But these variations of tonality can only be detected intermittently, when they have accumulated enough for our ear to observe them. If the acceleration is very slow, the variation will never exceed the smallest perceptible difference and after a while we will realize that the sound has become acute without our ever having heard it ascend. Melodic movement will therefore be better perceived by sudden variations that carry the sound from one degree to the next of the musical scale without any transition; and it is on that condition only that our ear will appreciate correctly the value of the intervals leaped. A further help in perceiving intervals is to have a point of reference in some fixed sound to which the different positions of the mobile sound can be related. Such is the usual role of the bass. In this case, almost infinitesimal variations of tonality can be perceived; and even the smallest intervals are detected with greater clarity than the larger ones, because of the physiological effect of the pulsations produced.

Finally, it is only due to the persistence of auditory images that we have the immediate perception of the melodic movement. We have a series of notes rapidly ascending or descending the musical scale, such as that produced by drawing the thumb from left to right or from right to left over the keys of a piano. Without the persistence of auditory images, I would, in order to judge whether a sound is ascending or descending and by how much, have to constantly compare the actual level of sound with its preceding one, which assumes both attention and memory. But if we take persistence into account, the explanation is much simpler. At the instant when the F note sounds in the ascending scale, the E note is still vibrating at a certain intensity, the D note a little less; and if the damper of the piano mutes the sound at once, the sensations emitted by each note subsist no less in the shape of consecutive sonorous images, and in that same category of intensity. If I had reached, on the contrary, that same note F by going down the scale, I would hear at the same time as F a clear G, a weaker A, an almost imperceptible B.

The nature of my current perceptions changes therefore according to the nature of the melodic movement which preceded it; that is to say, I have actual evidence of this movement. The sound as it ascends or descends leaves behind it a sonorous trail of deeper sounds in the ascending movement and of more acute sounds in the descending one. The duration of this trail can even indicate the rapidity of the movement by an immediate perception, since consecutive notes are clearer and less numerous in a slow movement, less clear and more numerous in a rapid one. If the melody, instead of going up or down uniformly, describes the most capricious arabesques, our ear will follow it in the sonorous space, just as our eye follows in the visual space those motile, ephemeral images traced by a moving light. If one had to be aware of a vocal line by perceiving it note by note, it would be as difficult as it is to realize the shape of a line by looking at it point by point; but thanks to the permanence of auditory images, we embrace at one hearing the ensemble of the successive notes.[3] And this explains why the motifs of a very slow movement are more difficult to grasp than the others: the impressions are effaced as they are produced and we can only reproduce the motif by a necessarily laborious effort of memory.

Thanks to its faculty of analysis, still incompletely explained, our ear can follow several melodic movements simultaneously, as we would follow with our gaze several lines, intertwined without overlapping. The complexity of our perception then becomes a marvelous thing. But to facilitate our ability to distinguish each of the parts, the composer takes care to entrust them to voices or musical instruments of a different timbre; he also gives them movements of different speed and directions. It is a rule of harmony that in four-part choruses one

must avoid direct harmonic movement; one also avoids unison, except on a weaker beat and between two parts that form a secondary harmonic movement. Finally, it is good, from time to time, to include dissonance, not only to quicken the general movement by making us await the chord that will eventually resolve this dissonance, but also to make us more aware of the independence of the various melodic movements and prevent them from melting into one another in a kind of resultant harmony.

One might wonder, in truth, why the prolonged resonance of all the sounds does not produce an intolerable cacophony in the brain where they meet. But one should note that the physical reasons that make us find certain alliances of sound unpleasant no longer exist as soon as it is a case of purely subjective sensations, of purely imaginary sounds.

As to the limitations of this ideal synthesis, they vary a great deal according to the character of the melody heard and to individual predilections. For my part, I can only picture as a whole a very short musical phrase, forming a single rhythmic period: the subsequent periods erase that first impression and leave me only with a confused notion of the anterior movement of the melody. But musicians need to assimilate with ease a large number of measures by mental audition. We have Mozart's testimony on this point. In a known letter in which he displays great sincerity, he speaks of his method of composition and declares that when he has finished a piece in his head, he views it at one glance like a beautiful painting; he hears it in his imagination in its totality, not in the details of its parts.[4] This seems to surpass immeasurably the limits we have assigned to

---

3   I am sure that this is the way we hear the human speech: we would not understand the meaning of words if we heard them syllable by syllable. We have to perceive them as a whole, and even several at a time, by this recapitulatory audition which presents them to us simultaneously.

4   Cited by Eduard von Hartmann, *Philosophy of the Unconscious*, trans. William Coupland (New York: Harcourt and Brace, 1931), 1:279.

the duration of consecutive sonorous images when dealing
with rhythm. But the melodic movement, by its variety, must
engrave itself more easily on the memory than rhythmic
movement, whose units, being homogeneous, tend to blend
together.

We now have a glimpse of the applications that can be made
from this study of auditory perceptions to the aesthetics of
sonorous movement. It is evident, in fact, that, all things being
otherwise equal, it is the rhythms and melodies susceptible to
being perceived with the least effort of attention that make the
most favorable impression on the listener. But we cannot
attempt to undertake here the study of musical beauty. It is too
important a question to be treated lightly and as a postscript, so
to speak.

I only wish to note, in ending, that if new research on this
difficult problem is attempted, it would be useful to proceed as
I have in this work: seek the rationale for musical aesthetics in
the determination of sonorous movement rather than in its perception. At least, that is the area in which there would be most
to discover.

# Index